Samora Machel: An African Revolutionary

Samora Machel: An African Revolutionary

Selected Speeches and Writings

Edited by Barry Munslow

Translated by Michael Wolfers

Zed Books Ltd.

Samora Machel: An African Revolutionary was first published
by Zed Books Ltd., 57 Caledonian Road, London N1 9BU,
in 1985.

Copyright © Samora Machel, 1985
Translation copyright © Zed Books, 1985
Cover design by Jacque Solomons

Printed in Great Britain
at The Bath Press, Avon

British Library Cataloguing in Publication Data

Machel, Samora
    Samora Machel: an African revolutionary:
    Selected speeches and writings.
    1. Socialism — Mozambique
    I. Title II. Munslow, Barry
    335'.00967'9   HX449.A6

    ISBN 0 86232 339 8
    ISBN 0 86232 340 1 Pbk

US Distributor
Biblio Distribution Center, 81 Adams Drive,
Totowa, New Jersey 07512, USA

Contents

Abbreviations and Glossary

ANC	African National Congress
ANP	Popular National Action — the official and only political party allowed under the Portuguese dictatorship
APIE	State Housing Authority
DETA	Mozambique Airline
DGS	General Directorate for Security
Flechas	'Arrows', a counter guerrilla unit
FPLM	Popular Forces for the Liberation of Mozambique
FRELIMO	Front for the Liberation of Mozambique
GE	Special Groups (in the colonial army)
GEPs	Special Paratrooper Groups
Machila	A litter used for carrying colonial officials
MANU	Mozambique African National Union
MPLA	Popular Movement for the Liberation of Angola
NESAM	Nucleus of Mozambican Secondary Students
OAU	Organization of African Unity
OJM	Organisation of Mozambican Youth
OMM	Organisation of Mozambican Women
ONP	National Teachers Party
OPVs	Voluntary Police Organisation, a colonial militia force
PAIGC	African Party for the Independence of Guinea and Cape Verde
Palmatória	A heavy wooden bat used to inflict corporal punishment
PIDE	International Police for the Defence of the State
SNASP	People's National Security Service
SWAPO	South West African Peoples Organisation
UDENAMO	National Democratic Union of Mozambique
UNAMI	National Union for Mozambique Independence

Introduction

Early Life

A small boy herding his father's cattle was frequently to be found perched on a hill under the shade of an exceedingly large and very splendid tree, around five or six kilometres from his house in Xilembene, in the Chokwe district of Gaza Province in Mozambique. Not far from the tree his mother had a *machamba* (cultivated field). The tree was rather a special one, not only because of its age and remarkable size, but because it had a history. It was here, in the middle of the 1890s, that Maguiguane Khosa, the head of Ngungunhane's army busily engaged in a fight with the invading Portuguese army for control of the territory south of the River Zambezi, used to receive his visitors. That struggle was a bitter one. Even after Ngungunhane was taken prisoner in 1895, Maguiguane continued the fight for a further two long years. It was the stories told of the invasion by his father and other relatives and of that heroic resistance which drew back the young Samora Moises Machel time and again to that particular spot. Indeed his own grandfather had been one of the leading warriors in the struggle. He knew none of his grandparents directly, but through the stories of one battle-scarred centenarian, he learnt of his grandfather's exploits. The spirit of resistance to foreign occupation never died and was rekindled anew when the boy grew into a man. For he was to train the guerrilla army of the Front for the Liberation of Mozambique, FRELIMO, for its decade of war which finally ousted the European invaders eighty years after that fateful defeat of Ngungunhane. Like Maguiguane, he was to lead the army against the Portuguese, but this time to victory and not defeat.

When the original armed resistance was finally silenced by a mixture of political guile, technological superiority and internal division and weakness, the spirit of resistance continued in many other forms. These too were to have a profound influence on that young boy born on the 29th September 1933, the third son of a peasant farmer, Moises Machel. In particular, there was the influence of Pastor Abel Tchambale of the Free Methodist Church. He introduced this church to the area as early as 1903 and later a school. He was already advanced in years when the young

Samora, whose father was an early convert to the church, began to frequent his house. Pastor Tchambale's home was near Samora's school and sometimes the boy would stay there, as his own home lay a good distance away. The Protestant churches were constantly persecuted by the Roman Catholic Portuguese colonial administration. Indeed, the tie-up between church and state was such that a formal Concordat was signed with the Vatican in 1940, following which, responsibility for education in the Portuguese colonies was handed over to the Catholic Church.[1] The Protestants were viewed, correctly in part, as a threat to the colonial order. They genuinely encouraged education and a certain independence of mind, both of which offered a potential challenge to the regime – for in effect there was no serious educational effort undertaken, which was a deliberate policy to maintain control.

Some time after independence, when President Machel returned to his birthplace, he spoke freely on this rare occasion, of the early influences on his own development.

> These old Protestants were always persecuted. They took part in the war of resistance against the colonial occupation of our country. When they became Protestants, it was a form of resistance. It was they who inspired us, these elders from here. We did not grow from nothing. A constant spirit of struggle, struggle, struggle . . . it was these elders who taught us. They spoke with us and said: 'It's necessary to fight these Portuguese, they are foreigners' . . . No book by Marx ever arrived here, nor any other book that spoke against colonialism. Our books were these elders. It was they who taught us what colonialism is, the evils of colonialism and what the colonialists did when they came here. They were our source of inspiration.[2]

Given the dominant hold of the Free Methodist Church within the area, the Catholic Church, which ran most of the schools, was anxious to make converts. Hence, much of the school curriculum consisted of religious education, which usually meant that it took six or even more years to pass beyond the third grade of what was termed 'rudimentary education'.[3] After a much interrupted passage, given all the difficulties, Samora Machel finally completed his third year. His father then sent him to study for the fourth class at the mission of São Paulo de Messano. Much of the disdain for the church that turned Samora Machel personally against religion emerged during his time here. For the children were expected to wake early and work until lunchtime in the fields. Only in the afternoon could they commence their schoolwork. Again after several interruptions to his studies, Samora was about to take the examination for his fourth grade when the priests laid down an ultimatum: either become baptised as a Catholic or you cannot take the exam. Effectively, within the Portuguese colonial system, those without fourth grade qualifications were denied access to most jobs above the level of simple manual labour – it was *the* vital hurdle. With no possible alternative, he accepted, and in

1950, shortly before he turned seventeen, he sat and passed the exam.

The entire colonial system was based upon a denial of education to Africans. Only the tiniest fraction of the population could hope to move beyond four years of primary education. Even those who completed four years were few indeed. The only real hope in continuing education lay in 'opting' for a religious career. He applied to go to secondary school but in spite of his acknowledged high intellectual abilities was turned down and urged to go to a seminary instead. He politely refused the offer. He trained instead to be a nurse (at the 'Miguel Bombarda' Hospital in Lourenço Marques), one of the higher positions available to Africans under a Portuguese colonialism which professed multiracialism but erected instead 'culture' barriers through the *assimilado* system. According to one author, 'The intent of that policy was to ensure cooperation and compromise, and to segregate the African intelligentsia from the "native" masses.'[4] From the money earned as a nurse he was able to continue his studies but was never to have the opportunity to advance very far within the formal educational system. Instead, he was to study privately and within the liberation movement. Essentially he was self-taught in the fire of the national liberation struggle.

The stories of the resistance of the past and a continuing spirit rejecting colonial occupation, permeated the early life of the first president of independent Mozambique. But beyond these lessons, there were also the direct experiences of what colonial rule meant for his particular community. The story of his home area in the Limpopo Valley is an important one in this respect. It is a measure of the weakness of Portuguese colonial capitalism that the prosperous Limpopo Valley with its narrow band of fertile soil was relatively ignored during the first decades of this century. Effectively, the south of the country had become designated a labour reserve for the South African mines, and according to agreements worked out between the two countries, Portugal received a fee and foreign exchange earnings for every Mozambican miner that was sent.[5] Samora's own father went to the mines prior to becoming an established farmer. His first contract was in 1912, and like many others who were to follow him, his meagre earnings enabled him, with judicious management, to save up enough to marry in 1917, purchase a plough in 1921 and finally cease migrating in 1926. He was lucky to survive the ordeal, unlike his eldest son, Samora's brother, who died whilst on the mines. It is a measure of the level of repression and exploitation practised, that Moises Machel did not even receive the derisory sum promised by way of compensation for the loss of his son, instead only a fraction of the amount arrived.

In the 1940s the relative tranquillity of the valley was shaken by two events. Forced cotton cultivation was introduced, with fearsome corporal punishment for those who tried to evade it. Necessarily food production was reduced, leaving little to store from each harvest by way of provision against years of drought; thereby making the population more vulnerable to physical disaster and hunger. Secondly, forced labour was employed to build an elaborate irrigation system in preparation for the settlement of Portuguese peasant farmers. The new scheme led to the dispossession of the African farmers from the fertile river valley land and their displacement to the drier, more sandy soils of the interior. This seriously affected the well-being of all the families involved as production declined. Inevitably the combined effects of these phenomena were to form a lasting impression upon Samora Machel, whose awareness of exploitation had already been aroused by the activities of the local Portuguese shop-keepers/traders.[6]

First-hand experience of colonial capitalism fuelled his spirit of resistance and the flames were fanned by the sadly, all too typical racial discrimination experienced when Machel first went to work. In an early interview with Basil Davidson, he explained what happened whilst working as a nurse:

> We were together with whites during our training, but it was only after graduating that we really discovered the very different treatment, the different attitudes to them and to us. And then, of course, we discovered the different level of wages.[7]

He then went on to tell of a turning point in his own thinking:

> Gradually, I saw that nothing would help but collective action. A man on his own couldn't achieve anything. At that stage – it was after 1956 – I began to understand what the key problems were, the key economic and political problems, and just why it was that we Africans were handicapped. Then 1960 taught me more – the independence of the Congo and its tumults. I began to think seriously about the possibilities of Mozambique becoming independent . . . Then it was that the consciousness of being oppressed, deprived, exploited, began to have its effect, as well as those ideas about independence.[8]

The wave of independence which swept across Africa from the late 1950s to the early 1960s had an important influence upon Samora's thinking. First the breakthrough with Ghana's independence under Kwame Nkrumah, then Sekou Touré in Guiné. Whatever the barriers of silence imposed by the Portuguese dictatorship of António Salazar, the word still spread of the changes transforming the countries to the north. The radio brought news, as did visiting sailors to the port of Lourenço Marques, and returning migrant workers from neighbouring countries, where nationalist parties were busily organising. There was the scent of change in the air, a hint, an expectation. The massacre of six hundred unarmed peasants in the northern town of Mueda in 1960 whilst making a peaceful protest, revealed Portugal's intention: opposition to any meaningful representation. No political parties were permitted, and the secret police were always on the lookout for any sign of rebellion. But in February 1961 the bubble finally burst when in Angola, colonial rule was met by force of arms. The challenge to the Portuguese empire had begun. A further rapid blow was delivered with the Indian invasion of Goa in December of that same year, which followed the independence of the first country actually to border on Mozambique – Tanzania. In addition to all of this external impetus there was the catalytic visit of Eduardo Mondlane to Mozambique that same year. This man had uniquely defied all the anti-educational policies of Portuguese colonialism to obtain a doctorate in the United States and then work for the United Nations. He was to become the first President of FRELIMO at its founding Congress held in Dar es Salaam in the middle of 1962. Albeit heavily monitored by the secret police, Mondlane was able to hold a series of meetings with people in many parts of the country, and he and Samora Machel met for the first time.

The Struggle Begins

In 1962, upon hearing of the formation of FRELIMO, Samora Machel màde preparations to leave the country. He eventually left, following a period of clandestine political activity, via Swaziland, South Africa and Malawi, finally arriving at Dar es Salaam in Tanzania in 1963. Whereupon he immediately volunteered for military training and was amongst the earliest recruits sent to Algeria. His elder brother, Alexandre Jossefate, took a nursing course as well as receiving military training and he returned to the south of Mozambique on a mission, just prior to the start of the armed struggle, and was captured and imprisoned. It is significant that unlike many of the other young people who flocked to join the new nationalist movement in exile, Samora Machel did not opt to continue his academic studying, but rather to engage in the study of struggle. This he was to learn through the experience passed on to him of the Algerian revolution, along with other military leaders within the movement who trained in that country.

Initially, they were very much influenced by the Algerian revolution, but very soon the Mozambican 'model' asserted itself. Once the armed struggle began, it was the reflections upon their own experience which were to be decisive. This is not to say that there were not powerful intellectual influences on the evolving thought of Samora Machel. Notably in his role as a political-military leader, he studied profoundly the theory of peoples' war in the works of General Giap, genius of the Vietnam war, and of course the classic texts of Mao Zedong. From these works the central message of the primacy of political and human factors over purely technological ones was drawn, with the need to mobilise and maintain popular support being the decisive factor.

Upon his return to Tanzania, he was given a senior post of responsibility at the first FRELIMO training camp at Kongwa in Tanzania, where serious preparations were undertaken for the start of the armed struggle, which finally began on 25th September 1964. The people who took part in those first attacks were trained at this camp, situated about sixty kilometres from Dodoma. It was built by hand, they had neither money nor machines. Almost from the very beginning they began growing food, pursuing a policy of self-reliance which was to become a cornerstone of Machel's own thinking. On a final visit to the Kongwa camp before leaving for Mozambique and the independence celebrations in 1975, he reflected upon its importance, 'When we arrived here in 1964, we came divided and it was the unity which we managed to obtain here that permitted us to win in Mozambique.'[9] Machel was soon charged with initiating the opening of a new front in the eastern part of Niassa Province, before being placed in overall command of the newly-established training camp and the movement's main rear base at Nachingwea, in southern Tanzania.

It was here that, in his role as head of training, he imposed his political authority upon the movement, and all the cadres most active inside the country passed through his hands. He was to instill into them the high moral principles and political orientation which came to win such widespread respect, admiration and support for FRELIMO, not only inside the country but also abroad. One of the standing orders given to all militants was 'Respect the people, help the people, defend the people.'[10] The success of the political mobilization effort was a reflection of the conduct and quality of the cadres produced at the camp.

The overall military commander, Filipe Samual Magaia, was killed in the second week of October 1966 and Samora Machel was nominated to replace him.[11] As Secretary for the Department of Defence, he was automatically drafted on to the Central Committee, which met that same month. Amongst the points noted at the meeting were that some of the political and military structures were not sufficiently strong and that there were also deficiencies in the co-ordination of general action.[12] In the following year, under his overall command, there were noticeable improvements in the political-military effort.[13] President Mondlane was to give fitting praise for Machel's work at the movement's Second Congress, held inside the newly liberated areas in 1968. He said:

> The political line and military discipline which Comrade Samora was able to inculcate in the fighters is instilled in the life of the Mozambican guerrillas who now serve as the basic elements of the national liberatory struggle, without which perhaps, our struggle would not have proceeded as such during the latter three and a half years.[14]

Internally, developments within the movement had not always gone smoothly. Indeed, virtually all of the Central Committee elected at the First Congress had been replaced by 1970. Many left in the first couple of years, unable to break out from the malaise of exile politics which they carried over from their earlier membership of the three nationalist groups that combined to form FRELIMO.[15] There was much in-fighting, especially in Dar es Salaam, which Machel managed to avoid in the early years by concentrating his attentions on the key task at hand – the spread of the armed national liberation struggle inside the country.

Effectively it was the military wing of the movement which proved to be the driving force inside the country, taking responsibility for establishing the base camps, population centres, health posts, schools, etc. Samora Machel's attention was always directed inside the country, to winning the struggle and building a new society in the process. But the ability to do this rested upon the firm commitment of the movement as a whole to such a goal. Inevitably there was a growing struggle between the right and left within FRELIMO, which led to a period of intense crisis between 1967 and 1969.[16] The revolutionary caucus within the leadership of FRELIMO coalesced around Samora Machel and the army, together with key revolutionary intellectuals based in Dar es Salaam, foremost amongst whom was Marcelino dos Santos, whose influence on the theoretical development of the movement was profound. But it included others such as Jorge Rebelo, who worked so successfully within the information department. Samora Machel's leadership qualities blossomed during this period, for it was he who genuinely welcomed and wished to deepen the crisis, so as to resolve the contradictions that had developed within the movement and thereby create a deeper and more profound unity around a common set of revolutionary principles. These contradictions had become deep-seated and bitter and were clearly hampering the development of the struggle. Several cadres were assassinated by the right wing, including Samuel Paulo Kankhomba, the military Chief of Operations, and President Eduardo Chivambo Mondlane himself.[17] This was the most difficult period for the movement and it was at this time that Samora Machel came into his own. He faced and fought the internal struggle, realising that only through its resolution could the liberation struggle itself develop and the revolutionary transformations, documented in the speeches of this volume, be truly set in train.

That period of crisis is too complex in its detail to rehearse on this occasion. But suffice it to say, as one example, that Samora Machel was in the forefront of the weeding out of the student malcontents in the FRELIMO secondary school in Dar es Salaam, many of whom had fallen under the racist influence of one of the teachers – Father Mateus Gwengere. Samora was quoted soon after the event as saying:

> When this priest arrived, FRELIMO gave him the responsibility for teaching. But instead of teaching what he should have taught them he slowly began to inject poison, stimulating reactionary ideas among our students, such as racism, saying that we should not have whites in our organisation because we are fighting the white man.[18]

It appears that Eduardo Mondlane had himself earmarked Samora Machel as his successor should anything happen to him, and President Nyerere was aware of this. Nyerere proved an important and loyal friend of Mondlane and then Machel, and the support given by Tanzania to Mozambique, by anyone's assessment, was of great importance. Both FRELIMO leaders had open access to President Nyerere, which was of considerable benefit. Samora Machel was officially elected on to the Central Committee at the Second Congress, and following the assassination of Mondlane, was elected on to the hurriedly formed three-man Council of the Presidency. That such a body was created reflected the deep internal rift within FRELIMO with Uria Simango, the Vice-President, being effectively blocked from automatic succession. He had increasingly come to represent the right within the leadership and it was a measure of the growing strength of the left that they outnumbered Simango two to one on the Council, with Samora Machel and Marcelino dos Santos aligned against him. Simango lost the struggle and left FRELIMO. In May 1970 the Council was dissolved and Samora Moises Machel was elected the new President of FRELIMO, *ad interim*.

Keen to orientate the movement more and more towards the inside of Mozambique, he had been instrumental in getting most of FRELIMO's functions moved out of Dar es Salaam. The medical centre was moved to Mtwara, general education to Tunduru, and the Secondary School to Bagamoyo. By early 1970 in the Tanzanian capital, there was only the information department, the Mozambican Institute and FRELIMO's official representative. His energy was inexhaustible. One Scandinavian journalist who visited the liberated zones and observed Machel over a considerable time period commented, 'he is always on the move between different operational zones.'[19] Even after becoming President he was a regular visitor inside the country and took personal responsibility for conducting the FRELIMO response to the massive Gordian knot counter-insurgency thrust by the Portuguese army in June 1970, which involved 10,000 troops.

FRELIMO grew in strength under Machel's leadership, and the liberated zones expanded. In 1970 the Zambezi River was crossed and the armed struggle was opened up in the southern part of Tete province. In 1972 a new front was opened in the strategically significant central province of Manica and Sofala. Less than two years later, under the impetus of the national liberation struggles in the colonies, the Armed Forces Movement in Portugal had overthrown the country's dictator, and the path was laid open for negotiations.

This was a demanding period for President Machel, not least because Josina, his wife, died at a tragically early age. She had been a leading militant within the movement and he was devastated by her loss. Soon after the event, he wrote this poem to her memory:

JOSINA, YOU ARE NOT DEAD

Josina you are not dead because we have assumed your responsibilities and they live in us.

You have not died, for the causes you championed were inherited by us in their entirety.

You have gone from us, but the weapon and rucksack that you left, your tools of work, are part of my burden.

The blood you shed is but a small drop in the flood we have already given and still have to give.

The earth must be nourished and the more fertile it is the better do its trees flourish, the bigger are the shadows they cast, the sweeter are their fruits.

Out of your memory I will fashion a hoe to turn the sod enriched by your sacrifice . . . And new fruits will grow.

The Revolution renews itself from its best and most beloved children.

This is the meaning of your sacrifice: it will be a living example to be followed.

My joy is that as patriot and woman you died doubly free in this time when the new power and the new woman are emerging.

In your last moments you apologized to the doctors for not being able to help them.

The manner in which you accepted the sacrifice is an inexhaustible source of inspiration and courage.

When a comrade so completely assumes the new values she wins our hearts, becomes our banner.

Thus more than wife, you were to me sister, friend and comrade-in-arms.

How can we mourn a comrade but by holding the fallen gun and continuing the combat.

My tears will flow from the same source that gave birth to our love, our will and our revolutionary life.

Thus these tears are both a token and a vow of combat.

The flowers which fall from the tree are to prepare the land for new and more beautiful flowers to bloom in the next season.

Your life continues in those who continue the Revolution.

Three years later President Machel led the FRELIMO delegation in independence negotiations with the new Portuguese government, held in Lusaka, Zambia. On 7 September 1974 an agreement was finally reached that power would be handed over to FRELIMO within the year. An interim Transitional Government was formed with FRELIMO's Joaquim Chissano as Prime Minister. Finally, on 25 June 1975 independence was declared and Samora Machel became President of the People's Republic of Mozambique. It had cost the blood and sacrifice of many men and women.

Theory and Practice

The quality of a great leader is measured not merely by the ability to comprehend underlying societal movements. Important as this may be, what is ultimately decisive is the ability to shape the destiny that these might imply. Samora Machel's upbringing was such that he was touched by many of those forces which together make up the broad brush strokes on the canvas of Mozambique's history in the 20th Century. If his life provides a marker of the continuities it is also a measure of the changes. In this respect the histories of the revolutionary movement FRELIMO and of Samora Machel the person are intimately connected. His analysis grew from personal experience and the struggle to find new ways of comprehending and transforming that experience. He grew in stature and leadership qualities within the movement, and the movement in its turn grew as a result of the leadership that he imparted. It was a vibrant, down-to-earth, enormously vital leadership that animated the cadres and displayed not only a political line, but a personal *method* of political action that was regarded as being of equal importance. Individual example provided the key to this, requiring an inner struggle to internalize new revolutionary values and thereby personify in everyday life and habit the future goal for Mozambican society as a whole. As he writes in the first text of this volume, 'Our working methods are not of secondary importance, as it is through them that we apply our decisions.' Such a philosophy inevitably places an enormous burden upon the shoulders of the figure-head of the revolution. But it has to be said that few have carried the mantle so easily, with such good humour and with such constant energy that all around are kept enthused and above all optimistic.

For in the course of the Mozambican Revolution there has been and will undoubtedly continue to be many a dark hour. When the forces of opposition seemed dominant and even appeared within the movement's leadership, that challenge was faced head on, with determination and a will to succeed.

Above all, what is asked of a leader is guidance as to the route, and the will to embark upon and complete the journey. With the achievement of independence in 1975 an important milestone was reached, but this was not the ultimate goal. Development and socialist transformation had still to be completed, a far more difficult and challenging task, and that was much more than a lifetime's work. The world has been replete with leaders who upon attaining power have been solely concerned with how to maintain it in order to reap the benefits. The luxury and privilege of office have gradually corrupted even where such corruption was not present before. It takes a deeply-held moral and political commitment to withstand the undermining effects of such influences – the kind of commitment that Samora Machel shares with but a few of his fellow African leaders, but with a distinguished few, who remain his firm friends and allies.

Throughout the protracted armed struggle, he was to lead from the front, setting the pace of the marches across the endless kilometres of sparsely-populated Niassa Province, through the heartland of FRELIMO's liberated areas on the Mueda Plateau, in the province of Cabo Delgado. But not just walking, all the time discussing the problems of the zone with the local people who gave their support, not least by literally shouldering the logistical burdens of the struggle. Talking and walking, sometimes all day and half of the night. And then after independence, there was the chauffeured car with motorcycle escort speeding out from the former governor's palace on the promontory overlooking the bay, with the whole city of Maputo sprawling out to the west, in an enormous crescent shape.

How to maintain the simplicity of lifestyle, the strict morality of self-sacrifice in such a surrounding? This was the new challenge. Most difficult of all perhaps, how to maintain contact with the base and people's everyday problems and pressing concerns, when surrounded by the temptations of relaxing and reaping the benefits after suffering the deprivations of that decade of war? There was the justification of success in defeating Portuguese colonialism and actually coming to power; there were some sycophants in both party and state apparatuses, but especially the latter, eager to appease and lull. Yet the new President of the People's Republic of Mozambique met the challenge full square, tried to maintain the revolutionary dynamic, and struggled to maintain also direct contact with the people – not always with ease, given the encumbrances of office, with its protocol, heavy schedules and duties, and the ever-present demands of running a continuing war. But it will remain a lasting testament that the President and the top leadership of FRELIMO have remained uncorrupted, have not succumbed to the temptations of self-enrichment, resorting to a mere lip-service homage to the aims of the revolution.

The inner leadership core has remained virtually the same since 1970, although numbers have expanded. It has maintained an internal democratic openness that has proved to be its greatest strength. When I talked with Joaquim Chissano,[20] Samora Machel's longstanding compatriot – they had trained the cadres together in the camp and he is now the country's Foreign Minister – back in Dar es Salaam in 1972, the nature of this intimate and refreshingly democratic relationship shone through. He said quite plainly:

> Samora Machel is someone with whom you may discuss programmes and opinions, together we make the policy of FRELIMO – not only with me, but with the other leaders, and the militants as well. The rank and file discuss with him . . .[21]

During the national liberation struggle, the *collective* nature of the leadership was overwhelmingly apparent. An interesting anecdote which illustrates this point relates to the time when Samora gave an interview to

John Saul. Having been shown the draft version of the interview, Samora went through it and meticulously crossed out 'I' wherever it appeared, to substitute 'we'. The revolution was clearly considered to be a collective process. [22] Hence in the first text of this collection, the secret of success in maintaining substantial leadership unity is seen to be the nature of the movement's inner democracy: 'For a leadership body to work with the masses it must be united . . . when we feel a companion is falling behind, we must make an effort to help him progress.' Concerning the basis for this unity, practice again is considered the key. Machel writes, 'It is not by words that we are bound together, but by the many activities we share when serving the people.' The stress in his writing is on working together and helping people along. With many more violent and more bloody means to resolve differences being practised elsewhere in other revolutionary situations, this is no mean achievement.

At FRELIMO's Third Congress, held in February 1977, the party's open commitment to Marxism Leninism was espoused, the Front was transformed into a party, and Samora Machel's Presidency of the Party was officially confirmed. [23] The theoretical development of the President and of FRELIMO was not the result of borrowing anyone's ready-made formula or book of divine truth. Hence, we read in the second text of this collection, 'Granted that ideological drafting owes an immense debt to the theoretical and practical contribution made by the revolutionary movement of other peoples, *ideology is always the creation of a specific struggle by a people and its revolutionary classes.*' Examining the development of Machel's own thought reveals just how important he considered starting from a study of one's own reality to be. In a brief interview given in 1969, he stated that like Mondlane, he believed that the theory and ideology of the revolution should come from practice and not dogma. [24] As he observed in the above-mentioned text, 'ideology is not formed in a simple reading of the masters of revolutionary thought.' At the same time, he also carefully noted that the Mozambican experience confirms yet again that without revolutionary theory there can be no practice. But importantly he goes on to assert the validity and contribution of Mozambique's experience and the theorizing that emerges from this for the wider world.

The original text of *The People's democratic revolutionary process in Mozambique* was drafted for an audience in the Soviet Union, where the national liberation experience best understood was that of the classic model of a Communist Party existing within a broader front. In this text, Samora Machel is trying to explain why and how the Mozambican experience is different, and the contribution made thereby. Hence we read: 'our practice does offer some original features in this sphere, in particular how a broad front without an established vanguard party relates to revolutionary ideology.' He goes on to explain that there was a *de facto* vanguard within the Front, but that the vanguard was formed in the process of the struggle itself. As it was the army who were in the forefront of that struggle in practice, what was more natural than that this component should provide the vanguard? This passage is of particular importance because it genuinely reflects the problem that Samora Machel confronted as the military commander in the mid-1960s, faced with an important political administrative section of the leadership that saw the military wing as merely an instrumentality for their accession to power. He was able to accelerate the success of the armed struggle precisely because of his insistence upon the *essentially political nature of the armed struggle*. As a result of the crisis and its resolution, the political mobilization structure of the movement was incorporated within the new political-military structures established in the liberated areas. These were subordinate to the Defence Department, and an integrated approach to people's war was thereby operationalized. The success that ensued is a meaure of its effectiveness.

The Power of Human Will

'The launching of the struggles and the victories we have won reveal concretely that there is no such thing as fateful destiny: we are capable of transforming society and creating a new life.'

These few words, in the text *Establishing people's power to serve the masses*, sum up perhaps best of all the need for the power of human will in revolutionary transformation – a political leadership determined in its attempt to overturn the old and build the new. His words convey the power of human agency, rebelling in organized manner against the mammoth and seemingly invincible forces of repression. In the fulfilment of this task, we find one of the most important contributions made to revolutionary political thought by Machel, and it concerns the sphere of *internal personal struggle* – for he took opposition to the colonial capitalist system to its logical end, incorporating every aspect of a person's life. The party had to create an entirely different world vision. His speeches and writings reveal a profound sense of the cultural and psychological dimensions of the revolutionary process. These ideas grew during the armed struggle when ever greater stress was laid upon the totality of the distinction which needed to be drawn between 'the life of the enemy' and that·of the revolution. This entailed more than the creation of new structures, although these in themselves were important. But alone, these would inevitably fail if a new mental outlook was not also developed to consolidate and animate that change. They would otherwise remain hollow shells.

This process was perhaps most coherently formulated during a speech that Machel gave at the Symposium in Homage to Amilcar Cabral, held in Conakry in January 1973. As we have not included that particular text in this collection, the relevant passage bears repeating now in full:

. . . the previous dividing line between colonizers and colonized has to be further completed by an even deeper dividing line between exploiter and exploited. This dividing line affects every field, and primarily the ideological and cultural fields. Ideas, values, habits, usages and customs, all the unconscious standards which regulate the everyday behaviour of the individual, are expressions of the ideology and culture of the existing society.

It so happens that we were all born into an exploitative society and have been profoundly imbued with its ideology and culture. This is why an internal fight against what we believe to constitute our moral framework is difficult and may at times seem impossible.

Divesting ourselves of the exploitative ideology and culture and adopting and living, in each detail of everyday life, the ideology required for the revolution is the essence of the fight to create the new man.

It is not the personal fight of one man wrapped up in himself. It is a mass struggle in which we accept criticism and do self-criticism, purifying ourselves in their fire, which makes us conscious of the path to be followed and fills us with hatred for the negative values of the old society.

When we launch this process, on the one hand the establishment of popular structures of political power and, on the other, the fight to acquire a new mentality and behaviour, we are opening the doors to serious contradictions in our midst.

Discontent will arise. All those who were hoping to exploit the people, to step into the shoes of colonialism, will oppose us. Erstwhile companions of ours who initially accepted the popular aims of our struggle, but who in practice reject the internal struggle to change their values and customs, will move away from us to the extent of deserting or even betraying.

The successes achieved militarily, the feeling of the imminence of victory, will hasten the process of the discontentment of a handful of elements frustrated in their ambitions and corrupt tastes. In this way, a breach is made in our ranks through which the colonialist and imperialist enemy will penetrate.

The reactionary forces, the disgruntled elements, will see in an alliance with the enemy a way of safeguarding their petty and anti-popular interests, while the enemy will find in such an alliance a golden opportunity to strike a blow against the Revolution.

In the critical phase through which we are passing of the sharpening of the internal class conflict and the military and political defeat of the enemy, the protection of the Revolution and of its leaders, the survival of the revolutionary structures and of their cadres, depends now more than ever, on the masses.[25]

The power of human agency then, but one informed by a materialist analysis, is a dominant theme running throughout his thought. Mozambique, and indeed all of Africa, should seek nothing less than a modernity free from traditional superstition and ethnic, regional and racial complexes – but a modernity that does not merely ape the lifestyles of the West. In this regard, education is seen as having a vital role to play. This is reflected in an early talk that he gave to the second conference of FRELIMO's Department of Education and Culture, back in September 1970; the title sums it up: *Educate Man to Win the War, Create a new Society and Develop our Country.*[26]

The Selected Texts

The works compiled together in this volume reflect only a small selection of Machel's thought. In their entirety, a collection of his speeches and writings would run to many volumes (see the *Bibliographic Note* by Colin Darch). But represented herein are some of the most important, which touch upon many of the dominant themes that keep re-emerging in his thought. Each contribution produced at a particular stage in the movement's history provides a reflection on the previous experience of struggle and gives direction for the future. There is change and development expressed throughout, mirroring the new agendas set by differing circumstance. For anyone who has seen President Machel deliver one of his speeches, the inadequacy of the written text alone becomes all too apparent. When he speaks in front of an audience, the words come alive and are much more meaningful as the message is acted out. This can be readily appreciated, for example, in the opening passage of the third text of the collection. Throughout his speeches there is an acute attention to the detail of people's lives and living circumstances. He addresses the day-to-day realities that Mozambican people themselves will understand, and frequently this is hard for the outside observer to fully comprehend. At the same time there is much of universal value. In this, Machel stands alongside his distinguished companions in the sister movements which together fought Portuguese colonization – Agostinho Neto of the MPLA (Popular Movement for the Liberation of Angola) and of course Amilcar Cabral, leader of the PAIGC (African Party for the Independence of Guinea and Cape Verde) who was assassinated in 1973.

In part one of the volume, the focus is on liberation, the state and party. The first text, completed in 1974, lays the basis for the movement's analysis of Mozambican reality, providing an important pointer towards the Marxism declared as the official ideology at FRELIMO's Third Congress. With wit and devastating sarcasm, Machel deflates the myths of Portugal's 'civilizing mission' and the outrageous claims made by certain leading members of the Church in support of this. The early part of the text, with its ringing indictment of the colonial system, echoes the force and passion of Fanon's accusations over a decade before:

> It is our taxes that pay the police who arrest us when we disobey the company, our taxes pay the army that massacres us if we rebel against oppression. We and our labour pay for everything, but those who receive service and disobedience are the exploiters.

The stress is laid continually upon the *system* that exploits, not upon individuals within it, and the dangers of neo-colonialism warned of by Nkrumah as well as Fanon, are powerfully underlined.

The nature of state power and how it should be transformed, occupies a central place in his thought. The key concept in the revolutionary transformation initiated by FRELIMO is that of *people's power*. The interrelationship between vanguard leadership and mass democratic participation and control at the base, provides the creative tension that is to run throughout the entire post-independence experience.[27] In so many ways, it proved far easier to destroy the colonial bourgeois state in the liberated areas precisely because it was only there in shadowy form. The movement as the counter-state, in its manifestation as popularly institutionalized mass mobilization in those zones that became liberated, was so entirely different from the post-independence situation. Then one found the Front and later the Party, grappling with the infinitely more complex heart of the (state) beast, when power was taken in Lourenço Marques (renamed Maputo), site of all the ministries and the state bureaucratic stratum. It was then that the cruellest legacy of Portuguese colonial rule was most keenly felt with the extreme shortages of technically and educationally qualified cadres to run the state machine.

The first two long texts review FRELIMO's experience of and reflection upon power and the need to transform the state. Both were written before Mozambican independence, when a new set of circumstances presented themselves. The third, *Make Beira the Starting-Point for an Organizational Offensive*, dramatically paints the picture that FRELIMO found when it entered the country's second largest city and in particular, the dangers to the integrity of the movement are laid out. The text which follows is concerned with the problems of coming to terms with the reality of running a state and economy given the particularly invidious colonial inheritance. It is a sobering, down-to-earth assessment. Following the brief period of relative calm at the end of the Rhodesian war, with the gaining of Zimbabwe's independence in early 1980 – at the cost, it must be said, of enormous sacrifice to the Mozambican economy and people – an internal *Ofensiva* was announced. Texts 3, 4 and 5, written in the first three successive months of that year, chart the analysis of the problem and the proposed remedies.

Whilst the texts have been divided into two parts in this volume, with part two concentrating on national reconstruction, frequently the contents of the texts spill over these boundaries. Hence texts 4 and 5 touch upon economic matters, including the need to link salaries to the economic performance of enterprises and the continuing important role envisaged for small businesses and private traders, with the clear implication of the limitations on the state's capacity that this implies. The final short text in part one emphasises that even in a country with a weak industrial base and with a small proletariat, a socialist revolution is still possible over time. When the force of human will meets the force of circumstance a titanic struggle is inevitable, the outcome being far from certain.

Production is an act of militancy, the text that opens part two of this collection, provides a cool appraisal of the limitations of existing working-class consciousness inside Mozambique. Given the terrible economic problems besetting the country, the need to improve productivity was paramount. This has to be understood in the context of an economy which was built upon forced labour and forced crop cultivation. When these key forms of colonial exploitation were abolished (a major gain of the armed struggle) productivity and overall production declined, dramatically hastened on by the skills-drain occasioned by the settler exodus. This text expresses well the problems of the early transition period, bringing with it the uncertainties of the new situation. It displays a subtle and complex understanding of the class forces and their mode of operation at this time.

The second speech on economic matters expresses many of the themes which were to be crystallized much later at Frelimo's Fourth Congress, held in 1983 (four years after this speech was originally given). These include the need to decentralize decision-making, the need to use the technology most appropriate to the skills of the people and the need to put the best cadres into production rather than lose them in provincial capitals 'behind desks loaded with papers'.

The speech on education reinforces the earlier theme of the need to create a new society with new values, morals and standards of conduct. Two speeches are included on health, in part because they concern much more than health alone, important as this is. Above all, these two speeches reflect the ongoing tension between centralized managerial authority on the one hand and popular power on the other. Although in the second speech the emphasis is given to the need for clear managerial hierarchy and responsibility, in the eight-day meeting of health workers which followed the speech, the important role of the workers' council was defended.[28] There is an ongoing debate within the party on this fundamental issue, and corrections of course are required from time to time as the balance perhaps swings too far one way or the other. This particular inner tension is likely to remain for some considerable time. The President has of course a close interest in and knowledge of the health sector, as he worked in it during the 1950s. In the first of the two hospital speeches his profound understanding of the prevailing attitudes and working practices of the hospital are revealed. Here again one sees his ability to get to the heart of the matter in the eyes of the person on the ground.

There follow speeches addressed to women and youth, both of whom have their own mass organizations linked to the party. Women in

Mozambique as elsewhere in Africa have a long uphill struggle ahead of them; this much is apparent from the speech and it is the one where the perspectives of those living in the industrialized countries are likely to differ the most. In addition, a vigorous debate upon these questions is continuing inside the country. Finally, there is the important statement on the defence and security forces – openly admitting the mistakes and abuses that have occurred and signalling the launching of the *ofensiva* in this quarter also. No one is infallible, mistakes are made by everyone at all levels, but what is vital is the ability to realize these and make the necessary changes. There is strong evidence that this spirit is still alive within the leadership of the party and this bodes well for the future.

Machel's contribution to revolutionary thought is marked by a peculiarly rich fusion between patriotism and Marxism.[29] It also manifests a profound concern with the importance of practice and theoretical reflections upon the lessons that can be drawn from it. Living out the revolution in everyday life is seen to be a necessity and this demands personal inner struggles and firm resolve. Without it, the people as a whole will never be prepared to believe the messages being projected. For Samora Machel, an African revolutionary, mobilizing the people is what creates the movement for change within society and the chance of shaping historical destiny. The ways of achieving it in the detail may differ with circumstance, but its importance remains central. People's power in its essence is about people first seizing and then determining their own destiny in an organized way. Samora Machel has made an important contribution to that goal.

Notes

1. A Missionary Statute of 1941 made Catholic missions the official arm of the state for the education of Africans.

2. *Tempo*, 2 October 1983, p. 45. This commemorative issue on the occasion of President Machel's fiftieth birthday is an invaluable biographical source.

3. Under law number 238 of 15 May 1930 and of the subsequent Concordat of 1940 the goal of this 'rudimentary education' was clearly spelt out, it was to 'lead the *indigena* gradually from a life of savagery to a civilised life.'

4. R. H. Chilcote, *Conflicting Nationalist Ideologies in Portuguese Africa: The Emergence of Political and Social Movements, 1945-1965*, a paper given to the Annual Conference of the African Studies Association, Montreal, October 1969. It is significant to note that by 1950 only 4,554 Africans in Mozambique had been granted *assimilado* status (E. Mondlane, *The Struggle for Mozambique*, Zed Press, London, 1983, p. 60).

5. For a detailed study of mine labour from the south of the country see R. First, *Black Gold. The Mozambican Miner, Proletarian and Peasant*, Harvester Press, Brighton, 1983.

6. See *Tempo*, 2 October 1983, pp. 45-6.

7. Quoted in B. Davidson, *In the Eye of the Storm. Angola's People*, Longman, London, 1972, p. 178.

8. Ibid.

9. *Noticias de Beira*, 22 May 1975.

10. *Mozambique Revolution*, No. 21, September 1965.

11. Filipe Magaia was a former leader of the student movement NESAM. He had been a prime mover amongst political groups working clandestinely inside the country and was imprisoned several times, on the last occasion between April 1961 and February 1962 (see *Mozambique Revolution*, No. 27, October-December 1966).

12. *Mozambique Revolution*, No. 27, October-December 1966.

13. See the report given in *Mozambique Revolution*, No. 32, December 1967-January 1968. For a summary of the restructuring undertaken in the defence department at that time see E. Mondlane, *op. cit.*, pp. 152-3.

14. Quoted in Panaf, *Eduardo Mondlane*, Panaf, London, 1972, pp. 34-5.

15. These were UDENAMO, UNAMI and MANU.

16. For a full account of the national liberation struggle and the internal crisis see B. Munslow, *Mozambique: the Revolution and its Origins*, Longman, London, 1983. See also, Frelimo, *Central Committee Report to Frelimo Third Congress*, Mozambique, Angola and Guiné Information Centre, London, 1978.

17. For an account of the background to the assassination of Eduardo Mondlane see Ibid. The early texts of part one of the book explain the political divisions between the 'right' and the 'left' within FRELIMO at this time.

18. *The Standard* (Tanzania), 6 November 1969.

19. *The Sunday News* (Tanzania), 1 September 1968.

20. Joaquim Chissano was a close companion of Samora Machel from the early days. With the reorganization of the Defence Department during the armed struggle he was charged with heading security, hence liaised closely with Machel.

21. Author's interview with Joaquim Chissano, Dar es Salaam, April 1972.

22. I am grateful to Iain Christie for bringing this to my attention and placing his not inconsiderable archive at my disposal over the years.

23. The accepted usage has now come to be *FRELIMO*, for the designation of the Front until the Third Congress in 1977, and *Frelimo* for the vanguard party. At the Fourth Congress held in 1983, the statutes were changed to rename it the *Frelimo Party*.

24. *The Guardian*, 3 February 1969.

25. See S. Machel, 'Sharpening of the Class Conflict' in A. de Bragança and I. Wallerstein (eds), *The African Liberation Reader*, Volume 2, Zed Press, London, 1982, pp. 104-5.

26. For the full text see S. Machel, *Mozambique: Sowing the Seeds of Revolution*, Committee for Freedom in Mozambique, Angola and Guiné, London, 1974, pp. 37-45.

27. See B. Egero, 'People's Power: the Case of Mozambique', in B. Munslow (ed), *Africa: Problems in the Transition to Socialism*, Zed Books, London, 1985, for a full discussion of this theme.

28. See J. Hanlon, *Mozambique: The Revolution Under Fire*, Zed Books, London, 1984, p. 68.

29. See A. de Bragança, 'La Longue Marche De Samora', *Afrique Asie*, No. 133, 18 April-1 May 1977.

Part I:
Liberation, State
and Party

1. Establishing People's Power to Serve the Masses*

This year, 1974, we are celebrating the tenth anniversary of the launching of our armed struggle. During these ten years countless militants and the people as a whole have accepted every kind of sacrifice and hardship, and in the ten years we have overcome difficulties and shown that we are capable of achieving victory.

We are already beginning to know the meaning of victory. In increasingly large areas of our country the people already make comparisons and speak of 'before the revolution' and 'today'. Our people are beginning to savour the fruit of their struggle.

But at the same time we are all aware that the final victory will not come tomorrow and that there is still a long way to go.

What is the reason for our sacrifices? Why is the enemy so stubborn and cruel? Why does the enemy, in the face of condemnation by all just men of the world, still find the necessary support and assistance to carry on with his crimes?

Is all this happening merely because we seek our independence? After all, in 1143 and 1640 Portugal also fought for independence. The United States which is now supporting Portuguese colonialism waged war in the eighteenth century to free itself from British colonialism and become independent. France and Britain which are financing and arming Fascist and colonialist Portugal were only a few years ago, in the period from 1939 to 1945, fighting against Hitler's Fascism and enduring heavy losses and sacrifices to preserve their own national independence.

We find close to Mozambique many independent countries: Madagascar, which was a French colony; and the former British colonies of Tanzania, Zambia, Malawi and Swaziland. All these countries became independent through negotiations between the colonizing power and the colony.

Why did Britain and France agree to grant most of their colonies the right to independence, and yet today support a colonial war? Why these

*This text originated in President Machel's talks given during a reorganizational offensive in a FRELIMO education centre in November 1971. It was later expanded and amended, to appear in its present form in 1974.

1

ten years of colonial war, ten years of shelling, ten years of massacre of the population, ten years during which NATO and the Western countries have done all they can to help Portugal?

We often say that in the course of the struggle our great victory has been in transforming the armed struggle for national liberation into a revolution. In other words, our final aim in the struggle is not to hoist a flag different from the Portuguese, or to hold more or less honest elections in which Blacks and not Whites are elected, or to put a Black president into the Ponta Vermelha Palace in Lourenço Marques instead of a White governor. We say our aim is to win complete independence, establish people's power, build a new society without exploitation, for the benefit of all those who identify as Mozambicans.

Here lies the explanation for the war. Just as a man infested with lice has to plunge his clothes in boiling water to destroy the lice irrespective of their colour or origin, so we were obliged to plunge our country into the flames of war to destroy exploitation, whatever the origin or colour of its agents.

What is at stake is the establishment of a people's power that asserts our independence and identity, and destroys exploitation. This entails destroying the power of those who foster exploitation. That is why the imperialist countries which live by exploitation come to the rescue of Portugal since it is in their interests that the exploitation goes on.

Today thanks to our struggle a new power is being built in our country.

Ten years of FRELIMO's power is not long. Young as we are we have taken on responsibilities that would overwhelm older people. Hundreds and thousands of years of experience underlie the exploiters' power, whereas our power is young and yet has to solve problems that the millennia-old rule of the exploiters never managed to deal with.

The new power is not something abstract. The new power is ourselves, who with all our shortcomings must wield it. The New Man able to wield the new power will not step down from a cloud. Our responsibility is great although our capacity is still limited. But we have one great and decisive advantage: we have a correct political line, and the masses are with us.

But in building and using our power, we bear within us, in our ideas, habits and customs, all the disfigurements created by the old power.

We must therefore constantly correct our working methods, and apply the scalpel of criticism and self-criticism to lop off the enormously weighty and destructive burden bequeathed by the ancient society.

For the tenth anniversary we shall shortly be celebrating, we want to analyse our power, rethink our actions, study what we have done and what is still to be done, and above all correct the deviations.

We shall begin with an initial study of what power is, what it expresses and what values it embodies. We shall analyse the difference in origin, character, methods and aims between colonial capitalist power and people's power established under FRELIMO's leadership.

By tackling this crucial question we shall be able to understand why the conflict between us and the enemy is so antagonistic that only war can settle it. In fact the establishment of people's power that entails the ascent to power of a new class is possible only through the overthrow of the previous class and its power. And once we have grasped this concept we can see how impossible it is to reconcile our interests with those of the enemy, through bogus autonomies and independences that safeguard the essence of the colonial capitalist state.

The popular character of the power that is being built implies a genuine and profound democracy such as has never been known in our country's history. And like power, democracy is not something abstract: if it is to be used and to be tangible, we must create conditions for it to come into effect. So our second theme is a study of democracy, the new experience our people are enjoying for the first time.

Finally, since people's democratic power is already practised in our various centres, they provide a test bed for our experience, and broadcasting centres for our political line and its practical results. So we must indicate how our centres should fulfil this task and what are the essential preconditions for them to succeed in their historic role.

The Exploiters' Power Is to Oppress the People. Our Power Is the Power of the People

In the process of societies' historical development, various kinds of social relations were forged between men. At the dawn of mankind, when the change from ape to man occurred, pre-humans lived in nomadic bands governed by the concern for survival. The entire productive effort was consumed immediately, and often failed to satisfy basic needs. These pre-humans lived on roots, wild fruit and animal corpses.

Mankind's forebears lived like this for hundreds of thousands of years. At a certain stage these forebears began to use bones or sticks to dig up roots, to hunt animals. They began to use tools to produce their food, production albeit highly primitive began, and the ape gave way to man. Production distinguishes man from the beast, unleashes his brain, and opens the way to progress.

With the emergence of production, initially gathering and hunting, and in a second phase agriculture and animal husbandry, mankind begins to develop. A division of labour arises and an improvement in tools for production and production techniques. So man's productive effort can now yield more than he himself needs for subsistence. Production generates a surplus.

The existence of surplus production provides the material basis, the objective conditions, for forces to emerge in society that seek to appropriate the surpluses to the detriment of those who have produced them.

The society divides into opposing classes, with differing interests: some want to appropriate the fruit of the labour of others, while the latter

3

object. Human relations which have until now been co-operative become relations of conflict between exploiters and exploited.

Obviously this whole process took hundreds of thousands of years; opposing interests, antagonistic classes did not grow overnight. But the process is fundamental.

Once differing and antagonistic interests had appeared in society, the fundamental issue in that society was one of 'power': who could make decisions, on what criteria, and in whose favour.

A given group can impose its interests and project its aims only if it controls the society, or in other words rules that society.

Ruling a society means organizing the society to serve the interests of the ruling group, imposing the will of this group on all other groups whether they agree or not. With the passage of time, the ruling group makes the other groups regard its domination as the best, the fairest and the wisest, and one that corresponds to the interests of all.

This goes on until the moment when new forces within the society, realizing that their interests are prejudiced by the ruling group, unite, struggle, overthrow the former power, and establish their new power, reorganizing society to satisfy their own appetites.

Until a recent period of mankind's history it has been the various exploiting classes – slave-owners, feudalists, bourgeoisie – who have successively dominated society and organized its politics, economics, ideology, culture, administration and legal system for their own benefit.

This was possible because the exploited masses did not have sufficient class consciousness to unite them, or an ideology able to give them an overall view of their interests and provide the appropriate strategy and tactics for the struggle to win and exercise power.

Historically speaking, the first occasion when the exploited masses did, after various failed bids, win and exercise power, was in Paris in 1870. The Paris Commune was smashed after a few months by a coalition of French and German reactionaries, and 30,000 workers were massacred.

Finally, in 1917, under the leadership of Lenin, the exploited masses achieved power in Tsarist Russia and created the Soviet Union, the first state in the world with the people in power. After the victory of the democratic forces in the anti-Fascist war, people's power spread to new countries such as China, the People's Democratic Republic of Korea and the Democratic Republic of Vietnam in Asia. In Europe, people's power was established in many countries such as the Romanian Socialist Republic, the German Democratic Republic, the Bulgarian Socialist Republic, etc. The first people's state on the American continent was established with the victory of the popular forces in Cuba in 1959.

People's power has become a reality for about one-third of mankind. The areas where the working masses have won power are known as the 'socialist camp' and today comprise 14 countries.

In our country, slave-owners, feudalists, kings, emperors ruled society until the colonial conquest. The colonialist bourgeoisie then established itself in power and imposed its wishes upon all strata in the country until the time when our struggle began to overthrow it.

The successive domination by the various exploiting minorities – dictatorship over the masses – is always exercised in a more or less camouflaged manner so that the masses do not appreciate their real situation and do not perceive that they are subject to oppression.

In our country, before the colonial conquest, the tribal chieftains and chiefs who held sway asserted that their power represented the will of the ancestors. In some kingdoms, for example, the people were not allowed to look upon the king's face, and in others it was forbidden to speak to the king – one could only listen to his voice.

Even in our own times in some areas where the power of the chieftains has remained relatively untouched, such situations are quite common and the brutal reality of oppression by feudal lords is cloaked in myth and superstition.

The colonialists, in order to give a better camouflage to their domination and to prevent the masses understanding and resisting their wretched situation, encouraged superstition. So they spread numerous religions among us that weakened the masses by dividing them. And all the religions preached resignation to the people.

The missionaries to our country taught us that disobedience to the government and the settler was a sin, that we must be deeply grateful to Portuguese colonialism since it had brought us the true faith. In the last century, the church defended the criminal slave-trade by saying it was a good thing because it enabled the slaves to be baptized. The present Archbishop of Lourenço Marques, Custodio Alvim Pereira, has often stated publicly that the Mozambican people should not demand independence, since this would merely serve Communism and Islam, or in other words that independence is a sin against God. In a speech he made in June 1961 to seminarists of the archdiocese of Lourenço Marques, when he was still an assistant bishop, he laid down the following principles:

1. Independence is irrelevant to man's well-being. It could be desirable in certain geographical and cultural circumstances, but these do not yet obtain in Mozambique.

2. So long as such circumstances do not obtain, founding or participating in an independence movement is to act against nature.

3. Even when the circumstances do exist, the mother country has the right to oppose independence, provided that freedoms and rights are respected and that the welfare and civil and religious progress of all is pursued.

4. Any movement that uses violence goes against natural law, since if independence is desirable it should be obtained by peaceful means.

5. If there is a terrorist movement, the clergy must in good conscience not merely abstain from it but also oppose it. This is the logical corollary of their mission.

6. Even if the movement is peaceful, it is advisable for the clergy to

abstain so as to give spiritual guidance to everyone. The Superior can impose this abstention, as has been done in Lourenço Marques.

7. The native peoples of Africa have a duty to be grateful for the benefits conferred on them by colonizers.

8. Educated people have the duty of openly battling against the illusions about independence among the less educated.

9. Present-day African independence has almost always been born out of revolution and Communism. The Holy See has expressed firm doctrinal opposition to atheistic and revolutionary Communism: the great revolution is that of the Gospel.

10. The slogan 'Africa for the Africans' is a philosophical monstrosity and a challenge to Christian civilization, since current events show that Communism and Islam wish to impose their civilization on Africans.

The current head of the church in Mozambique closed the same speech by saying: 'Love your land which is Mozambique integrated with Portugal, just as an inhabitant of the Algarve is concerned for his province without forgetting the common fatherland . . . the present African liberation movements are against the church.'

In short, according to this prelate, we should show gratitude for colonial exploitation, forced labour and the sale of men to the mines, the plunder of our lands and compulsory crops. We should be grateful for oppression with the *palmatória* and the whip, and deportations to São Tomé. We should be grateful for the humiliation of racism and raped women, for the abandoned and fatherless children and for our transformation into a nation of errand boys. We should be grateful for obscurantism, a lack of schools; for superstition, a lack of hospitals and social welfare. We should therefore show gratitude. To rebel against this is a sin. To take up arms when they come to massacre us, as at Mueda, Xinavane, Lourenço Marques, Wiriyamu is a sin. It is to go against the church.

We know of many homilies from Catholic bishops and priests, many preachings by Muslim sheikhs, many sermons from all the Protestant churches, and until very recently all of them were telling us that we must be submissive, that we should accept and be thankful.

We should, however, note that in the face of the mounting crimes committed by the enemy, more and more voices have been raised in religious circles in the past three years to condemn the colonial war and its massacres. But such voices still appear in isolation and we cannot regard them as a clear public and official stand taken against colonialism by the churches in Mozambique.

The colonial bourgeois society uses other arguments than superstition to camouflage and justify its dictatorial power. They say we are an inferior, backward race with primitive customs, an ignorant people that must be educated by the superior, advanced race with its fine customs and wisdom. The Portuguese Constitution expressly states that the essential task of the Portuguese nation is to 'civilize' the 'barbarians' that we are.

They constantly repeat this argument, although everyone knows that Portugal has more than 40 per cent illiteracy, that the wretchedness of the Portuguese peasants and people is extreme, their obscurantism is no less than ours and that they have as many, albeit different, superstitions, or even more than we do.

They say this when they want to persuade us. But in practice and when they are expressing their policy, they speak and act very differently.

The late Cardinal Archbishop of Lourenço Marques, Teodósio Clemente de Gouveia, in a pastoral letter of 1960 establishing policy in the schools, wrote: 'Schools are necessary, it is true; but schools where we teach the natives the path of human dignity and the grandeur of the nation that protects them.'

Coming to 'educate' us clearly means making us submissive mental slaves to colonialism.

General Kaulza de Arriaga, who was ignominiously defeated in Mozambique, said in a course to the High Command of the colonial Fascist army in 1966–67:

> If there were 20 or 30 million Blacks in Angola or Mozambique, we would have a very serious problem; so it is useful that these populations are small. I don't know if this is the result of the export of these people to Brazil, but if so it is a good thing that such exports occurred.

Following his approval of the infamous slave-trade – the most degrading of all forms of human exploitation and humiliation – Kaulza de Arriaga, the 'civilizer' who used to hold forth in public on winning 'African hearts' and on 'multiracialism', envisaged at the same time the annihilation of our people. Thus he stated: 'Another highly significant aspect is the demographic: first, White population growth; then, limitation on Black growth.'

The meaning of 'racial equality' and the task of 'promoting African advancement' are made quite clear when the general writes:

> Multiracialism must be authentic and remain so, even if under its umbrella we have perchance to put a slight brake on the advancement of the Black populations. We must then convince these people that we are bringing them forward at a reasonable pace . . . There is of course another problem: we must also not be too efficient in advancing the Blacks, since we must indeed advance them, but should not overdo it.

In short, 'civilization', 'education', and 'advancement' are merely to camouflage the actual reality of exploitation and plunder, oppression, brutalization and humiliation. They are pretty words to fool us and put us to sleep. So, behind every watchword of the oppressive regime we must see the reality it masks.

Oliveira Salazar, the mastermind of Portuguese colonial-Fascism,

7

expressed this principle clearly (F.C.C. Egerton: *Salazar, Portugal and Her Leader*):

> The hierarchy which exists between the work of planning, organization, management and implementation, properly speaking, reflects not only a need inherent in production, but also the naturally imposed inequality of individual ability which is something which society cannot and should not seek to go against.

One of the greatest Portuguese writers, Eça de Queiroz, in *O Conde de Abranhos*, a masterly work where he denounces and unmasks the bourgeoisie, explains the mentality of the exploitative and oppressive bourgeoisie as manifest in the system of university education:

> Thus the student remains forever imbued with the great social idea: that there are two classes – one which knows, the other which produces. Naturally the former, being the brain, governs; the latter, being the hand, works to clothe, shoe, feed and pay for the former . . . Graduates are the politicians, orators, poets and by tactical adoption, the capitalists, the bankers and big businessmen. The small fry are the carpenters, the plasterers, the tobacco workers, the tailors . . . This conception of a division into two classes is salutary, because those who are educated in it do not when they leave the university run the risk of being contaminated by the opposite idea – an absurd and godless idea destructive of universal harmony – that the small fry may know as much as the graduate. No, he cannot: it follows therefore that the intellects are unequal, which destroys the pernicious principle of equal intelligence, the sinister base of a perverse socialism.

The oppressors, particularly the colonial bourgeoisie, in the hope of masking their activities and keeping us in ignorance, spend their time drumming in our ears that they exercise power for the benefit of everyone, or of the majority, and they do it to spread progress, civilization and the Christian religion. They are always telling us what a great sacrifice the exercise of power is, how heavy their responsibilities, how willingly and happily they would give them up, if they were not a matter of duty.

The speeches we hear, the newspaper articles, radio propaganda and the entire machinery of colonialist intoxication tries every day to persuade us that the power of the oppressors is the best in the world, that we should be content with domination and only ungrateful people, lunatics and Communists could think otherwise. However, the reality behind the splendid words is very different.

From the governor general down to the local administrator, the entire administrative apparatus has a single aim: to do everything it can to ensure that the companies, the wealthy, the capitalists exploit the people.

The laws passed, the taxes collected, the orders given in no way serve the people, but are always for the benefit of the bosses. If occasionally a law seems to benefit the people it is because the people's revolt was particularly fierce, and something was done to appease the people's anger so as to demobilize the masses and thus maintain colonial domination.

One example of this was the Lourenço Marques dock strike in 1963. Before the strike the stevedores were paid between 12 and 15 escudos a day, but after the strike and despite the repression, the rate was raised to 28 escudos, for fear of a more serious revolt by the stevedores. Now wages are being raised everywhere, on account of the war, and the aim is to corrupt people and make them forget they are colonized, exploited, oppressed and humiliated. In the same way, in places where the colonialists fear that people are beginning to support the struggle, and that it may spread to their area, they soon drop some of their arrogance and distribute large photographs of Blacks and Whites together, apparently happy. It is, however, nothing but a mask, as PIDE continues to arrest, torture and murder individuals, while for propaganda purposes sweets are handed out to children.

The nature of the oppression remains the same. The government's laws still order our arrest and sale for the mines in South Africa. Those who gain are the owners of the gold mines, and we are the ones who lose life, or come back with tuberculosis or missing an arm or a leg.

The government's laws compel us to grow cotton and sell it to the companies. The companies profit, but we never have clothes to wear despite having produced the cotton.

The government's laws hand us over as work-horses to the sugar companies and the tea companies. The companies make millions of escudos, but in our homes we and our families do not have tea or sugar in the mornings.

It is the administration that arrests us if we refuse to obey the company's will, and the administration that compels us to go and work for the plantations, the mines and the factories.

It is our taxes that pay the salary of this administration that oppresses us, our taxes pay the police who arrest us when we disobey the company, our taxes pay the army that massacres us if we rebel against oppression.

We and our labour pay for everything, but those who receive service and obedience are the exploiters.

The bourgeoisie and the colonialists say that the courts are impartial and dispense justice. Propaganda says justice is blind and so does not distinguish between rich and poor, the grand gentleman and the humble workman, and thus finds the truth, rewards the just, and punishes the guilty. Certainly they say this. But nobody ever heard of the courts of the bourgeoisie and colonialism ordering the return of land to peasants who have been dispossessed. As is happening now for the Cabora Bassa dam, where 25,000 people have been robbed of their land and evicted, and no court says we are in the right. Nobody has ever heard of a court condemning PIDE for murdering and torturing prisoners or for keeping them in prison for months and years without trial. The courts convict those who struggle for the people, and give their approval, support and praise to those who massacre the people.

These very concrete examples that everyone knows, that each of us has experienced as a daily fact of life, show quite clearly the effect of the power of the colonialists and capitalists, and who benefits from it. When power is in the exploiters' hands, it is used by them to impose their dictatorship.

To exercise power in the exploiters' society one must belong to the exploiting group and give oneself body and soul to serving the exploiters.

In the traditional society not just anybody can be a chief. To be a chief one must belong to the feudal stratum, belong to the chief's family, that is be a son or a nephew. The new chief is designated by the predecessor or a body of feudalists. The same thing happens in bourgeois society, where power belongs to the companies, to the big capitalists, and is exercised by the faithful servants of capital.

Everyone knows that a governor general or minister, as well as milking his office, will as soon as he is replaced find a high position in the banks and companies. Deputies, governors and ministers move from the companies and banks into the government, and from the government into the companies and banks.

Take, for example, Pimentel dos Santos, now the Governor of Mozambique, whose various positions before his appointment in October 1971 included being chairman of the board of directors of the Lobito Mining Company. Obviously although he is a governor, he is still connected with his company and serving it. So in September 1972 his company, in association with Bethlehem Steel of the United States and the Mozambique Uranium Company, was granted a concession for mineral prospecting and mining in an area covering tens of thousands of square kilometres between Chioco and Changara in Tete Province. We could give similar examples for each of the ministers, governors, deputies, etc.

In the context of a colonial society such as exists in Mozambique under colonialism's control, there is, in addition to the 'qualities' required in the usual bourgeois society, the need for the individual to belong to the colonizing race or at least to be totally submissive to the colonizer and thus become a total puppet.

These familiar facts show clearly that power and the state are not technical and neutral instruments, but rather weapons used by the exploiting classes against the exploited masses.

The oppression does not come about because the local or senior administrator or governor is an evil, hard-hearted man who takes pleasure in exploiting us. Generally speaking and in individual, human terms they are no better or worse than anyone else, of any other race. They are what they are by virtue of the position they hold.

If by chance there is a senior or local administrator whose conscience is troubled by the crimes he is obliged to commit, and if he dares to object to his task, he is immediately removed, replaced and punished. That is why we are always saying that the struggle is against a system and not against the individuals in it.

The practice of Portuguese colonialism and the war of aggression were not altered in the slightest by Marcelo Caetano's better or worse qualities when he replaced Salazar, just as the criminal and murderous practice of PIDE continues under its new name of DGS.

The existence of exploiting classes, White, Black or any other colour, produces an exploitative power and state.

That is why we always say that we are struggling against the exploitation of man by man, and that Portuguese colonialism is its principal manifestation in our country today. In other words, this means that our aim is to overthrow the power of the exploiting classes in Mozambique represented mainly by the colonial and imperialist bourgeoisie, and to destroy the colonial state as the quintessence of colonialist and imperialist domination of our country.

We must be very clear on these points. Some nationalists, either innocently for lack of a developed class consciousness or because they are involved in exploitation, think that the objective of our struggle should be to install Black power, instead of White power, and to appoint or elect Africans for the various political, administrative and economic positions now held by Whites. The former category of nationalists, once they are actively involved, understand and accept the need to destroy the exploitative state, while the latter category who identify with the system refuse its destruction. In short, for the latter nationalists who are not entirely satisfied with colonial power as it is foreign, the final aim of the struggle would in fact be to 'Africanize' exploitation. So they reject our revolutionary ideology – just as they particularly reject the changes of outlook and behaviour we demand, and which they claim have no bearing on the fight against colonialism. That is a reactionary standpoint that jeopardizes the nature and purpose of the struggle.

In their view, our struggle should be between Black power and White power, while in our view the struggle is between the power of the exploiters and people's power.

We have already seen that in an exploitative state, the entire apparatus of power – its laws, administration, courts, police, army – have the sole aim of maintaining exploitation, serving the exploiters. The state, power, laws are not neutral techniques or instruments that can equally well be used by the enemy or by us. So the decisive issue is not that of replacing European personnel by African personnel.

Just as the colonialists have their way of fighting and we have ours, they have their military science and we have ours, so we have our power and they have theirs. There is a contradiction between us and them over the origin, character, method and objective of power.

We cannot found a people's state, with its own laws and administrative apparatus, on the basis of a state whose laws and administrative apparatus were totally conceived by the exploiters to serve themselves. It is not by ruling through a state designed to oppress the masses that one can serve the masses.

'Africanizing' colonial-capitalist power would rob our struggle of all meaning. What would be the point of struggling if we continued to be subject to forced labour, to the companies, to the mines, even if everywhere was chock-full of African managers and foremen? What point in the sacrifices if we were still forced to sell cattle and cotton in markets that benefit only the traders, even if these traders were Africans? What would be the purpose of so much bloodshed if at the end of the day we were still subject to a state that, though governed by Mozambicans, served only the rich and powerful? How could we maintain a police force that arrests and tortures workers, keep an army that fires on the people, even if all its generals were Blacks?

A state for the rich and powerful in which a minority takes decisions and imposes its will, whether we like it or not, and whether we understand it or not, is the continuation in a new form of the situation we are now fighting.

The question of people's power is the essential question in our revolution.

In this context it is absurd to talk of autonomy, or even consider the independence that Caetano or his successors could offer us. The mass of the people have understood this, their class instinct has enabled them to grasp this point: independence, autonomy, as conceived by imperialism and colonialism, are tactics designed to preserve everything as it was before – to maintain exploitation.

Hence it is that since the masses have taken up the defence of their power, they accept the most heroic sacrifices to spread and struggle and consolidate the liberated areas. All enemy offensives, however rabid and violent, have been smashed in the face of this unyielding determination of the masses to defend their power.

When a new group of exploiters in our midst was able from 1967 to 1969 largely to paralyse our leadership and to begin to distort the meaning of our struggle, in the hope of reintroducing a dictatorship of exploiters, it was the people, the class instinct of our working masses, that responded to the risk we were running and gave the revolutionary forces within the leadership the decisive support that led us to victory.

Our power represents the interests of our working people, and expresses our determination to drive out colonialism and imperialism, and create a new society without exploitation. Our power is the revolutionary expression of an alliance which, by defending the interests of our peasant and working class, unites all social strata and groups who feel a sense of patriotism and democracy: workers, peasants, labourers in the plantations, sawmills, concessions, mines, railways, docks and industries, mechanics, intellectuals, technicians, civil servants, clerks, petty and middle-level traders, etc.

This power which is coming into being reflects the new balance of forces emerging in our country and is favourable to a people's alliance. The exploiting minority's former dictatorship over the people is being replaced by the power of the people, which is being imposed on all colonialist forces and reactionary classes, the overwhelming majority prevailing over the tiny minority and destroying exploitation.

Our power is different in form and content from anything that has previously existed in our country.

Our power belongs to the people and is exercised by its genuine representatives to serve the interests of the people.

The Central Committee of FRELIMO, in a document issued at its May 1970 meeting, defined the qualities required of a Central Committee member:

> It is from among the militants who show the most outstanding militant qualities that members who are to lead the organization, and in particular members of the Central Committee, must be selected. A Central Committee member must come from the ranks of the struggle. A Central Committee member must distinguish himself by his dedication to the national liberation struggle and by his own self-denial in devoting himself to the struggle and to serving the people's interests.

The same document expressing the qualities required of a FRELIMO militant stresses: 'He serves the masses and sacrifices himself for the majority.'

This means that whereas in the other area, the exploiters' area, a leader is required to serve the exploiters and come from within their ranks, in our area the leader comes from the masses, from the ranks of struggle, and is a servant of the masses ready to sacrifice everything, including his life, on behalf of the majority, in defence of the majority.

We are the majority, we peasants, workers and labourers born of the exploited and dominated people, and our aim is to liberate ourselves, to build a new society, a society that reflects our interests.

Our struggle has already established our power over vast regions of our country. In these regions ours are the interests that prevail. FRELIMO's political line, which reflects these interests, is daily implemented in all sectors of work for the benefit of the majority. FRELIMO's political line, which guides our power, is daily transforming social relations, the relationships between people, and changing society. Our line is transforming nature, putting the resources of our land at the disposal of the majority and mobilizing nature's laws for the benefit of the broad masses.

From the moment when our power was exercised in education, we stated that its task was to educate men and women to win the war, build a new society and develop our country.

Our teaching is aimed at making science serve the people and the revolution, and at making pupils, students and intellectuals into workers at the service of other workers.

When we took power on the health front, we stated that hospital work should put into practice the principle that the revolution frees the people.

We do not want hospitals for the rich staffed by technocrats who are rich and serve the rich. The luxury of bourgeois and colonialist hospitals is of no interest to us, since what we want is to make our hospitals into bases, operational detachments in the struggle against both physical disease and disease that subverts the mind – superstition, ignorance, tribalism and the bourgeois mentality.

In Cabo Delgado, Niassa, Tete and Manica e Sofala the companies and rich landowners are abandoning our areas and fleeing.

Hence our power is being established in production. It is no longer the companies and landowners who determine the aims of labour and production or who benefit from our efforts.

Today, since we have power, production is liberating man and giving him his identity as the transformer of nature and society. We produce in order to learn, and we learn in order to produce and struggle better; we produce to supply our needs, feed our children and families, and live better.

Our power creates collective production at the service of the people and the revolution, destroys the exploitative system of production and transforms individual producers into producers integrated into the community. Production, instead of dividing men into the exploited and exploiters, now unites them all, and makes them all the people's servants, promoting the welfare of the people.

In our liberated areas the colonial bourgeois state has been destroyed and feudal structures have disappeared. A new democratic form of power is emerging, which is our own.

Those who exercise power enjoy the genuine confidence of the masses, since their political growth has been within the struggle of the masses. They constantly discuss with the masses. New guidelines and directives, which come from discussion with and the practical experience of the masses, are adopted by the masses to be put into effect.

From the circle to the locality, and from district to provincial and national level, the people for the first time in our history have their own power which they do not regard as something alien to which they are subject.

Power that belongs to the exploited majority and imposes the will of the latter on the whole nation: such is our power.

Organizing Democratic Life

The exercise of power, its form and methods, must correspond to its content.

But often new wine is kept in old bottles – that is, new power may be expressed through old forms.

Our Statutes, in laying down the working methods of FRELIMO –
from Chapter VII, paragraph (a) – give a series of points which can be
summarized as follows: free discussion, the submission of the minority to
the majority, collective responsibility, and criticism and self-criticism as
regards work and behaviour.

Our Statutes, the content of our action, demand genuine democracy,
true freedom of opinion, and thorough discussion on any decision we
take.

That is why we give so much attention to meetings with the masses and
the fighters. These meetings enable us to sound out the true feelings and
awareness of the rank and file, discover the contradictions, and explain
and instil both the political line and the concrete directives for each
specific situation.

Our decisions must always be democratic in both content and form.
Democratic in content means that they must reflect the real interests of
the broad masses. Democratic in form means that the broad masses must
take part in reaching a decision, feeling that it is theirs and not something
imposed from above.

Obviously there are practical and emergency situations when someone in charge has to take it upon himself to make a decision on his own
without consulting anyone. In an ambush a commander cannot assemble
all the fighters so that they can take a vote on when to fire, when to attack
or retreat.

But, on the other hand, the more discussion a commander has with the
fighters before an action, giving them a grasp of the meaning and objective
of the battle they are undertaking, the difficulties they face and the best
tactics to adopt, the more disciplined they will be under fire and the more
prepared to make sacrifices, since victory depends on the fine fighting
that results from fine leadership that releases the initiative of the rank and
file.

Sometimes in the course of discussion a comrade may express himself
badly or even put forward an erroneous argument. We might be tempted
to use our authority and tell him to keep quiet. This will have a negative
result: first, because the speaker will feel misunderstood and will persist
in his error even to the extent of grumbling outside the meeting, and
second, and even more important, in order to oppose an erroneous
argument it is essential that everyone, or at least the great majority,
should understand how and why the argument is mistaken.

Democracy within the party is an essential precondition for each and
every one to feel committed and responsible for a situation, since the
creation and development of the situation are always closely tied.

Naturally there are different echelons within structures. In practice,
the type and character of each discussion will vary according to the level
at which it is being held; this is only natural. But the principle of discussion
and collective decision-making must always be maintained.

A bureaucratic decision, that is a decision taken purely and simply by the command or leadership without prior debate and explanation among the masses, may be excellent in content – though this is unlikely – but will not mobilize the masses who, in the final analysis, are the ones who have to adopt, implement and defend it.

A bureaucratic decision, however good its content, runs the risk of being unrelated to the masses' level of understanding; in other words, it may be unrealistic and set up a contradiction which would have been avoided if discussion had taken place.

Democratic discussion requires rigorous preparation. Before the discussion we must make a careful study of the subject, ascertain the general feeling on the issue, and be quite clear as to the party line on the matter.

Thus prepared, we are in a position to guide the discussion and formulate correct guidelines and precise watchwords.

We must always bear in mind that even if a guideline is correct in principle, it can often have a negative effect to seek to impose it if it does not correspond to the masses' level of understanding. In particular, guidelines that go against traditions should be introduced gradually, and only after thorough mobilization especially of the sector or sectors which are most affected by the tradition in question.

In guiding a discussion, we should use the tactic of uniting the enlightened sector, isolating the recalcitrant forces, and winning over the hesitant majority to a correct view.

We must not be abstract in our discussions, we must deal with concrete issues, and we must dig deep into the most painful facts so that everyone feels the real need to settle the problem.

A discussion should therefore be prepared in the same way as we prepare for a battle: carry out strategic and tactical reconnaissance of the items to be discussed, understand our weak and strong points and those we want to combat, and organize and deploy our arguments correctly, knowing how to advance and how to retreat if need be.

In order to carry out an offensive to democratize our working methods, we must pay special attention to political, economic and military democracy in our midst.

When working, we must always bear in mind that power belongs to the people, that we are all equally oppressed, humiliated, sold, exploited and massacred, and that we are brothers of the same class with one purpose: to serve the people. This is the basis of our unity, the starting-point for our democracy.

Political democracy is based on collective discussion, on a collective solution of our problems. Each and every one of us is expected to express his views on how best to serve the people in each specific situation. Each and every one of us is responsible for the life of our organization, for the development and consolidation of the struggle and the revolution. Each and every one of us has a duty to develop our political line creatively by drawing on the rich experience we have gained in political and armed struggle against the enemy, by transforming society and mobilizing nature's laws on behalf of collective progress.

Mistakes that are made, whether individual or collective, and violations of our political line and discipline, should serve to educate us. The lessons we learn from these mistakes should be discussed by the masses, so that they can acquire this new experience. Violations of our line and breaches of discipline should be the subject of discussion and public criticism by the masses. In so doing, on the one hand, we use our mistakes to deepen our political consciousness and, on the other, we put the defence of our line and discipline where they belong, in the hands of the people.

The tendency of certain comrades to hide the mistakes of those with responsibilities from the masses reflects a lack of political democracy and a lack of confidence in the masses. Power belongs to the working people. The political line reflects the interests of the mass of labourers, and discipline is the watchdog that defends the line. It is therefore clear that the defence of our line and discipline is first and foremost the task of the masses of the people, since this defence is the defence of their lives.

To entrust the masses with the task of criticizing mistakes, deviations and violations of our line and discipline is also to affirm that mistakes, deviations, violations and crimes are first and foremost political acts which reflect either inadequate understanding of our line or opposition to that line. Within this context, public criticism and denunciation provide political lessons that educate both us and those who contravene our line.

It is for this reason that we have generally opposed secret trials and any immediate concern with drawing up penal and disciplinary codes. When secret trials are brought in as a system it prevents the masses from exercising their power and opens the way to possible abuse. Moreover, legal codes tend to freeze dynamic development and the process of ceaseless change in which we are engaged, and can therefore easily depoliticize and bureaucratize justice.

Military democracy is ensured by the participation of everyone in absorbing our combat experience, in collective study of our country and of the enemy, in the lessons learned together from each operation, and in constant discussion on ways of spreading the armed struggle to new areas and consolidating our rear.

Economic democracy is an integral part of our fight to destroy the system of exploitation of man.

We ensure economic democracy by first abolishing the power of the companies and the exploiting colonialist-capitalist or traditional-feudal classes. By preventing these classes from exploiting the workers we are laying the foundations for economic democracy.

Our work of mobilizing and organizing the masses to transform individual and family production into collective production consolidates the process of economic democracy. Indeed, by doing this we prevent individual and family production from degenerating into exploitative ownership which would give rise to classes of new exploiters. At the same time, we give material form to the just principle that all our country's wealth and our efforts belong to the community, serve the community and are intended to advance and improve the living standards and welfare of the people.

In this context, work, participation in production, is not only a duty but also the right of each and everyone.

For the revolution there are no unemployed, no useless or disqualified, no talents that cannot be used. Everyone has both the duty and the right to take part in the common struggle to transform society and use natural resources for the benefit of the community. Taking part in production unites us with our class, and a refusal to participate reflects opposition to our line and support for the exploiters.

Collective discussion on ways to increase, diversify and improve our production, constant and collective synthesis of our positive and our negative experiences, and decisions taken jointly on the way to share out the fruits of production, taking into account the requirements of the war effort and of raising the living standards of the broad masses – all guarantee the development of economic democracy.

Within this framework, we can see that laziness in our midst and lack of respect for the property of the people and movement are serious infringements of both our political line and economic democracy, reflecting a parasitic and exploitative attitude.

The process and experience of democracy are new in our country. Our people have never known real democracy because they have always lived under the domination of various exploiting classes.

The revolution has brought democracy, which is already being asserted at several levels: political, economic and military. It is also exercised within the framework of the organization. In the present phase it is vital to broaden its field of application, thereby putting further into practice the principle that power belongs to the working masses.

In this context an important need, corresponding to the consolidation of power in the liberated areas, is gradually to extend the system of elections, starting at the lowest levels, to appoint civilian heads of the population, in other words the creation of truly democratic basic structures of administrative power.

It is clear that such elections cannot be anarchic, but must be guided in such a way that the choice of the masses falls on those who have internalized the party line in their thinking and behaviour, and who show initiative and organizing ability.

Here it is important to use great vigilance to prevent the election of people with exploitative tendencies, even though they may enjoy some popularity for subjective reasons or because of demagogic actions.

Old and young, men and women, all must take equal part in the choice and must show responsibility by fighting the archaic tendency to discriminate against women or young people.

We must realize that as the revolution advances and is consolidated, and life is reorganized, an ever clearer division of labour is established between political organization, administration and military structures.

The increasing involvement of elected representatives of the population in administrative tasks encourages the initiative of the masses and by accustoming them to a democratic life creates a sense of collective responsibility, and leads the masses to exercise power.

In the final phase, the definitive task of the political party is to lead, organize, guide and educate the masses; the task of the administrative structure is to put into practice decisions taken in the various fields of economic and social life; and the task of the military structure is to support and protect the masses, drive out our country's enemy, defend the country, and play an active part in its reconstruction.

The party leads and guides the reorganization of the life of the masses and national reconstruction, just as it guides and leads the army, setting the goals to be achieved and heightening political consciousness. The army creates the conditions for liberating the people and the land. The administration puts into practice directives on national reconstruction.

At the present stage, where administrative tasks are increasing and diversifying, we must progressively democratize our methods of working and of appointing officials.

Our working methods are not of secondary importance, as it is through them that we apply our decisions.

For a leadership body to work with the masses it must be united.

When there are contradictions in a leadership body, this gives rise to rumours, intrigue and slander. Each faction tries to mobilize support for its views, dividing the masses. When we are disunited we divide the masses and the fighters, causing the rank and file to lose confidence in the leadership, demobilizing it and making it inactive, and opening breaches through which the enemy penetrates. We ultimately divide our own friends.

To be united and to unite with the masses, we need to know ourselves well.

To know ourselves well is to be sure that we are correct in thinking and behaviour and, when something is wrong, to be ready to assume responsibility for it, submitting ourselves to criticism and self-criticism.

Unity within the leadership behind a correct line, at whatever level, is the driving force of any sector and the precondition for success in a task.

Just as a person must feed himself daily so that his body is able to cope with his tasks and difficulties, so does unity need daily sustenance.

Collective living, work and study, criticism and self-criticism, and mutual help are the food, salts and vitamins of unity.

Members of the leadership should not therefore live separately from one another, each absorbed in his own private world, only coming together when there is a meeting.

With due allowance, of course, for the tasks each of them has and for the fact that they have to travel about, the members of the leadership ought to make an effort to live together, to know one another better in day-to-day life and to understand each other's failings, so as to be in a better position to offer mutual correction. Working together, producing together, sweating together, suffering the rigours of the march together and overcoming the challenges of the enemy and the environment creates strong bonds of friendship and mutual respect. It is not by words that we are bound together, but by the many activities we share when serving the people; it is unity fed by sweat and suffering and blood that binds us together.

So when we feel that a companion is falling behind, we must make an effort to help him progress.

We must understand that the ignorance of one is a corporate weakness and affects the work of us all.

How, for example, can we accept the fact that a companion remains illiterate and unable to speak Portuguese when many of us can read and write and speak Portuguese? To make this comrade literate, to teach him to speak Portuguese, must the Central Committee meet and pass a resolution on the matter?

One person's weak point can never be anyone else's strong point, since the weakness of one, the mistake of one, makes everyone's work more difficult, jeopardizes our task, and weakens the community.

Our aim is to advance like the waves of the sea, advancing together, and leaving no one behind in ignorance or error; to organize political, scientific and literary studies so that we can jointly rise to the situation and avail ourselves of the techniques that will equip us to overcome difficulties; to use criticism and self-criticism frequently, as much to rectify our working methods as to correct individual errors and deviations.

However, we must be wary of making criticism and self-criticism a pious routine, a kind of confessional where we admit our sins, are absolved, receive penance, and then prepare to repeat the same acts.

We must vigorously combat the triumphalist spirit of complacency. Nothing is more absurd and bogus than to hear a comrade say that 'everything's fine, it's all going well'. Statements such as this reveal self-satisfaction and a routine approach, as well as lack of analysis and an inability to spot weak points and organize the fight against them. Lack of analysis and study leads to ignorance of problems and indecision in the face of concrete situations; and a ditherer has no authority in the eyes of the masses.

An individual is not made responsible, a leader, simply because he has been elected or appointed to perform a task. The real authority that makes a leader is political authority.

When a leader does not have the confidence of his colleagues and the masses, or has had it and lost it, he falls into the trap of administrative authority, authoritarianism.

To have political authority is primarily to reveal through one's behaviour and thinking that one has internalized the party's line and consistently lives by it.

A leader is at all times the representative, defender and examplar of FRELIMO's political line.

If a contradiction arises between the line and a leader's behaviour, he will be in no position to represent, defend and exemplify the line to the masses.

We have a common saying that he who has steak in his mouth cannot speak. In other words, however much an undisciplined person in a position of responsibility talks about discipline, he will in fact teach only indiscipline and through his own indiscipline foster liberalism and anarchy.

An official who misappropriates property of the party to satisfy his own interests and indulgences may make a thousand speeches on the importance of respecting the party's and the people's property and on the price paid in blood to acquire this property. The only effect will be to teach people corruption, and they will fight among themselves to see who can most benefit from the party's property, who can best turn the blood and sweat of the people to his own advantage.

An official who will not let his own hands become calloused may hold hundreds of meetings on production, but he will not persuade one person to be productive or set up a single co-operative.

An official who talks about collective production and wants to keep his own farm plot or livestock will continue to teach that we should retain private property.

An official who organizes the fight against traditions that oppress women but is the first to allow his sons and daughters to be subjected to initiation rites will actually mobilize the masses to remain submerged in reactionary traditions.

An official who comes to explain the importance of hygiene and health yet cannot dig a single latrine or clean his house and rid it of flies and mosquitoes, who does not boil his drinking water and continues to frequent medicinemen and witch doctors, leads the people to do the same by the example he sets.

In short, the masses will always say: he's saying this because he was told to say it, but his words are as empty as the wind – let them blow by and everthing will go on as before.

The end result when such a person is in charge is that he creates chaos with his behaviour and as he is afraid of being reprimanded by his superiors, and afraid of being dismissed from the post that he has surrounded with privileges, he will impose a kind of dictatorship over the masses in order to create an elegant façade when everything is in ruins.

Instead of using discussion and persuasion, he will shout his orders and impose punishments and yet at the same time, since his way of life creates obligations, he will not be able to punish his accomplices, so provoking a general atmosphere of injustice, and he cannot punish those who know his weak points, so encouraging liberalism.

Such an official will create all the conditions for fostering contra-dictions among the masses, divisions, and a door wide open to rumour and intrigue. In short, he establishes an enemy base where there should be a broadcasting centre for FRELIMO's way of life.

Political authority demands high discipline of an official – that is, his ideas, determination and conduct must be totally identified with FRELIMO's line and the decisions of the competent bodies. In addition, political authority requires competence, willingness to learn, ability to recognize one's own limitations and determination to overcome them.

An incompetent is in no position to lead or organize. To maintain his position he will have to impose decisions, and as these will inevitably be erroneous ones, he will have to block discussion and criticism. At the same time, he will oppress all those in whom he sees higher qualities, since he is conscious only of his own ambition, ignores the needs of the community, and sees the competence of others as competition.

The more competent someone is the more willing he is to learn from others, and the easier it is for him to recognize his own limitations and overcome them. He will always foster a collective spirit and discussion, encourage the initiative of his subordinates, and fight the bureaucracy that hinders progress.

A leader must have an overall view of things, since only this will enable him to understand how his task or field of activity fits into the general process of struggle. In this way, he will be able to decide what are short-, medium- and long-term objectives and what are priorities in his work.

Establishing correct priorities means that work can be planned. Plan-ning means organizing material and human resources, creating the politi-cal and material conditions for achieving the planned objectives within the time set, and establishing the right strategy and tactics to make optimum use of the resources to meet the plan.

A final quality demanded of a leader is: constant concern to improve the living standards of the masses and fighters. The aim of the revolution is to raise living standards.

This implies material changes which will provide an objective basis for raising the standard of living. This in turn demands explanation and education, so that the need for change as well as the ways of benefiting from and using change are understood.

For example, it is not enough to make a vegetable plot; people must also understand the benefits of eating salad and how to prepare it. It is not enough to dig pit latrines in a village or base; their necessity and use must also be explained.

In the final analysis, those responsible for leadership express our political line.

Their main qualifications are their defence of our line, and concern for the life of our political organization and for the life of the masses and fighters.

This is the supreme criterion for assessing the value of our work, the touchstone for distinguishing between correct, effective leadership and incorrect and incompetent leadership.

In the colonialist and capitalist area, leadership is judged in terms of the benefits its activity brings to the exploiting classes and its capacity to impede and repress the demands put forward by the mass movement.

Since our aim is to serve the people, and power belongs to the people, our criterion is the change effected in our society and the use of our natural resources for the benefit of the broad masses.

Broadcasting Centres for Our Line

Any one of our centres – educational or health, child-care or trading post, co-operative or detachment, base or district – has in addition to its particular task the fundamental role of being a broadcasting centre for our line and new life-style, of being a model for the new society under construction and for the new social relations between people.

Like a light on a dark night showing the way to follow, our centres show the masses how our new society is being built. This means that the centres must be dynamic agents in changing people's outlook and must be driving forces in mobilizing nature's laws and resources to raise the living standards of the masses. In the process of changing man and society we encounter numerous obstacles.

Our task is to transform the vast, diverse and valuable mass that from the Rovuma to the Maputo and from the Tete borders to the Indian Ocean constitute our people. There are old people encrusted with archaic traditions and young people corrupted by the false values of colonialism and capitalism. We have women who have been oppressed by society for centuries and had their initiative stifled. Our ranks are joined by lawyers and engineers, sociologists and economists, technicians and intellectuals, often brainwashed by the bourgeoisie into despising manual labour and seeing themselves as a ruling élite with nothing to learn. But we also find illiterate peasants with a knowledge of the world limited to their village horizon, where colonial domination has instilled the notion that they form an ignorant and brutish mass incapable of rational thought or initiative. From the factories and mines, from the sawmills and the plantations, from the transport industry comes an embryonic working class whose class consciousness is low and which is not yet ready to play its leading role in the process of transforming society. From the administration and offices, from business and the banks we are joined by civil servants and clerks riddled with petty-bourgeois attitudes.

The rural and urban areas send us a continual stream of new supporters with their particular defects. Life in the rural areas is especially disorganized, with no sense of planning or punctuality, and deeply affected by routine and obsolete traditions that hamper progress and paralyse initiative. To the peasant, power means the hostile, foreign government whose presence is felt in identity cards and taxes, through forcible recruitment and the low prices set for the sale of painfully gathered crops, through the *palmatória* and the *machila*. Fear stifles initiative. Man lives in constant contradiction with unknown nature that he dreads, with a state that exploits, oppresses and humiliates him. His social relations go little further than the village where he lives and at best to the language group to which he belongs.

In the colonial-capitalist city there is a fierce struggle for survival and this forces people to be selfish and competitive. Over-ambition and the struggle to exploit others more effectively destroy confidence between people and turn them into rivals. Civil servants and employees foment slander and intrigue against colleagues to be promoted over their heads. They fawn on their superiors, pull strings, form cliques of some against others, and humiliate themselves just to hang on to their daily bread. The degenerate colonial-capitalist culture glorifies decadent and corrupt tastes that dehumanize man. A desire for power and luxury built on the exploitation and humiliation of fellow beings is instilled into each individual.

The wave of colonial-Fascist oppression swamps the countryside and, still more, the towns. PIDE activities aim to keep people in permanent terror so that they will resign themselves to the fateful destiny of exploitation and domination.

The launching of the struggles and the victories we have won reveal concretely that there is no such thing as fateful destiny: we are capable of transforming society and creating a new life.

That is why people are seeking out FRELIMO. They all loathe the enemy, oppression and humiliation, exploitation and terror, even if their definition of the enemy is not always very clear. They all yearn for freedom and are ready to sacrifice themselves for it even if they do not yet fully know how to describe its content. They all aspire to a different world although they would be hard put to spell out what the difference would be.

So, lacking clarity, with their doubts and uncertainties, their vices and defects, with moribund traditions and decadent tastes, in the grip of tribalism or individualism, with initiative stifled and a fear of using their brain, with inherited and imposed complexes, they come one by one to the struggle, come one by one to FRELIMO seeking a clear answer, the right path.

Our task is to integrate them all and transform them into servants of the people, into fighters who defend the interests of the exploited masses, into militants in the cause of the country's liberation.

There will be no miracles to help us in this gigantic task. The transformation process is made by the men and women we are through continual struggle against our own limitations.

For us to transform ourselves and those who join us every day, we must be organized, in other words have the machinery and structures capable of putting the political line into effect. Unless we are organized we shall not be able to transform ourselves but, on the contrary, we shall be held back by the habits and tastes of the other area.

Being organized means first of all having structures. The structure provide FRELIMO's organized presence among us. They show us what our task is and how we are integrated into the body of FRELIMO. Without structures, or in other words without integration in FRELIMO, we shall be isolated like limbs without a trunk.

It is obvious that however intelligent, dynamic, hard-working and dedicated a person is, he cannot on his own do all the work of the centre where he is. It is the structures that provide suitable mechanisms for sharing out the tasks among us. The structures provide the appropriate channels for solving problems we face in our work and lives.

Through the structures we ensure discussion of our problems, find how to apply the line creatively to every concrete situation we face. It is within the framework of our structures that we correct our working methods.

Structures are the instrument for democratizing our life, since they lead to everyone's participation in an organized manner and to a collective solution of problems. When we involve everyone in problem-solving, when we make everyone feel responsible for solving the problems that arise, we are collectivizing our leadership, collectivizing our lives.

Structures do not drop from the sky; they are the product of specific situations and answer specific needs. This means that structures must be operative, that is must meet the particular needs and circumstances of a given centre. They must allow for the centre's tasks to be shared out and co-ordinated, both for the main task and for other revolutionary tasks.

Clearly we are not in a static situation: the development of the struggle and the enemy action are constantly changing our situation. A changing situation and circumstances require the structures to adapt themselves. The structures must adapt themselves to life, and life must not be subordinated to the structures. This means that structures must be flexible, must always be responsive to the actual situation.

The function of the structures is to ensure continuity and development of work, to permit our tasks to be carried out correctly in all circumstances; in other words they must be dynamic as they are the transmission belts that drive the machine.

But structures are also human beings, for without them they become dummies drawn more or less skilfully on a sheet of paper or a board.

In the revolutionary process, errors and deviations are frequent, even when the line is clear and the structures adequate. And we must blame such errors and deviations on our own shortcomings.

The development of our revolution, the spread and consolidation of our armed struggle provoke new contradictions. Each advance brings a reaction, revolution is always opposed by counter-revolution.

The principal contradiction arising among us in the current phase is that between the demands of the situation and our capabilities. The struggle and the establishment of people's power are developing more speedily than the consciousness and capacity of cadres, who bear the burden of the task of guiding, channelling and stimulating the overall process.

The main aspect of this contradiction is visible in the inability of cadres in some centres to find their own correct answers to the different problems that crop up. It is seen in the difficulty they have in defining and planning tasks, and the failure of the centres to integrate and transform the growing numbers of personnel and the increasingly large population for which they are responsible.

But we all have a clear guiding line, a line that has stood the practical test: the FRELIMO line, which covers all aspects of our life and all sectors of our struggle. Creative analysis of the line enables us to find the appropriate response for each particular situation we face. Our structures have been following the changing situation, we are always organizing ourselves. We have the masses with us, we have the structures and the line.

So what is the cause of the contradiction? How shall we resolve the contradiction and move on to a higher stage? The answer lies in the cadres who are the decisive factor in the application of the line and in the effectiveness of our structures.

We ask: why is it that veteran cadres in the struggle, who through immense sacrifice built what we have today, are now letting themselves, in a manner of speaking, be overtaken by events?

The prime cause of this situation is the spirit of triumphalism. The great victories we have won, on the battlefield, and in eliminating reactionary forces and enemy infiltration among us, and in national reconstruction, have led certain comrades to see only a string of victories, and to underestimate the enemy, by looking always on the bright side and never learning from setbacks or studying how to overcome our limitations.

So those comrades stop studying our line and think they already know it well enough: the proof is there in the victories. The outcome is the abandonment of political analysis, a blunting of our awareness of deviations from and attacks on the line, and so we fail to detect and nip in the bud the enemy's ideological, moral and physical infiltration.

They neglect scientific study, thinking they already know enough; and there again the proof is in the victories. But development of the war and national reconstruction demand increasingly sound and more advanced scientific knowledge that we still lack. As a result of this attitude, our own ignorance hampers progress, and anything that does not progress stagnates and rots.

They stop studying the enemy, believing that they know him well enough, and that the proof is there in the victories. But the enemy's manoeuvres are constantly changing, and his criminal and desperate intent hardens at each defeat. If we do not constantly study the enemy, if we underestimate him, we fall into routine and then we are caught on the hop by new enemy manoeuvres, by his new crimes. So instead of us keeping on the offensive, instead of destroying the snake in the egg, we fall back on the defensive and we find the snake full-grown and rearing its poisonous head to destroy us.

Little by little internal struggle is abandoned, as we are already purified enough, we are sufficiently distinct from the enemy since we have no physical contact with him. Little by little the old life, the life of the other area creeps in, liberalism is introduced, corruption starts, obligations begin to paralyse us, mistaken ideas are rife, superstition spreads. This creates a lax atmosphere, so mistrust and injustice worm their way in, then there is division and the enemy finds that the soil is becoming fertile ground on which to act.

The triumphalist spirit is a manifestation of ultra-leftist opportunism: it leads us to underestimate the enemy, and into adventurism. Sooner or later triumphalism will be paid for in sacrifice, and the mistakes we are making will cost us dearly in heavy and unnecessary losses.

Triumphalism is twin brother to defeatism, ultra-left opportunism is the other side of the coin of rightist opportunism.

When we suffer setbacks as a consequence of the errors of triumphalism, the adventurists then become defeatist, overestimate the enemy, and begin to consider only the failures, and overlook advances in the struggle. As they had been expecting a quick victory, the war now seems 'endless' to their minds. The past victories were in their view fortuitous and isolated.

In this mood they begin to carry out their tasks with an obvious lack of enthusiasm, totally lose sight of the whole, are quick to spot mistakes in the work of other comrades but refuse to point out and discuss these mistakes and propose remedies. They prefer grumbling to criticism and self-criticism, intrigue to open discussion. They form their cliques, their allies.

Merely studying failures, merely seeing mistakes becomes a way of justifying and concealing their abandonment of a revolutionary stance, their loss of appetite for work. They invent imaginary illnesses and problems, and present themselves as being misunderstood, persecuted, martyrs to conspiracies and enemies that exist only in their fevered and idle imagination. Their bodies remain in our area, but their spirits have already moved to the other area, with their dream of comfort and corruption as ideals.

Another shortcoming that is frequently linked to these other attitudes is the 'veteran' or 'old hand' spirit in war and politics, the know-all who has nothing to learn especially from the younger generations. The new generations in particular with their dynamism and eagerness to bring in new ideas and methods are treated as unwelcome competitors coming along to displace the 'veterans' from their set ways and privileges.

Such 'veterans' who are veterans only by virtue of long service and not in a wealth of absorbed experience to be passed on to new generations are mentally stagnant. They perform their tasks to a set routine and are not concerned with bringing in new methods inspired by the experience they have acquired. When they work they are not thinking about doing the task as well and as quickly as possible, and when they make mistakes they excuse them by saying that it is human to err. They are ashamed to admit to their own ignorance, and refusing to learn they stick to their old mistaken ways. Their long service is a pretext to claim privileges and to demand priority for their selfish personal problems. They expect special treatment because of their long service and they forget that we demand of veterans an especially exemplary morale and behaviour to educate us in the new life. They prevent the promotion of new cadres and forces, and try to create mistrust of them. They do this because they have lost their vision of the whole and the idea of the growing needs of the war and national reconstruction. They are concerned about positions, not about the tasks of the struggle, they want to preserve the privileges and routines that turn them into small capitalists.

Such manifestations reveal the permanent contradiction between the old and new, progress and routine, developmentalism and conservatism. This contradiction is characteristic of all revolutions and the right way to treat it is to train cadres in a progressive spirit, in a vision of the whole and in a sense of serving the masses by winning over new generations to build on the work.

The new generations too must be properly trained. The new generations, in our liberated areas and when they grow up in our centres, are often regarded automatically as 'revolutionaries', steeped in our line. They think that themselves too. So sometimes political work among them is neglected, as is the collective fight against the tastes, vices and defects of the other area. There is an unjustified assumption that the new generations are freed from the past simply by growing up away from the enemy presence.

This is a serious and dangerous mistake that could lead to the forming of petty reactionaries in our midst, when we fondly believe that we are training those who will carry on the revolution.

We must be aware that the new generations are growing up in contact with the old generations who are passing on the vices of the past. Our practical experience shows how children and young people in our own centres can be contaminated by decadent ideas, habits and tastes. In our situation enemy subversion too plays a key role in introducing and fostering values and practices from the other area. Lastly, so long as there is capitalism and imperialism in the world, its propaganda and subversion will make itself felt against us, and the winning of independence and power will be no guarantee of our invulnerability to degenerate values.

Indeed one cannot in ten or twenty years overcome the dead weight of a millennia-old inheritance. The values, tastes and ideas from the past, though contrary to our line, our life-style and progress, are still strong. The struggle has shaken them but it is still very early for us to hymn the victories. This political fight will have to be pursued for decades, until a new outlook has really won over almost the whole of society and new problems and contradictions come up that demand new battles. Moreover the new generations have grown up without direct contact with the exploitation, oppression and humiliation typical of colonialist and capitalist society. They experience the shelling, but have never known the *palmatória*, they have fought against helicopters, but have never been subjected to forced labour, they have wiped out enemy soldiers but were never arrested for non-payment of taxes, they have witnessed crimes but were never sold to the mines.

Within the broad masses there is a wealth of experience of suffering, an enormous store of hatred for the enemy. But the experiences are not sufficiently compared, not sufficiently absorbed for the knowledge and hatred of the enemy and exploitation to be deepened. It might be said that the experience of suffering that should serve to shape the new generations and consolidate the consciousness of the masses in general is being wasted.

An ideological and organizational offensive is required to overcome these shortcomings and resolve the contradictions of the present phase. This means acting at section and group level in respect of army organization, and at circle level in regard to mass organization.

But if we are really to transform the sections and circles into basic cells and centres of our political life, we must work on the cadres since they have the task of activating the rank and file.

We must lend dynamism to every work sector through those who in their behaviour and thinking demonstrate that they have responded creatively to our line and form part of our organization's vanguard. They have initiative and a vision of the whole, are ready to link their main task with other revolutionary tasks, engage in the internal struggle, study, and with sensitivity to the least deviation from, or attack on, the line, defend discipline as the sentinel of our political line.

Apart from the specific problems and ills affecting each sector, the leadership and the cadres must concern themselves with the following:

a) representing, instilling and defending our line in their sector;

b) projecting and defending our discipline as the sentinel of our policy;

c) putting politics in the commanding position in all our activities;

d) organizing the work sector, in the spirit of the conflict between two lines and the growing dividing line between us and the enemy, and acquiring a vision of the whole and the linkage of the principal task with other revolutionary tasks;

e) organizing and guiding militants in daily critical analysis of individual and collective activities, synthesis of experience, freeing of initiative and elimination of routine approaches in favour of an innovatory and progressive approach;

f) organizing and guiding the work sector in political study, the teaching of literacy and higher scientific knowledge, study and analysis of our own and the enemy's situation;

g) maintaining an intensive and permanent collective battle to purge our ranks of incorrigible elements who are impervious to the line and persist in corrupt tastes, vices and defects, refusing to change;

h) organizing and guiding study of the theoretical and practical side of other revolutions so as to derive useful lessons for our own situation and to train militants in the internationalist revolutionary frame of mind.

We might say in essence that the ideological offensive should build in us a strong political consciousness based on three central points: 1) thorough knowledge of our political line; 2) intimate knowledge of our struggle, in its evolution and in its significance for our people and the other peoples of the world; 3) total trust in the masses united and organized under the leadership of our correct line, in the consciousness that the masses in this framework understand and respond to the struggle with their creative energy, and are invincible to any enemy whatever its strength.

This activating process requires careful research to identify the concrete problems in the sector where we must act and to choose the activist nucleus who must genuinely comprise vanguard elements.

If we inspire the cadres who are the decisive factor in putting our political line into effect, we shall then be in a position to transform the sections and circles into basic cells for our political organization.

This action will enable us to structure and transform the life of the masses who in growing numbers are joining our organization, and will thus ensure the consolidated broadening of our front. This action will also create conditions for establishing among us the organized vanguard of our people and the labouring and exploited classes, as the indispensable instrument for developing the people's democratic revolution in Mozambique.

Within this context the character of relations between our centres and the mass of the people has a fundamental role. The masses are the source of life for our organization, they are the principal and decisive force in the process of our country's liberation and in the building of a new society. The fight is made and won by them and is intended to meet their interests.

Any centre of ours is a collective centre at the service of the masses, a centre that by absorbing the revolution's experiences brings those experiences to the broad masses in order to develop the process of social change.

We serve the masses by setting an example in implementing our line. When our behaviour as militants reflects the line, we are training the masses in the new life.

We serve the masses by setting an example of organized living, by teaching them the methods of organization and guiding them in organizing themselves more effectively.

It is by organizing the masses and creating democratic and popular structures among them that we shall be able to transform society. The structures created in the circle will guide the peasants, the cattle raisers, fishermen and craftsmen to organize collectively in production co-operatives, to improve their production techniques, to raise production and so in turn the living standards of the masses. Obviously the example of collective production in the centres and the results achieved – in fields and market gardens, orchards, and natural or artificial fishponds – will be the best testimony to the value and credibility of our collective capacity to transform society.

The structures created in the circle will lead the masses to organize detachments to counter any enemy attack against the village, its fields and workplaces. Organizational work will transform every village and field into a source of chastisement and casualties for the enemy. With the example of each of our centres as a defence against enemy aggression, with our work of military training for the masses, with our ability to arouse the imagination and initiative of the masses in combining traditional weapons and animal traps with modern weapons, it will be impossible for the enemy to consider any widespread action against our people.

The structures created in the circle will raise the political conscious-ness of the masses and draw a sharp dividing line between them and the enemy, and thus make the masses more acutely aware of enemy manoeuvres and infiltration which can be stopped at source.

In the final analysis it is this structuring process that makes the libera-tion of an area irreversible, and enables us to repel enemy invasion and aggression on whatever scale.

Clearly for our centres to activate life for the broad masses and change society, each centre and each militant assigned there must fulfil the mission of serving the masses and must always in an exemplary and unfailing manner show total respect for the interests of the masses.

We can never allow any militant of ours to dare to misuse the power or the weapon entrusted to him for the people's service, by violating the people's interests to the smallest degree. We must be intransigent about any liberties taken with women, any misuse of the people's property, or any injustice committed against the population. This is an integral part of our political line and discipline, and a precondition for the masses to be able at all times and without fail to distinguish our actions from those of the enemy.

Serving the masses by handing them the invincible weapon provided by our line and experience and guiding them to a higher ideological and organizational level is the mission of all our centres in their relations with the masses.

We are beginning the tenth year of our people's liberation war against Portuguese colonialism and imperialism. During these ten years of armed struggle, and these twelve years of FRELIMO's existence, the situation in our country and the world has undergone profound changes.

Our initial aim of national independence has gained in depth in the process of developing people's war, by creating the basis for a national and democratic people's revolution, for the establishment of people's power, the power of the broad labouring masses in our country.

The expansion of the armed struggle to areas where the substantial economic and strategic interests of imperialism predominate has brought a direct confrontation with the latter and brought to the fore the anti-imperialist character of our fight.

The heavy political and military defeats suffered by the Portuguese colonial forces and their manifest inability to halt the advance of the fight for liberation have obliged the enemy leadership to modify the pattern of aggression against our people in the hope of preserving basic imperialist interests: exploitation of the country's work-force, plunder of our resources and destruction of the revolutionary movement in southern Africa in particular and on the continent as a whole.

South African and Rhodesian entry into the war against us comes in this context of increased military, financial and technical support for the enemy, and the exchange of notes on aggression between the Portuguese colonialists and their allies and the imperialist states, notably the United States, France, Federal Germany and Britain. So the internationalization of aggression against our people has become a fact and the colonial war has already become an imperialist war of aggression.

The enemy command, with the aim of cutting down its alarmingly heavy casualties, has decided to change the colour of the corpses, by 'Mozambicanizing' the war, with the establishment of a puppet army forcibly recruited and led by Portuguese: the OPV, GE, GEP, etc. This procedure will also help conceal from world opinion the foreign aggression against our people.

The changes in the situation demand an appropriate response from us. We said in the past that our essential tasks were to intensify political work among cadres, to extend the struggle and consolidate our own areas. The Fifth Session (December 1972) of our Central Committee elected by the Second Congress, when giving us the watchword of generalizing the offensive to tip the balance of forces with the enemy in our favour, made it clear that this would require spreading our line to the people, that is seeing that the broad masses understand and adopt our line, and making our working methods more democratic and our leadership collective.

As more recently we studied the means of putting these directives into effect, we laid down two basic guidelines; intensifying the ideological offensive aimed at cadres, fighters and the masses, and intensifying organizational work in forming groups and sections as basic cells in the army, and in making circles the basis for our political activity among the masses.

The various FRELIMO centres – military, educational, health, child-care, production and marketing – have a decisive role to play: they are the broadcasting centres for our line. It is their job to provide a practical demonstration to the broad masses of the superiority and correctness of our principles and aims.

In short our centres have a duty to pass on FRELIMO's political line to the masses in a dynamic manner. Each of our militants has the responsibility of making our revolution take root in our country, and of ensuring its victory, which is the sole justification for the immense sacrifices already made and the sea of blood that has been shed.

The answers are found in our centres, and there we have the forges of the New Man, of the new society. So as we prepare to mark the tenth year of our people's war, we issue to all our centres and militants this watchword:

'DRAW A DIVIDING LINE BETWEEN OUR POWER AND THE ENEMY'S POWER, ESTABLISH PEOPLE'S POWER TO SERVE THE MASSES.'

2. The People's Democratic Revolutionary Process in Mozambique*

The Nature of the Enemy

For a long time and particularly for most observers in Western countries, Portuguese colonialism seemed almost a fossilized phenomenon, an anachronistic whim of a dictator still living in the time of the Conference of Berlin.

A well-orchestrated propaganda campaign about the unique virtues of a colonialism that purported to be multiracial and unfurled the supposed virtues of a recently invented Lusotropicalism contributed to the acceptance here and there of illusions about the benevolence of Portuguese colonial exploitation.

Strict censorship, ferocious repression, systematic cultural obscurantism, careful selection of visitors to the territories and even more careful choice of their itineraries allowed a heavy curtain of silence to be drawn around the Portuguese colonies, thus isolated from the world.

The launching in the period 1961–64 of armed struggles for liberation dealt a death blow to the propaganda campaigns that portrayed the peoples of the Portuguese colonies as content with their lot.

At the same time, the revelation of the increasingly sadistic, infamous and habitual crimes of the colonial soldiery tore away any pretensions as to the uniquely benevolent or virtuous character of Portuguese colonialism.

The replacement of Salazar and the continuation and expansion of the colonial war under his successor, the strengthening of economic and military alliances that have sustained the colonial war for more than a decade, the spread of aggression to countries bordering the Portuguese colonies, the increasing role of non-Portuguese personnel and weapons in the war – in sum the growing internationalization of the colonial war –

*This text is based on the first published version, which was prepared for the Soviet Academy of Sciences in February 1974, and published in 1975 in Moscow, under the following title: Samora Moise Machel, 'Razvitie narodnovo-demokraticheskoi revolutsii v Mozambique', *Borba za osvobozhdenie Portugalski koloni v Afrike 1961–1973*, Moskva, 'Nauka', 1975 ('Development of the People's Democratic Revolution in Mozambique', *National Liberation Struggle in the Portuguese African Colonies 1961–1973*, Moscow, *Science*, 1975).

have all compelled the various observers to place the Portuguese colonial war in its genuine context.

The nature of Portuguese colonialism and of the alliances supporting it has imposed armed struggle on us as the sole instrument by which to solve the contradictions that pit us against foreign domination in our country.

However, the process of the struggle's development in Mozambique has brought a qualitative change. The struggle is waged by masses who have precise interests, specific demands. These interests and demands are becoming clearer through the process of fighting and put a certain imprint on the struggle.

The creation of liberated areas brings to the fore the issue of who has power, who should wield it and who should benefit from it, in the same way as it puts at issue the kinds of social relations of production, whether those inherited from the traditional society or the recent colonial innovations.

So in the actual course of armed struggle for national liberation, there has been unleashed a process aimed at installing power based on an alliance of the exploited social strata in our country, and bringing to fruition the national liberation struggle by destroying the system of exploitation of man and building a new society.

In other words, the primary demand for national independence has been supplemented, in an initial phase, by giving real substance to independence and, in a further phase, by raising the essential question of the kind of regime to be built.

It was not a matter of a long-term abstract plan, which could as a complete package be imposed on the actual process, nor of constant improvisation resulting from some kind of spontaneity or other mechanism. In fact the evolution grows out of a dialectical relationship between on the one hand FRELIMO's political guidance, the development of the armed struggle and of mass consciousness, and on the other the kind of contradictions current between the exploited masses and the exploitative society.

Awareness of these contradictions has been accelerated by the war situation which on a day-to-day basis has stripped concealment from the forces supporting the enemy; the captured weapon, the aircraft brought down, the tank or lorry destroyed are invariably of non-Portuguese origin. Likewise consciousness of the sacrifice offered brings a demand for liberation to take the form of radical transformation of society and its internal relations and structures.

This combination of facts means that our liberation struggle is a people's struggle in the form and content of its demands against Portuguese colonialism and imperialism, against exploitation of man.

The Social Nature of the Front and Its Political Line

Mozambican people, workers and peasants, workers on the plantations, in the timber mills and in the concessions, workers in the mines, on the

35

railways, in the harbours and in the factories, intellectuals, civil servants, Mozambican soldiers in the Portuguese army, students, men, women and young people, patriots,

In the name of all of you, FRELIMO today solemnly proclaims the general armed insurrection of the Mozambican people against Portuguese colonialism for the attainment of the complete independence of Mozambique.

Our fight must not cease before the total liquidation of Portuguese colonialism.

Long live FRELIMO!
Long live Mozambique!
Long live Africa!

(The Central Committee proclamation of the launching of armed struggle for national liberation, 25 September 1964.)

Unification of the Nationalist Movement

The nature of the struggle, a struggle for national independence that destroys foreign domination opposed to the interests of all Mozambican social strata, explains the concern for unity that from the start has dominated the Mozambican patriotic movement.

The experience of wars of resistance against colonial conquest (still fresh in the population's memory – the Barue revolt ended in 1918) shows clearly that the essential explanation of the colonialist victory lies in the disunited and dispersed character of the resistance. But these objective facts were not discovered automatically and a long struggle was needed to bring the triumph of unity.

From the end of the 1950s, patriotic movements were formed outside Mozambique, essentially among groups of economic exiles settled in neighbouring countries.

UDENAMO, the National Democratic Union of Mozambique, was formed in Southern Rhodesia by recruiting members among workers and emigrants mainly from Manica e Sofala and Gaza Provinces and from Lourenço Marques.

UNAMI, African National Union of Independent Mozambique, was established in Malawi, finding its members particularly among those originally from Tete, Zambezia and Niassa Provinces.

MANU, originally called the Maconde African National Union and later the Mozambique African National Union, was formed in Mombasa by bringing together members particularly of Maconde origin from Cabo Delgado Province.

This activity, as we see, was unable to free itself completely of tribalism and regionalism, and was unable to unite broad masses for the task of national liberation. There are various explanatory factors. Instigation by colonialism of tribal, religious and other rivalries, a lack of experience and political culture in the militants, most of whom were very young, are the essential factors.

However, the existence of several organizations does not really reflect a political and social cleavage. The organizations were established among *émigré* and exile groups, according to the place where they were living, and often they did not know of the others' existence. The fact is that a proliferation of organizations is not the kind of thing to mobilize the masses.

Events in the Congo, the launching of the liberation struggle in Angola, the independence of Tanganyika, acted as a stimulus to patriotic feeling. But it was above all the evolution within Mozambique that was to launch the unifying movement.

In parallel with patriotic agitation abroad, patriotic action was developed within Mozambique, particularly in the urban centres of Beira and Lourenço Marques and in the areas where there was an embryo of farming co-operatives as in Gaza, Cabo Delgado and Manica e Sofala. At the same time small groups launched a theoretical debate often through cultural, recreational and mutual aid societies. This is the case of the Nucleus of African Secondary School Students of Mozambique (NESAM), and the Negroes Association Centre of Mozambique, etc.

These groups, although numerically weak and subject to constant repression, appeared as an expression of patriotic feeling that above all stirred the urban masses. Their numerical weakness does not give a true picture of the significant and dynamizing impact they had on public opinion.

The 1961 visit to Mozambique by Comrade Eduardo Chivambo Mondlane, at the time a United Nations official, crystallized and accelerated the sense of unity and the aspiration for national liberation. The contacts he made during the visit and the simple, clear and sound platform he proposed to the various scattered forces were to launch the process that was to lead to the formation of the national liberation movement.

Action by Comrade Eduardo Chivambo Mondlane and by other comrades, with the support of groups inside, finally resulted in bringing together MANU and UDENAMO on 25 May 1962, for the purpose of discussing unification of the nationalist movement. A unification protocol was signed between the two organizations. UNAMI, feeling the pressure in favour of unity, was obliged to put its signature to the unification protocol.

In accordance with the protocol, the three groups disbanded on 25 June 1962 and established FRELIMO – the Mozambique Liberation Front. A provisional leadership headed by Comrade Eduardo Chivambo Mondlane was charged with organizing FRELIMO's First Congress and this was held from 23 to 28 September 1962.

FRELIMO at its founding defined itself as a mass organization open to all Mozambicans, without distinction of sex, ethnic origin, religious belief or place of domicile, provided that they accepted FRELIMO's Statutes and Programme and pledged themselves to follow FRELIMO's political line.

37

The First Congress spelled out FRELIMO's aims; total elimination of foreign domination and of all traces of colonialism and imperialism; the winning of immediate and complete independence; the building of a developed, modern, prosperous and strong Mozambique. FRELIMO outlined the work priorities to put its purpose into effect.

It was primarily a matter of mobilizing and organizing the broad mass of the people, whose objective interests and aspirations were expressed in the Front's Programme; and of bringing the masses to an understanding of the strategy and tactics of national liberation.

The then recent Mueda massacre, the brutal repression unleashed against Angola, the reinforcing of colonial military forces and the intro-duction of PIDE with its terrorist campaign of intimidation, all made it apparent that national liberation would demand the resort to armed struggle. So the second aim was to prepare for the launching of armed struggle for national liberation, notably by training the politico-military cadres necessary for the undertaking.

In the third place it was essential to launch an overseas campaign to unmask Portuguese colonialism and to mobilize international solidarity in favour of the Mozambican people.

Finally, in consequence of the particularly obscurantist nature of Portuguese colonialism, it was imperative to bring a rapid improvement in the level of scientific understanding: scientific and arts education was seen as a priority, a precondition for the eventual development of armed struggle and national reconstruction.

The simple and clear theses that FRELIMO put forward found a positive and almost instant echo in all social strata, in all regions of the country.

The mission of the first organizers FRELIMO sent on underground work did not in practice turn out to be persuading the population of the justness of the cause or of the need for struggle. It was rather to organize the people, that is to give them specific tasks in preparing the launch of the struggle. But the success FRELIMO encountered, the massive adherence of the population, and the enthusiasm that was awakened, did not in the least mean that the essential question of unity had been finally solved.

In fact, unity came out of a continual process of meeting the people's demands, and during this process there was rejection and absorption.

Unity in the Continual Process of Defending the Masses' Interests
The unity process is described, in many FRELIMO texts and in meetings and discussions among militants, as following three phases in constant succession: unity – criticism – unity.

One phase of unity reached is followed by practical experience which shows up weak and strong points of the unity that has been attained and indicates the demands of the new situations provoked by the development of the struggle and of awareness. There then follows a phase of criticism during which ideas, forces and forms of conduct are rejected if they do not correspond to the actual phase and have the effect of undermining unity by introducing obsolete values. A higher stage of unity is thus attained.

The transmission line of the process, the touchstone for discovering deviations, is the objective interest of the working masses and the consequent progress of the revolution. In the criticism process the question was constantly being raised: who is helped by this idea, this method, this conduct? Which area is represented by this phemomenon, ours or the enemy's?

Unity, therefore, is not something static, a supernatural and absolute value that we place on a pedestal to worship. In the process of struggling for unity we have always said: we must know with whom we are uniting and why.

We have experienced this process constantly since FRELIMO's foundation and – as it was put by the Central Committee in its April 1969 session – the revolution is like a river, as it goes along it swells by drawing in fresh strength, but it also gradually throws out on the bank the debris it carries.

When FRELIMO was established in 1962, its aim was to offer the masses an alternative to surrender. Almost the entire Mozambican people rejected colonial domination, but the consciousness of the masses was low, organizational experience almost nil, and repression strong. In this context it was a matter of showing that victory is possible through united combat against the common enemy, Portuguese colonialism.

Unity could be reached on this point in 1962 and serve as an initial platform for FRELIMO. But there then followed the question how to eliminate colonialism from our country. The clear answer was that the only way to liberation was through armed struggle. This was made clear by the massacres at Xinavane (1947) and Mueda (1960), the bloody and brutal repression of the docks and railway strikes in Beira and Lourenço Marques (1963), the contempt shown by Portugal for United Nations Resolution 1514 (XV) and other UN resolutions, colonialist rage in Angola, the steady rise in military and police forces posted to Mozambique, and clear and repeated statements by Portuguese colonialism.

The situation thus demanded a stand by everyone on the crucial question of armed struggle. A split began. Within the FRELIMO leadership there were many members of the old leaderships of MANU, UNAMI and UDENAMO. These members had been living for a long while outside Mozambique and had no direct contact with or real understanding of the actual situation. Their political experience was gained in contact with nationalist bodies in Rhodesia, Malawi, Zambia, Tanganyika and Kenya, bodies whose strategy was to organize the broad masses in demonstrations, strikes and other non-violent actions so as to create the conditions for the colonial power to negotiate initially on self-rule and later over independence.

These members confused the situation of a developed, industrialized and imperialist colonial power, such as Great Britain, with that of Portugal, underdeveloped, unindustrialized and virtually a semi-colony. These members overlooked the difference between a bourgeois democracy, where national and international public opinion have some impact, and a Fascist regime, where censorship and police repression prevent any expression of dissent.

Hence their opposition to the route of armed struggle. This mistaken analysis, which was prejudicial to the progress of the struggle and contrary to the objective interest of the masses, was in contradiction with the level of consciousness already reached by those masses. Opposition to armed struggle was blocking the process of liberation. For the contradiction to be settled in the interests of the masses, the mistaken ideas had to be overcome. The principle of armed struggle triumphed but had some opposition.

A first group including Baltazar Chakonga and other former leaders of UNAMI and MANU withdrew from FRELIMO, since they were opposed to the principle of armed struggle. Another group including Gumane and former leaders of UDENAMO and MANU underestimated the enemy's real strength which they did not know, and believed that a few violent terrorist actions would be enough to persuade the enemy to give in. This was in effect opposition to the principle of people's armed struggle, since it implied that the struggle should be launched immediately without any prior mobilization of the masses, without any preparation of cadres to guide and lead the process. These elements likewise withdrew from FRELIMO, while FRELIMO laid down objective and scientific methods that would lead to the launching of a people's armed struggle. The phase that had been reached demanded clarification of the fact that the elimination of opportunists and adventurists would allow progress in the struggle, and a strengthening of unity at the service of the masses and their aims.

Thanks to the unity acquired in the process of criticism, armed struggle was successfully launched on 25 September 1964 at various points of the national territory. The victories achieved, in Cabo Delgado and Niassa Provinces in particular, led to new developments in the situation.

From the end of 1965, we began to have areas where the colonial administration had retreated and the population had abandoned their villages to escape repression and live under FRELIMO's protection. This process gradually advanced and we had liberated and semi-liberated areas, that is areas where all aspects of the life of the masses depended on FRELIMO's guidance, and where our watchwords were day-to-day practice. A qualitatively new situation had been created with new demands.

How to organize production, how to administer the population, what kind of social relations of production should exist in our areas, what were relations to be between the population and the FRELIMO leadership structures, between the army and the population: these problems immediately came to the fore and required concrete and clear solutions.

Traditional society, as well, took oppressive and discriminatory forms, notably in regard to women and young people. So it was necessary that the liberating process should also reach the traditional society.

The rise in population in our areas brought a significant growth in the size of the army. It was no longer 250 members, but thousands of fighters and so the questions arose of what kind of army it should be, and what relations there should be between it and the masses and FRELIMO.

Questions about the organization of production and trade, the social relations of production to establish, the character of the army and of power were shown to be keys to the solution of a whole range of problems.

Once again two lines arose, one reflecting the interests of those who saw in the struggle a means of replacing the colonialist classes as exploiting classes, and the other reflecting the objective interests of the masses struggling to abolish exploitation of man by man.

In the liberated areas, once the colonial presence had vanished, the embryo of the bourgeoisie and the feudal survivors thought it was fertile ground for their advancement as exploiting classes. Control over the emerging power and the army seemed a precondition for the achievement of such ambitions.

Obviously the claims of the new class of exploiters were not formulated in such crude terms. They said they were against exploitation but that was exclusively an offence by the colonialists, or that the issues of power, the organization of production and trade, new kinds of social relations of production, etc., could be left for independence.

However, these problems did demand an immediate answer. Should we introduce a people's administration, people's power, or simply maintain the former administrative system by Africanizing it? Should we organize trade at the service of the people, who would control the domestic and foreign market, and launch the farming co-operatives movement, or on the other hand should we allow traditional chiefs and others to exploit farm workers or introduce profiteering in trade? These were not theoretical questions and academic debates and hypotheses. They were real and urgent questions, affecting every liberated village, every region, every area under our control.

It was clear that the issue divided the FRELIMO leadership. But it was imperative to know whether, in order to safeguard unity with a handful of components of the leadership, we should sacrifice the interests of the broad mass of the people, thus allowing the bloodshed and the sacrifices made to nourish the growth of a new exploitative and oppressive class.

A political battle was waged in our midst, a struggle that reflected contradictory interests, a hard fight in which reactionary elements often resorted to violence, as is evidenced by the murders of Comrades Mateus Sansão Muthemba, a member of the Central Committee, and Paulo Samuel Khankomba, a member of the general staff and deputy operations chief.

At a certain juncture, the reactionary forces, feeling they had lost the battle because of the consciousness of the masses, took the side of the Portuguese colonialists, in some instances designating the target to attack, as in the case of the murder of Comrade President Mondlane, and in others deserting to join openly with the colonialists, or initiating slanderous public campaigns abroad to run down the organization.

However, the rejection of these reactionary forces had a strengthening effect on the organization, as the masses were able fully to realize that their interests required the revolutionary line to be defended and that its defence was tied to fulfilling the people's demands.

The battle that was waged between 1967 and the second half of 1969 enabled us to reach the present phase of unity, the phase in which our unity helps the anti-colonialist and anti-imperialist fight, and destroys the political, economic, social and cultural structures of exploitation, so that we can introduce into our country a new society and authority of the people.

The phase of unity that we have reached now is by no stretch of the imagination its final form. New contradictions must arise out of the development and demands of the situation. Perhaps they will not be as serious as in the past. We have more experience in spotting and solving the contradictions at an early stage. The forces representing the interests of the exploitative strata have withdrawn from the struggle, taking off their masks and showing their true colours as allies of colonialism itself. But contradictions will arise, opposition to the revolution, counter-revolution will go on. This is the historical experience of all revolutions, an inevitable aspect of progress.

The Question of Ideology in a Broad Front

The net effect of these questions raises the issue of the role and need of ideology for revolutionary development. The classic assertion that without revolutionary theory there can be no revolutionary practice is amply confirmed by our experience. But our practice does offer some original features in this sphere, in particular how a broad front without an established vanguard party relates to revolutionary ideology.

To avoid any confusion it should be stated that the absence of a vanguard party from the broad front is not a result of a premise in our analysis or an aim or even a strategy of ours. It is the result of a web of historical circumstances we face, with characteristics including basically the non-existence of an organized working class and tradition, the lack of struggle experience by the broad masses, the burden of reactionary traditions and concepts imposed on the people by feudal and colonial domination, the isolation of communities, particularly in the countryside, before the founding of the nationalist movement, which has deprived us of the theoretical and practical experiences of the world revolutionary movement.

The need for a revolutionary ideology does not come as a bookish demand, just as ideology is not formed in a simple reading of the masters of revolutionary thought. Granted that ideological drafting owes an immense debt to the theoretical and practical contribution made by the revolutionary movement of other peoples, ideology is always the creation of a specific struggle by a people and its revolutionary classes. Ideology becomes a reality when it is taken up and experienced by the broad masses, when theory is renewed and materialized in day-to-day practice of struggle. Only in this way can it be transformed into the immense material force that leads the people to overthrow the old order and build the new society.

The political line, the ideology, arise as guidance for the specific problems raised by the development of the struggle and required for the progress of the whole process. The concrete needs we faced and still face are to replace obsolete loyalties to tribe, language, religion and culture with national unity and with a sense of belonging to an immense, exploited working class, to give a clear definition of the enemy and to make the masses conscious of its exploitative character, and hence to distinguish unambiguously our ideas, values, aims, methods and behaviour from those of the enemy.

National and class unity are indispensable weapons for the destruction of the enemy's powerful machine, and are our basic strength, our main strong point. Defining the target for our weapons cannot admit any ambiguity, all the more as in the historical context of our struggle, when we are mainly confronting the economic, political and military forces of another nation, it is all too easy to identify the enemy with a race. This denatures the sense of the struggle, allowing the reactionary forces to dig themselves in and losing us the political sensitivity needed to avoid mistaking friend and enemy.

So we still demand of each one of us an internal fight to rid ourselves of anything in our ideas, value system and behaviour that does not reflect what we need in our area where a new society is under construction. The war's development and national reconstruction demand a transformation from metaphysical reasoning, typical of our traditional society, to scientific and materialist reasoning. The latter is the only form capable of analysing and changing society and mobilizing nature's laws on our behalf. We need the liberation of the creative energy of the masses, who are suffocated by the conservatism and lethargy of the outdated society, and we need emancipation for women and young people, who are dominated by reactionary traditions.

A solution to these problems requires of us the formulation of a clear and precise line to guide cadres and militants. Destroying the colonial power structures, eliminating exploitative ownership and evolving individualist forms of production into collective forms, all necessitate that the leadership supply clear and concrete principles and guidelines.

The social diversity of our country is made more acute by ethnic and racial diversity. Our victory is the result of our ability to commit to the anti-colonialist and anti-Fascist struggle all forces and social strata of

Mozambique, with the evident exception of the tiny minority who control and handle large exploitative capital and the machinery of repression. But it takes clarity and firmness of principles to do this without putting at risk the interests of the majority comprised of the exploited working masses.

In other words, the central question is one of a balance between the broad front intended to overthrow colonial and imperialist domination on the one hand, and demands on the other of an ideology that can bring the revolution to its fruition, and already represents the claims of the broad working masses.

In our experience it has been a matter of safeguarding and constantly broadening the front by bringing in new forces and yet at the same time raising the general standard of consciousness in the masses and the ideological rigour of militants in such a way as to deepen the content of the people's demands and draw these demands into the process of changing society.

Hence one can understand the prime importance we attach to ideological work in our midst and among the masses, and the priority we give to the training of cadres, who are a decisive factor in the creative implementation of our political line.

It is through the same process, with ideological work intimately associated with revolutionary practice, that we are gradually creating the conditions whereby, within the broadening front, there should be taking shape an organized revolutionary vanguard of the mass of Mozambican workers.

The framework of national reconstruction and the setting up of new power structures in a war situation offer concrete and immediate pressures that the broad masses are able to understand and respond to, provided that we do the necessary work of political explanation.

This is the ensemble of circumstances, factors and aims that has allowed development of the national liberation struggle's content, and moved it in theory and practice into the phase of people's democratic revolution. That phase is typified by the destruction of the colonial-Fascist state and imperialist domination and by the installation of the power of the alliance of the broad mass of workers, with the aim of establishing the foundations of a new society, a society based on the interests of the labouring masses.

The process of people's liberation war and the creation of a people's army have given an enormous boost to the general process of deepening ideology and changing attitudes of mind, the indispensable preliminary to building a new society.

People's War and the Creation of the Army

The Political Line in the Armed Struggle
There is war, armed struggle in Mozambique. Everyone understands more or less that our strategic and tactical concepts of armed struggle are

different from those of the Portuguese army, given that our political aims are antagonistic and the character of our force is different. By contrast, quite a lot of people have difficulty in seeing that even within the forces seeking revolution there may be opposing strategic and tactical concepts.

There were some who envisaged forming a continental or international army that would invade Mozambique and liberate the territory from colonial domination. Some others argued that as the objective political conditions were ripe for the launching of the struggle, it would be enough for a group of convinced and determined professional revolutionaries, even if unknown to the masses, to initiate armed struggle in appropriate places, for the masses automatically to organize and mobilize themselves, give support to the struggle and so bring the revolution's triumph. In addition to the unreality and idealism of these concepts, they are based on false premises.

The first case starts from the principle that the people are incapable of freeing themselves. Hence the need for an external force – the continental army that would come and free them. At this level there remains the notion that a people's liberation is a question of military technique and hence the idea that a body of officers foreign to the political and concrete reality of the country would be able to lead the liberating process.

The second view, that a body of professional revolutionaries are in a position to set in train a revolutionary process by initiating armed engagements, reveals a spontaneous and mechanical outlook on the revolutionary process. This is an idealist analysis of the masses and how their consciousness is raised.

In contrast to these concepts is the people's liberation war. The people's war is made and won by the masses. What makes it possible to overcome the enormous material shortcomings and gain victory is the participation by hundreds of thousands, or millions, of individuals in the various tasks that are required, from armed combat to production, from transport of material to reconnaissance of the enemy.

However, to involve the broad masses in the fight for liberation, it is imperative that the vanguard forces in their midst undertake prior political work in mobilizing them and organizing them. It is essential to be constantly advancing this work in order to raise the level of political understanding of the masses so that they can more readily respond to the nature, aims and methods of the war, and can overcome the innumerable difficulties, as we gradually eliminate our weak points and reinforce our strong points.

On this view it is wrong and foolish to make any attempt to fool the masses with promises of quick, easy victories, or to lie to them about the failures or successes achieved. That kind of thing blocks the political understanding of the masses, prevents them studying and absorbing collective experiences, and thereby enriching and developing our political and strategic thinking, and improving our tactics.

The masses cannot be regarded as a band of passive individuals who carry out certain tasks that are dictated to them. Millions of men, divided and devoid of a clear awareness of their situation and the potential and means for changing it, are an amorphous mass that the enemy will dominate. When the masses have their consciousness aroused and are united on the right line, they make for a decisive force to transform society and annihilate the enemy.

The way to organize and mobilize the masses, the watchwords to devise, are specific matters that relate to the specific situation of each country and of each region within the country.

Mozambique is essentially a rural country, where more than 90 per cent of the African population live in non-urban areas. The urban areas are principally populated by settlers and were planned in such a way as to isolate and easily contain the African population found there. Hence the rural areas are easy for us to approach, while the urban areas, tightly controlled by the enemy, demand more time and energy-consuming work by the cadres and rapidly eat up the efforts of a large number of those cadres.

This explains our priority for struggle in the rural areas and why in the present phase we have not paid much attention to urban guerrilla activity. Although such activity would be spectacular, it would be fatal for us, above all for the heavy cost it would take in cadres.

Our struggle in the rural areas where the enemy is weak allowed us to liberate considerable proportions of the territory and the population. We are thus more and more isolating the enemy and reducing his capacity to carry on the exploitation of our country that is the *raison d'être* for his presence. We are raising the numbers of the free population and this means an increase in our personnel. This is the process that will in the end lead to the destruction of the colonial-Fascist state and the installation of people's power.

By struggling in the heavily populated rural areas, we are operating like the alligator who tries to carry his prey to the water where it is weak and he is strong. Guerrilla warfare forces the enemy to fight in the midst of a hostile people.

The enemy has at its disposal numerous well-equipped forces who can move about and regroup rapidly thanks to their aircraft and helicopters. As it has heavy weapons capable of destroying substantial targets, it constantly tries to secure a frontal engagement with our forces. Its propaganda goes so far as to describe us as cowards, because we refuse to wage a battle in which we and they would assemble our forces to engage in a single, heroic and final clash.

But we do not see why we should obey enemy generals and it is not they who should say where, when and how the fighting is to be done. The enemy in its bases, as a fixed target, and in its columns, as a mobile target, offers objectives for our weapons. Our concern at this stage is not with winning a big victory, a spectacular victory. The accumulation of small victories, possible for our few scattered personnel, provides, in sum, the effects of a big victory.

The destruction of the enemy's numerous small bases that protect the main base, forces the enemy to evacuate from positions and to group its forces at particular points where they remain isolated, unoccupied and useless. The ground is then left for us and the population are liberated. So the conditions are created for the large isolated base to be destroyed in the long run.

Some might think that in our kind of war, a national liberation war, all those individuals who have the enemy's colour or nationality are automatically the enemy. The child as much as the soldier, the old man as much as the policeman, the woman in the same way as the big bosses, the worker as much as the heads of the colonial administration; if they are White, or Portuguese, they should be targets for our weapons. The group of new exploiters in our midst who hoped to replace the colonialists as a dominant class did try to impose this definition of the enemy. Some circles regard these racist concepts as revolutionary radicalism, either through lack of ideological clarity or in a bid to confuse public opinion about the justness of our line and to discredit the genuine revolutionary forces.

Since ours is a people's war and defends the people's interests, we are well aware that there is no antagonism between the fundamental interests of the Mozambican people and those of any other people in the world, including the Portuguese people. For the same reason we always say that there is no reason for any antagonism between us and the Portuguese civilian population in Mozambique. It is the Portuguese colonialists who are putting settlers on land pillaged from our population, who indulge in the most atrocious crimes against women, children, old people and civilians in general, who are trying to provoke a racial war that would change the character of our combat.

FRELIMO's political action, the consciousness and sense of discipline of the masses and the fighters have destroyed this sinister manoeuvre of the enemy. We accept in our ranks without discrimination all Whites who identify as Mozambicans and want to fight alongside us. Our forces have shown scrupulous regard for the life and property of Portuguese civilians. FRELIMO has constantly appealed to the Portuguese community in Mozambique to support the fight against colonialism and Fascism.

We have constantly worked for an understanding by the Portuguese soldiers, the vast majority of whom come from the ordinary Portuguese people, that by turning their weapons against our people, they provide a bulwark to protect the authentic enemies of our people and of the Portuguese people themselves. But the army, police and colonial administration are the foundations of protection for the colonial state, and so necessarily must be destroyed.

By contrast and as a mark of our solidarity with the Portuguese people, we exercise a policy of clemency towards enemy soldiers captured in combat and sometimes we free them unilaterally. Obviously when it comes to deserters from the Portuguese side, they are regarded as our people's friends and our allies, and to them we offer not clemency but, rather, friendship.

So there is a clear line of distinction in Mozambique, even at the level of armed struggle, between us and the enemy. The enemy has his way of fighting and we have ours. He has his strategy and tactics, his terrorist methods that reflect the interests of the exploitative classes and the Fascist ideology he serves. We have our strategy and tactics, our methods that respect human dignity, since we serve the people's interests and are guided by the ideology that reflects the interests of the exploited masses.

Disciplinary Problems in the Army

Effective operation of an army, even a guerrilla army, above all in wartime, requires a high standard of discipline that preserves good internal morale and rapid and correct carrying out of orders. The colonial-Fascist army bases its discipline on fear imposed from the senior officers on the rank and file, on constant, brutal punishment, on the denial of any initiative and reasoning ability on the part of the soldiers, and on a strict compartmentalization of officers and soldiers.

It is obvious that this kind of discipline bears no resemblance to ours. Here, as in all other fields, there is a clear line of demarcation between us and the enemy. Discipline for us comes out of the fighter's understanding and the matching of our behaviour and ideas to the principles and rules that govern our approach as FRELIMO militants, combatants in the Mozambique People's Liberation Forces and servants of the masses. Discipline is like a sentry guarding the political line, alerting us to any attempt to deviate from or attack the line.

It is a particularly difficult task to integrate into our way of discipline individuals who come from a different way of life. The deserter from the colonial army or the civilian from the enemy area arrive with a habit of blind obedience to orders from the army or the colonial administration. They follow a discipline inspired by fear. Those who come from traditional village life bring with them values, ideas and customs that reflect the metaphysical reasoning and conditioning of feudal society – tribalism, superstition, worship of the past, and blind submission to tradition and the orders of the elders.

Integration of such individuals presupposes liberation from the spirit of passive obedience instilled by the chiefs, or by superstition, and then making the individual understand and love our way of life, so that he can consciously follow the principles and rules that guide it. Integration into a new discipline cannot be divorced from a change in the man's consciousness.

There is the further aspect of instilling collective values and a sense of collective responsibility. A collective sense means that the individual measures himself by the extent to which he can devote his energy to the progress of the masses and the revolution. A sense of collective responsibility means understanding that any mission we are given, any material entrusted to us, is intended in the final analysis for the progress of the masses and the revolution.

Within this framework, an order to us is a demand to carry out a task reflecting the interests of the masses and the revolution, so even an unjust order or the failure to carry out a just order are regarded as a serious breach of our discipline.

Since discipline is thus based on a profound adherence to the new society we are building, we attach a fundamental importance to internal debate and political study. Decisions are made after discussion and take account of the level of political understanding of the sector that must implement them. Implementation is preceded by a campaign of explanation and political mobilization. When the tasks are done they are analysed so that the new experience can be absorbed and we can thus advance our revolutionary consciousness and theory. In our army we do not have posts, although there are obviously varying levels of responsibility. The distinction is not merely semantic and demands some explanation. The concept of a post certainly includes the idea of varying levels of responsibility, but it also implies that the holder of a post permanently exercises responsibilities at a given level commensurate with his post.

We do not believe there are higher and lower tasks, since all of them are intended to serve the revolution. So a provincial head may be withdrawn from his task to take on an instruction mission, for example, without this implying a demotion, a drop in post. He was fulfilling one responsibility, he is now fulfilling another.

Our concern was to establish among rank-and-file soldiers, cadres and leaders, an atmosphere of total confidence and brotherhood in which the word 'comrade' should have its full value.

In our work in this area we had to contend with two kinds of deviation. There are some individuals with the sin of authoritarianism, a defect inherited from the colonial, or even the traditional, society, where there is no democratic way of life. On the other hand there were manifestations of ultra-liberalism, a lack of respect or consideration for the structures, artificial egalitarianism, and the building of bogus solidarity on the basis of vices or weaknesses, decadent and corrupt tastes.

Both tendencies are vigorously combated amongst us, since the first example violates the democratic spirit of our army, and the second breaches the principles of our unity and our structures, democratic centralism and our own discipline.

Revolutionary discipline is always one of the decisive factors in the fighting spirit and effectiveness of the revolutionary army at all stages.

Experience has shown us that in the difficult circumstances we face, any retreat from discipline results in a relaxation of vigilance, infiltration of ideas and behaviour that are alien to us, the growth of mistrust and the start of desertion, in sum the creation of an atmosphere favourable to defeat. That is why discipline expresses and protects the political line, the organization and its structures.

A vitally important aspect of discipline is concerned with relations with the population. Strict respect for the people and their possessions is a basic principle for everyone. The people do not in fact distinguish us from the colonial army by the colour of the skin or the vernacular or words we use. Our attitude towards the masses and our respect for them is the touchstone that marks us off from the troops of aggression.

The enemy army may use the same uniform and weapons as we do, may speak the same language and have the same colour, and may even purport to help the masses. But in reality everything it does is aimed at disorganizing and demobilizing the masses so as to drive them away from the struggle and make them give up their just demands, so as to integrate them into the system of exploitation. The exploitative mentality of the colonial army naturally leads it to pillage and robbery of the people's possessions. The enemy's corrupt mentality in regard to women leads him naturally to immorality and rape. The decadent tastes of capitalism lead to a taste for drunkenness and drug-taking, as a way of smothering and alienating consciousness. Fascist and colonialist logic, and its intrinsic contempt for human dignity, leads to systematic use of the most barbarous, inhuman and sadistic crimes, just as it provokes human degradation and bestiality in the repressive forces themselves.

A clear line of demarcation between our conduct and the enemy's matches the demarcation between our political lines. Respect for the people's possessions, respect for women and the struggle for their emancipation, the fight against alienating drunkenness and drug-taking, respect for human dignity and personality that precludes resort to crime, terrorism and torture: all these are essential characteristics of our army, a people's army.

In some circles touched by the decadent tastes of capitalist society, it is argued that such matters as sexual promiscuity and the abuse of drink and drugs are progressive actions, or at least trivial questions with which the revolution should not be concerned. We reject the idea that anything expressing corruption and decadence can be progressive. The revolution is incompatible with corruption, just as the war is irreconcilable with soft living.

For the militant there are no relaxed moments, moments when he abandons the line and discipline to rest. The line and discipline are air and blood, and we cannot expect to rest from the act of breathing or from the blood's circulation.

So these are not trivial matters, as it is argued, but fundamental issues that define our revolutionary personality, that condition good relations between the population and the guerrilla force or army, relations between the principal strength in the people and its armed wing. Relations between the army and the people are further affected by how the army sees its task.

Military Tasks and Politico-Military Tasks

FRELIMO has laid down as task and watchword for all its soldiers: Study, Production and Combat.

Through political, scientific and technical study, we acquire not only the knowledge needed to develop the war, economy and culture, but also, and principally, the basis for shaping a materialist consciousness free of all forms of idealism and superstition, a consciousness that is essential to objective analysis of the revolutionary process. Political study strengthens our awareness and analytical capacity, enriches the content of our struggle, raises our revolutionary practice and level of commit- ment, and teaches us how to change society. Scientific and technical study reconciles us with nature and enables us to use its laws to improve our living standards and make the best use of our resources.

Production, as well as meeting our material needs, leads us to a practical proof of the correctness of our ideas, brings us new ideas, strengthens our consciousness of our social origin, and so reinforces our unity. Furthermore the practice of production and the critical analysis and synthesis we make of it allows us to innovate and to spread new production methods.

The internal battle rids us of vices and weaknesses inherited from the past, destroys false values, notions and conduct passed on from the exploitative society, and brings us in touch with the values, notions and conduct of the new society.

The fight against the colonialist and imperialist enemy frees territory and men and women, and provides the preconditions for us to destroy the exploitative structures and establish people's power.

These tasks are an integral part of the day-to-day activity of fighters in the Mozambique People's Liberation Forces.

Instruction, political study and production are constant at military bases. In the training of new recruits, political classes, meetings and political debates along with production are just as much a part of the curriculum as military skills. So we are equipping the fighter to become an active and conscious agent of social change.

Political study, meetings and debates are accompanied by criticism and self-criticism, intended to stimulate the internal battle, to correct our working methods, to raise consciousness, and to pool our experience. Literacy teaching for the fighters and the raising of the standard of those who can read and write are part of the work schedule at all military bases.

Production, though not the principal task, is essential for our army. We say it is not principal, since the army's principal task is the physical destruction of the enemy.

All FRELIMO bases and detachments cultivate their own fields as well as helping the peasants produce. Our insistence on productive activ- ity by the army has several motives. The army must make an effort to be self-sufficient and not overburden the population. Obviously it will be difficult for the army in our situation to be self-sufficient in foodstuffs, but at least by producing it it cuts the burden on the population.

As we have pointed out, collective production consolidates our consciousness of our class origin and reinforces our ties of friendship. The
soldier who is away from production may forget his worker origin, his
duty to serve the exploited masses, and may instead tend to behave like a
petty armed despot and deploy his weapon to gain privileges for himself
or serve the exploiting strata. High regard for manual labour also reflects
the ideas of the new society we have built, where, in contrast to the
exploitative society, manual labour is not regarded as degrading and fit
only for the ignorant.

The army's fields also serve as experimental plots where we can
introduce new crops and farming techniques. The masses can come to
them to learn the new technique in practice and observe its results.

Higher military skills and the enrichment of the cadres' knowledge are
a basic necessity in developing the armed struggle and finding an adequate
response to the new tactics and weaponry deployed by the enemy.

Some think the best way to train cadres is to send them to some
foreign academy, where they will spend long years following the teachings of the masters and studying various military theories. Reactionary
forces among us tried to impose this approach. Such training divorced
from the concrete practice of struggle, not merely of the armed struggle
but more importantly of the political struggle itself and revolutionary
practice, seems wrong to us. In our case it would be liable to lead us into
dogmatism, a stereotyped attitude and mental servility to such and such
a foreign experience.

As we have stated, a fighter for us is not merely a man with complete
mastery of weapons and abstract military arts. This would make him no
different from the colonial and Fascist fighter.

The tasks we entrust to the army are politico-military, just as the
training is politico-military. Political training cannot be abstract and
bookish, but is effected through constant contact with the real struggle.

Our strategy and tactics, although deriving enormous benefit from the
theoretical and practical experience of other revolutionary struggles, are
more than anything else a product of our own struggle, of the particular
military, economic, cultural and social conditions we encounter in our
country.

For this reason the essential preparation of our cadres can be done
only by ourselves. Within this framework we also accept the need to take
fighters temporarily out of the firing lines, for refresher courses at our
own bases, or even to send them on relatively short attachments in
friendly revolutionary countries, where they can learn new techniques
and broaden their theoretical and practical experience of these revolutions.

Our training method thus appears as a system of permanent and
progressive education, closely linked to the practical side of political
struggle and armed combat, although it does entail short-term withdrawal
from the firing lines for refresher courses and new skills.

The formation and expansion of our army comes within this broad framework. It lends a fundamental dimension to relations between the army and FRELIMO, or if you like between the military and the political.

Politico-Military Militants
There are differing views on the relations between an army and a political organization, between soldiers and politicians. Broadly speaking bourgeois armies claim that they are apolitical or politically neutral, although they are of course the main repressive force in the oppressor state and an assurance of the survival of the exploitation of the labouring masses.

This bourgeois concept also found an echo among us, when in the 1967–69 period the group of new exploiters advocated a separation between 'politicals' and 'military', and imagined a FRELIMO comprising two groups, a political wing as leader and a military wing charged with fighting. Their intention was that the army should merely have the task of physically fighting the enemy, and they were against the production and study tasks. This group violently criticized political mobilization by fighters of the masses and demanded that political commissars should refrain from holding public meetings and raising political issues. The group also insisted that political education in the army be dropped and that one should teach only obedience to the 'politicals'. We regard these ideas as profoundly wrong and reactionary.

In our circumstances we cannot have any compartmentalization between one strictly political sector and another exclusively military sector. All tasks in the current phase have the effect of consolidating and enlarging the armed struggle.

An artillery base cannot shell the enemy, if the population have not for weeks before carried the shells needed to supply the forces. The child who spies out enemy movements, the old man who fires on the invader with his 'wait awhile' hunting shotgun, are not soldiers but they fulfil essential combat tasks. And in turn it would be impossible to cultivate a field, put a school or hospital into operation, or establish a local committee, if the enemy had not previously been destroyed, and the land and the men and women freed by armed combat. The teacher or nurse who wants to live without weapons will not survive long before being taken by the enemy, in the same way as a soldier isolated from the population is heading for disaster.

To deny the army production, on the grounds that it interferes with fighting, reflects a narrow view of what fighting is and, above all, it denies the political and formative influence of production on the army. Our battle is not merely one of firing off shots and killing enemy soldiers. The central aim of our fight is to change society. Society is based on productive activity and social relations of production.

The army's participation in production, and its experience and example of collective production, and of a new kind of social relations of production, have a profound impact on the transformation of society and mental attitudes. And this educates the army into a new spirit.

Production at the military bases is fundamental, as is participation by the army in the population's productive activity; such sharing strengthens good relations and unity between the mass of the people and their army.

Opposition to study in the army reflects an ignorance of the realities of war. An army that does not study does not improve its scientific and technical culture, is outpaced by the process of war, becomes incapable of absorbing experience and progressing, cannot spot and counter changes of strategy and tactics by the enemy, and cannot make the most of its weapons.

The further notion that the army should be reserved for the 'ignorant' while the 'knowledgeable' should devote themselves to policy and leadership also reveals profoundly reactionary tendencies about the role of the army. It aims at establishing the 'knowledgeable' as a 'leadership' class with an exploitative role to take the place of the former exploiting class.

Our army is a politico-military body comprising the most advanced forces in the masses. Within the army are to be found the most dynamic and enlightened representatives of the masses, those who have willingly offered the supreme sacrifice for the liberation of the people and the country.

The inevitably more organized and systematic way of life in the army allows for more intensive political work, accustoms the individual to collective work, teaches him collective values, frees him from obsolete loyalties based on tribe, language, religion and so on.

Within a framework such as ours, a broad front without a vanguard party, the army is seen as the most dynamic and enlightened sector in the front, the sector that offers tried and tested cadres not merely for the tasks of battle, but for all the other tasks as well. The army, by virtue of its social origin and what it has learned, and of its willingness to serve the masses, is a basic instrument in our endeavour to transform society. In this context, denying the army contact with the masses would be trying to isolate the army and annihilate it. Meanwhile, depriving the masses of the mobilizing action of the army and the educative action of the political commissars would mean taking from the masses the ideological weapon of which the army is the main bearer in our current military situation.

FRELIMO's fighter is a politico-military fighter; the FRELIMO militant is a politico-military militant.

Among us there are no politicians and soldiers, politicians and technicians; to try for that would be to distort reality and above all cloud the meaning of struggle.

Taking all these points together, we can assert that we are building a people's army. Our army in the making warrants the name people's army by virtue of its social origin and the political weapon it has, and of the trials in which it has been tempered. We began with a derisorily small force. We had on 25 September 1964 about 250 fighters, equipped with old repeater weapons, pistols and a few individual automatic weapons. In each province where the struggle was begun, and in the other provinces, the number of fighters varied between 15 and 25.

In front of us the colonial army ranged some 40,000 men, equipped with modern weapons, with air and naval forces, with a broad network of military bases and positions, easy communications, etc.

However, as we were armed with a correct line, from being weak and frail we changed into a powerful force that inflicts defeat after defeat on the Portuguese colonial troops, and the racist South African and Rhodesian troops. Our army now has at its disposal many, many thousands of fighters, moderately well equipped, already able to handle modern artillery weapons, able to attack and destroy strategic enemy bases, and with the ability to launch devastating and simultaneous offensives in various regions. Despite the fact that the Portuguese colonialists have brought from Portugal more than 70,000 men, reinforced by puppets and neighbouring racist troops, these forces of aggression feel increasingly frail and unready to face the enormous fire of the people's liberation war.

Our army is growing and shaping itself amid mass struggle, thanks to the correct guidance of FRELIMO. Our army is becoming invincible because it is rooted in the mass of the people, united and led by FRELIMO. In ten years of fighting and as the fight has developed, a Mozambican people's army has been forged, a servant of the people and the revolution, and an armed wing for the working masses and their organization.

Materialization of Power

Structures of People's Power
When we talk about liberated areas, we are not only referring to the absence of a military and administrative presence, since even before the war such a presence was not to be found in every hamlet or village of our country, and furthermore, since the enemy presence does make itself felt in our areas, at least through its aircraft.

The real meaning of a liberated area is an area which has been liberated from the structures of colonial capitalist and traditional feudal domination. In other words administrative power is no longer exercised by colonial administrators or by traditional chiefs, and the forms, methods and content of power have been transformed. The population is organized openly and publicly and passes its day-to-day life in accordance with our guidance and our watchwords.

In the liberated areas power belongs to the masses and is exercised democratically at the various echelons. At the lowest echelon is the circle, which may cover anywhere from a dozen to some hundreds of people, according to the area's population density. Leading the circle is a secretariat with a variable number of members, appointed by general assemblies or general meetings of the circle.

A locality comprises several circles and is led by two bodies, a local council and a local committee. The local council is formed by the heads of the circle secretariats and by other members appointed by the circles. The local council appoints the local committee which deals with day-to-day management of the locality.

The circle secretariats and local committees organize all the activities at local level. They encourage the formation of co-operatives, organize mutual help with farming, organize groups of porters for carrying materials, organize the local militia, the recruitment of young people to the army, supplies to schools, hospitals, children's crèches, military bases, etc. It is also they, or the councils, who settle the various local disputes. The population census, marriage, birth and death registration, are carried out by the committees and secretariats.

At the next level to the locality is the district, likewise led by a council and a committee headed by the district secretary. Sitting on the district council, in addition to those in charge of the local committees and other members appointed by the local councils, are the responsible officials in the various sectors of activity, such as education, health, production and trade, and the political commissariat. Also on the district committee are members appointed by the council, along with the political commissar and the district officials responsible for education, health, production, trade, etc.

At the top we find the province. The province is led by the provincial council and the provincial committee, with the latter headed by the provincial secretary and an assistant. The provincial council comprises the heads of the district committees, members appointed by the district and local councils, and the officials responsible for various sectors of activity, the army, education, production and trade, health, political commissariat, etc. This is the highest institution in the province. The provincial council appoints the members of the provincial committee, which includes also the officials responsible for the various sectors of activity, the provincial secretary and an assistant.

The provincial secretary is appointed by the FRELIMO Central Committee and represents the organization in the province. He is the senior official in the province. His assistant is appointed by the Defence Department, is a member of the general staff, and is the senior person responsible for the army at the provincial level.

This structure is democratic since at all echelons the members are appointed democratically, which allows the exercise of people's power through representatives chosen by the masses, from those brought up in mass struggle who have demonstrated their fidelity to the people's interests.

The introduction of these structures was made after an intense political struggle which reflected antagonistic class interests in our midst. There were individuals who were resolutely opposed to the installation of people's power.

Some, purporting to be the defenders of a tradition trampled upon by the colonizer, but in truth reflecting the interests of the feudal strata, proposed the survival and resurrection of the chieftaincy, an anti-democratic structure of a feudal kind that had degenerated under colonialism and virtually become the latter's tool.

It was the political work of raising mass consciousness, the reorganization of economic life on new foundations, and the appearance of people's armed power in the army and militias that gradually undermined and isolated the feudal basis and created the appropriate conditions for its annihilation.

Another trend reflected the interests of the strata with a capitalist bent, the group of new exploiters. This trend proposed maintaining the colonial administrative structures, with the mere replacement of European civil servants by African civil servants, and eventually changing the titles of the positions while retaining their anti-democratic and exploitative content.

The partisans of this group put forward as their main argument the thesis that exploitation was only possible when it was carried out by the White against the Black and never by Black against Black. They argued further that the question of power was secondary, and should be settled after independence because in the current phase it brought the risk of dividing us, given that there were different points of view on the matter. It was further said that their position truly corresponded to the interests of the masses, since it was advocated by civilians with political responsibilities, all originating from the particular province, whereas the contrary thesis was espoused by soldiers, often from other provinces, who were seeking to impose a military dictatorship.

This position was entrenched in Cabo Delgado Province, thanks to the support of Kavandame, provincial secretary and ringleader of the group, who established his supporters in positions of responsibility at various levels in the province.

Here again, political mobilization of the masses was necessary, and an explanation of the new exploitation that was being introduced, in order to bring the masses to rebel against the exploiting strata that were trying to sidle into power. The fact that the new power brokers had already used their power to exploit the peasants, through private trade which exploited local difficulties and was playing the game of profiteering, created conditions conducive to a mass revolt against the new exploiters.

We say that after the sacrifices made and the blood that has been shed we cannot permit new parasites to come and feed on our sweat and sacrifice. Our weapons are not used to defend the interests of a handful, but of the majority. And it is on this principle that we are introducing and defending our power, and the masses are making every sacrifice to defend this power that is genuinely theirs.

57

Economic Reorganization

Under colonial domination, the rural mass was subject to a variety of forms of exploitation. The monopoly companies occupied vast tracts of land cultivated by legions of forced labourers, recruited and supplied by the colonial administration. At the same time in the concession areas, the companies forced the rural mass to cultivate annual quotas of certain crops, such as cotton, which the company later bought at starvation prices that it enforced in collusion with the administration.

The colonial administration, on the pretext that the African must provide a labour input, as well as the – exorbitant – taxes already being paid, forced men and women to give months and months of unpaid work on the construction and repair of roads, in the cultivation of fields belonging to administrative personnel, etc.

The small settlers likewise used African labour on land and in shops and their homes. The chieftains, and the occasional prosperous African peasant who was on good terms with the administration, also had the use of forced labour.

With the launching of armed struggle, exploitation by the companies, the administration and the small settlers began to crumble with the withdrawal of an enemy military presence. The need to change the siting of villages and the disorganization of life that followed the early stages of the struggle brought a temporary halt to production. But the population led by FRELIMO quickly resumed production. Initially the basic aim was to ensure the minimum for the subsistence of the population and the army. Mutual help was a matter of course.

Once this target had been reached and thanks to the development of the armed struggle, conditions were ripe for an increase in farm production, and the organization of crafts and an overall rearrangement of production. Agriculture was organized in various patterns: collective fields which were an offshoot of the organization and were intended to supply schools and crèches, hospitals and centres for the disabled, as well as the army; agricultural co-operatives in which the fruits of collective labour are shared out in proportion to the amount of work put in; and individual fields, but farmed on the principle of mutual help and non-exploitation of another's labour.

Production has already begun to produce a substantial surplus, thanks to the consolidation of our areas and the efforts made to bring in new, improved and more varied production techniques. The surplus is used for internal barter as well as for export to neighbouring countries. The appearance of surplus production excited the greed of certain strata of a capitalist inclination. They tried to introduce a private internal marketing network, based on unbridled profiteering that exploited the serious shortage of certain essential items, such as cloth, soap, salt, etc.

The same elements tried at the same time to recruit labourers for their fields, offering in exchange for a month's labour a few kilos of salt, or a few metres of cloth. This group was particularly powerful in Cabo Delgado

Province, where it was backed by the then provincial secretary, Lazaro Kavandame, who was himself deeply involved in these activities.

To have a better chance of introducing a system of exploitation they sought to sabotage the co-operative movement and destroy the internal and external trade network created by the organization. A struggle against this handful of new exploiters had to be unleashed to safeguard the interests of the people and the aims of the struggle. This lasted from the end of 1967 to the beginning of 1969, at which point these elements, totally isolated and unmasked and denounced by the masses, deserted.

Production, once rid of the new exploiters, could make a noteworthy advance. At the start we had to replace the crops intended for the colonial economy – cotton and oilseeds – with food crops; production had been subject to the principles of the colonial order, that is it was intended to meet the interests exclusively of the colonial metropole.

Current agricultural production is mainly of: four kinds of cereals, three of root crops, six of beans, eight of greenstuffs, nine of fruit. The factor of finding markets in friendly countries has enabled us to restart production of oilseeds and we are now producing six types of these seeds in our areas.

FRELIMO has also made an effort to diversify agriculture. An example was the introduction and extension of vegetable production in Cabo Delgado and Niassa, and the introduction of certain kinds of oilseeds in Tete and Niassa. A constant effort is made to improve farming techniques and introduce new ones, such as the fertilization of ground with manure.

It is noticeable how, in response to progress in agriculture achieved in the liberated areas, the enemy has resorted to all kinds of devices to destroy and sabotage our efforts. After incendiary and napalm shelling of our cultivated fields and granaries had failed, and after the enemy suffered severe casualties in attacks with troops brought in by helicopter, the enemy began in April 1972 to use chemical warfare against our crops, with the help of the South African racists who supplied aircraft, pilots and chemicals for the purpose.

Agriculture includes livestock breeding. The keeping of chickens has become widespread. Pig-farming and goat-herding have been developed in Cabo Delgado and Tete, and in the former province cattle-raising should be noted. Bee-keeping has also made its appearance in all the provinces.

Craft organization began in 1967. Extraction of salt from sea water has become an activity in several areas of Cabo Delgado. The manufacture of household utensils, pottery and basket-weaving has become general in all the provinces. And production of farm tools has been begun with the use of metal from enemy vehicles. Fishing and fish-drying has become common in coastal areas and where there are pools and rivers rich in fish. We have thus continually increased the volume and amount of production, although it would be difficult now to give precise figures.

FRELIMO has further organized under its direct control an internal trading network that enables the population to barter its surplus production without being exploited. Exports have also risen. Cabo Delgado has in the past year exported more than 1,000 tons of various products. In the near future the volume of exports will rise considerably, as external trade has been reorganized for Niassa and Tete Provinces. Exports go towards the purchase abroad of various manufactured goods, such as textiles, shoes, washing materials, tools, household goods, etc.

The organization monopolizes external trade. Cereals and foodstuffs cannot be exported. The main exports are oilseeds, sesame, castor oil, groundnuts, cashew nuts, and tobacco, wax, honey, hides, ivory, etc.

The New Education Pattern
When we took up arms to overthrow the old order, we felt the need to create a strong, healthy and prosperous new society in which men, free from all exploitation, would co-operate for the progress of all.

In the course of our struggle, in the fierce battle we had to wage against reactionary elements, we gained a very clear understanding of our aims. We felt particularly that the struggle to establish new structures was in danger of failing without the creation of a new mental outlook. This new outlook would depend largely on the education we offered, especially to the new generation who would carry on the revolution. So in education a political battle had to be launched which would distinguish it from traditional or colonial education and transform it into an instrument of revolution.

By this we are trying to say that for us, education does not mean teaching reading and writing, and forming an élite group of 'doctors' at the service of themselves and the privileged strata. In other words, just as it is possible to wage armed struggle without making a revolution, so it is possible to teach without educating in a revolutionary mould.

The FRELIMO leadership, in this context, laid down that the principal task of education, in teaching, textbooks and curriculum, is to instil in each of us the advanced, scientific, objective and collective ideology that will enable us to make progress in the revolutionary process.

Education must give us a Mozambican personality which, in no way subservient but steeped in our own realities, will be able, in contact with the outside world, to assimilate critically the ideas and experiences of other peoples and to pass on to them the fruit of our thought and practice.

In view of the burden of our society's traditions, a particular effort was made to create a new attitude in women, to emancipate them in understanding and behaviour, and at the same time to instil in men a new attitude and outlook towards women.

In short, it was a matter of making everyone feel the need to serve the people, to take a share in production, and to respect manual labour, to free initiative and develop a sense of responsibility.

For the first time in our history, there are children, young people, who are growing up away from colonialism, away from static and dogmatic traditions. There is a generation, the first, which is being shaped in the heat of revolution. They are the nursery from which will come the choice plants ensuring the triumph of the revolution.

Scientific study in our schools is therefore seen as closely linked to political study and the battle against the ideas, values and behaviour belonging to the enemy society. In the same way, study is closely tied in our schools to practical production.

We have now organized various kinds and levels of education. We have primary schooling, which covers four years. The number of children in school in the various provinces is well over 20,000. The number may seem insignificant, but it should be pointed out that when FRELIMO was founded in 1962, the official – colonial – primary schools in Mozambique had fewer than 5,000 Black and mixed-race pupils. And in practically all the places – more than 200 of them – where we have set up primary schools, there had not even been one.

Secondary schooling has been reorganized so that in six years the students can be prepared to enter any university faculty or higher education institute. In the 1974 school year, fifth-, sixth-, seventh- and eighth-year classes will be in operation with an attendance of more than 300 students. It should also be noted in this context that when FRELIMO was founded, there were scarcely 100 Black and mixed-race students in the official grammar school system in the whole of Mozambique.

We have, furthermore, in the Americo Boavida Hospital a nursing auxiliaries school, whose second course was formed at the end of 1973 with more than three dozen members. In the various hospital centres there are also courses for first-aid workers and many hundreds of these have already been trained. In 1972 training courses began for primary teachers.

We have in socialist countries, and in others, more than 100 young people on higher or intermediate courses, and in the past two years we have had back about a couple of dozen who have finished their higher studies and are to be found occupied in various tasks for the struggle.

Here again we should not omit a comparison with the situation obtaining before the foundation of FRELIMO. In the Portuguese universities in 1962 there were fewer than a dozen Black Mozambican students. The entire number of Black Mozambicans who obtained higher education diplomas under Portuguese colonialism was less than a dozen.

If these meagre numbers showing colonialism's systematic obscurantism have seen a change in the enemy-occupied areas, this is entirely due to the pressure created by the launching of armed struggle for national liberation and the international community's condemnation of Portugal's obscurantist policy.

The credit side of FRELIMO activity in the education field is already superior to that of Portuguese colonialism before the creation of our front and despite the enormous difficulties encountered, the shortage of materials, the absence of cadres, the shellings and attacks against the schools.

In the field of education too, our struggle is a liberating action, the decisive step towards the creation of a new culture at the service of mankind, for the utilization of science for the benefit of the working masses.

Social Welfare at the Service of the Masses

Social services for the masses, in the most essential forms of health care for mother and child, support for the war disabled and others, are a recent phenomenon in our country and came into being as a direct consequence of FRELIMO's political line.

The starting-point for our action is the essential principle of serving the masses. And it is this principle that determines priorities and guides the general pattern of our work. In the colonial area, the range of activities is subordinate to the twofold principle of serving the exploiting classes and permitting exploitation.

Social welfare, and health in particular, comes into this perspective. Illness and pain make man utterly docile in the face of the demands of the exploitative society. Medical treatment and specialists and adequate care are not there for those who need them, but for those who can pay. The geographical location of health services in the country does not match the real needs of the masses, but only the prospects of profit.

If we find more doctors and hospital beds, more specialists and laboratories, more nurses and analysts in the cities of Lourenço Marques and Beira, and if the overwhelming majority of staff and services are concentrated there, this only means that this is where the people with the money are. The unbridled advertising for greater consumption of pharmaceuticals, the duplication of effort in the production of a variety of medicines that have the same ingredients and different packaging, and each more costly than the other, reveal capitalist profiteering over human health.

We do not find health care in the plantations and the mines, in the factories and the villages. The rural areas are completely abandoned to tuberculosis, leprosy, malaria, to children dying of diarrhoea and mothers dying in labour. Although there are no exact statistics, it is likely that infant mortality is higher than 600 per 1,000. Life expectancy for a Mozambican is scarcely more than 30 years. Crèches and maternity clinics, convalescent homes for the industrially injured, social security, family subsidies are forgotten. Thousands of Mozambicans return each year, disabled in the mines of South Africa and condemned to a lifetime of poverty and charity. Victims of industrial accidents in factories or on plantations are simply left to their fate.

Social and medical welfare for mother and child, and family subsidies are discouraged in regard to the African population with the deliberate aim of reducing our population growth. General Kaulza de Arriaga, one of the principal formulators of Portuguese colonial policy, had this to say in lessons he gave (to the Military High Command, 1966–67):

> Even if in the metropole the family subsidy has to be as large as possible to encourage a high birth rate, we cannot do the same thing for the blacks, or they too will have a high birth rate.
>
> If there were 20 or 30 million blacks in Angola and Mozambique, we would have a very serious problem, so it is useful that these populations are so small. I don't know if this is the result of the export of these people to Brazil, but if so it is a good thing that such exports occurred.
>
> As for demography, the strong point in Portugal's structure is the limited demographic potential of the black populations.

This situation explains the deliberate colonial policy of neglecting the population. A recent event provides clear evidence of the neglect and unconcern of the colonial authorities for the population: the current outbreak of cholera in Mozambique, which has already affected neighbouring countries, originated in the areas occupied by the enemy, and spread out from Lourenço Marques, the colonial capital.

FRELIMO's political line puts welfare provision at the service of the masses. This means to us in the first place giving priority to preventive medicine for the masses, with the aim of removing the causes of the many endemic diseases. We have carried out vaccination campaigns that had never existed before in our country. More than 200,000 people in our area have already been vaccinated against smallpox and hundreds of thousands have been protected against cholera. We have created leprosaria to help lepers in areas where there had never been any colonial action against this evil. There are constant public campaigns in favour of hygiene, so as to prevent a range of diseases. Entire regions that had never known a medical post or health care now enjoy such care. Mothers are being taught how to look after children, about cleanliness and dietary rules.

Our concern is to preserve and improve the immense capital resource represented by the health of the masses. So in the health field we have achieved a genuine revolution, by establishing structures and laying down aims and methods to serve the masses in a way that had never happened in our country.

Our success depends on the active and conscious participation of the broad masses: hence the importance of our health services following a correct political line in mobilizing and organizing the masses in the fight against disease, by explaining what is to be done and why, and making them aware of their own interests. In other words the fight against disease proceeds from the conscious commitment of the masses to this fight, under the guidance of health services that function as a driving force.

If we are to speak of the battle between two lines in the field of health and social welfare, this area reflects the practical experience of our people. That we have achieved greater successes than those of the colonial health services, despite our material and technical difficulties, reflects the correctness of our principle: technical and material conditions, although important, are secondary in relation to the essential, the political line. In the final analysis, that is what determines who benefits from the action; if better technical and material conditions are put at the service of exploitation, this does nothing to benefit the masses.

The sole explanation for our success is that our hospital belongs to the people and serves them, and this is a fruit of the revolution. We have categorized the hospital as a centre where our political line of serving the masses is put into effect, a centre in which we put into material action our principle that the revolution frees the people. Our hospital is a centre of national unity, a centre of class unity, a centre of revolutionary and organizational propaganda, a combat detachment.

Production is linked to hospital work, not only to provide the necessary foods, but also to encourage the convalescents to feel reintegrated into useful activity, and to strengthen the ties of unity and collaboration between hospital staff and patients.

Our hospitals are also centres for political and educational training. Hospital staff act as a political and educational propaganda team with patients on the wards and with out-patients.

Our line is reflected in the same way in crèches and in the centres for aid to the disabled. Our aim in regard to children is to integrate them from the earliest age into the life-style and the values that form part of the new society under construction. Our crèches use organized games and songs, and the guidance and discipline they instil, to encourage in children a spirit of initiative and responsibility, a collective sense, love for one another, appreciation of manual work and study, a hatred of exploitation. We are also building in them an attitude free of any superstition and a belief in the equality of the sexes. So our children have given themselves the name of 'continuers' of the revolution.

The centres for assistance to war disabled and others were designed in such a way as to reintegrate these sufferers in activity consistent with each one's potential and to avoid anyone feeling incapacitated, useless or invalided. There are no invalids in the revolution, since there is always some contribution one can make to the common cause. These centres offer education, literacy instruction, and general training.

Production is organized there too. Large kitchen-gardens, for example, are prepared and worked by the disabled themselves, who rediscover a feeling of usefulness in their existence, and lose any complex of being a dead weight or burden on society. Tailoring, cobbling and other crafts are made available to the disabled who can thus integrate themselves into the general process of socially useful work.

Certainly there is a lot more we must do in various fields. We do not have enough material, our personnel are not yet up to scratch, and suffice it to say that we do not yet have a single doctor in our liberated areas. These difficulties are aggravated by the enemy's criminal actions, its attacks and sadistic shelling of hospitals and crèches. But our work goes on and precisely because of its success, provokes great venom on the part of the colonialists.

A new people's order is gradually being introduced, with the foundations of an apparatus of power that will express the new relation of forces in our country, one which is favourable to the labouring masses. Society is thereby being transformed into a new society in which man is in harmony with himself and with nature.

The process of change that is occurring in our country is essentially the outcome of our people's struggles, but also receives a significant contribution through the combat and solidarity of all other peoples.

The Mozambican Revolution in the World Revolutionary Process

The Mozambican people's struggle at its current stage has three aspects. It is an anti-colonial struggle aimed at destroying the colonial-Fascist state; an anti-imperialist struggle aimed at destroying the control by multinational companies and ending imperialism's use of our country as a launching pad for aggression against progressive African regimes and protection of the bastions of racism and Fascism; finally it is a struggle aimed at destroying the system of exploitation of man by man and replacing it with a new social order at the service of the labouring masses of the people.

These varying aspects of our struggle are a real factor in our day-to-day fighting: the enemy troops we are fighting are armed by the imperialist powers, notably the United States, Federal Germany, France and the United Kingdom. We face, in addition to the Portuguese colonial army, the armed forces of Rhodesia and South Africa which are equipped by the same powers. An element of the Portuguese troops, notably the air force and the senior officers, are trained or retrained in the United States and Federal Germany, and they attend courses given by American, British and French officers, who are specialists in colonial wars of aggression. Military 'advisers' from these powers take part, albeit unofficially, in the planning of operations and sometimes even control their implementation. The colonial war of aggression is financed by the economic activity of the large-scale companies that exploit our people and plunder their wealth.

In the liberated areas of our country, the colonial-Fascist state has been ousted, and with it has gone the companies' control. People's power is being built in the free areas.

The fight against colonialism, Fascism and imperialism and against exploitation of man is the fight of all mankind for a new social order, peace and brotherhood between peoples. FRELIMO has always believed that our struggle forms an integral part of the general struggle of peoples for a new world, free of all forms of exploitation and oppression, free of war. FRELIMO's external activity in accordance with our situation is part of our overall political line and reflects the reality of our fight.

Accordingly, FRELIMO's external policy is aimed at isolating the enemy and strengthening international solidarity with our people.

Portuguese colonial-Fascism is seen today as one of the most degenerate and despised forms of exploitation of man. Its obscurantism, terrorist practices, and systematic recourse to the most sadistic of crimes and even to genocide have horrified all mankind.

Even the governments allied to Portugal are forced by public opinion to condemn Portuguese colonialism: witness the unanimous vote in the United Nations Security Council on Resolution 322 (1972) on 22 November 1972. This resolution, after condemning colonial aggression, demands that Portugal enter into negotiations with the liberation movements, implicitly recognized as their people's representatives, on the basis of recognition of the right to self-determination and immediate independence.

The December 1972 massacre in Wiriyamu and neighbouring villages has obliged even the Vatican to abandon its customary policy of silence on the colonial war, and has led many member governments of NATO to call for an international inquiry. The political disgrace inflicted on Prime Minister Caetano in London when about half the British Parliament accused him of murder is clear evidence of the isolation of the Portuguese regime.

The Lisbon regime is making a frantic effort to avoid its inevitable isolation by playing on the atmosphere of *détente* in Europe, and notably the European Security Conference, by relying on its submissiveness to the logistic needs of American imperialism for the Azores base, and by taking advantage of its own accomplices in the multinational companies and some member governments of the EEC.

One of the central tasks of international solidarity with our people is to neutralize colonialist attempts to break out of the isolation facing Lisbon. It is essential to broaden the international movement against colonialist use of NATO. The facts provide ample testimony that maintenance of the colonial war is closely tied to the military, financial and technical assistance of NATO in general, and of the United States, Federal Germany, France and Britain in particular.

An end to foreign economic activity in our country is an urgent necessity: all wars are fought with the support of the economic machine. The imperialist circles that argue that these activities are of benefit to our people, or have no direct bearing on the war, are showing utter disregard for our people's views as expressed by their legitimate representatives, and are revealing their own duplicity. During the Second World War, the allied powers always gave as one of the main targets of their attacks the enemy economic centres, including those in territory occupied by the Nazis. Many governments, like that of France, took penal measures against national enterprises that carried on their economic activity during the occupation.

Of particular significance is the giant Cabora Bassa project, financed and under construction by American, British, West German, French and other finance houses and companies. One should again note that dams were significant targets during the Second World War.

The excuse that economic relations with colonialist Portugal are necessary does not stand up to any examination. Since the underdeveloped Arab countries have decided to halt supplies of petrol to Portugal as a mark of solidarity with Africa, since the underdeveloped African countries have managed to break their economic ties with Portugal, it is impossible to believe that the developed industrialized countries depend for their advance on trade with colonialist, Fascist, underdeveloped Portugal.

FRELIMO's external policy, as well as seeking the isolation of the enemy and the strengthening of the solidarity movement with our people, is an expression of our fundamental principle of internationalism. Our external policy, therefore, seeks to express our own people's feelings of solidarity, brotherhood and friendship towards the fight of all peoples against colonialism and imperialism, against exploitation, and in favour of the building of a new society based on social justice, democracy, progress and peace.

The defence of a wider unity and broader front at each stage of the revolutionary process is a constant factor in our internal policy as well as being one of the basic principles of our external policy. We believe that when it is a question of people's fundamental interests in their fight against colonialism and imperialism and for the revolution, there must be no contradictions dividing the revolutionary forces. It is inevitable that contradictions will arise and they are a necessary part of progress in revolutionary thinking and practice. But their correct resolution must always take into account that our basic aim is victory for the people's interests, and this is inseparable from our unity.

In view of the character and objective of our fight, our natural allies are essentially: the national liberation movements, and in these there must naturally be included countries recently liberated, especially in Africa; socialist countries; the labouring masses, especially the working class; and the progressive anti-colonialist and anti-Fascist forces in the capitalist countries.

A logical corollary of the struggle is the close alliance with the brother peoples of Angola, and Guinea-Bissau and Cape Verde, who under the leadership respectively of the People's Movement for the Liberation of Angola (MPLA) and the African Party for the Independence of Guiné and Cape Verde (PAIGC), along with us, take up arms to fight the same enemy.

The recent proclamation of the Republic of Guinea-Bissau, which FRELIMO hails as a victory for the peoples struggling against Portuguese colonialism, has given a powerful boost to the diplomatic isolation of the Lisbon regime and has helped to reveal the aggressive nature of the Portuguese colonialists.

We give total solidarity and support to the nationalist forces who in Rhodesia, South Africa and Namibia are fighting against the Salisbury and Pretoria regimes. The national liberation struggle of the southern African peoples has direct and immediate impact on our own fight, and explains the close ties between us. The current intensification of the armed struggle for national liberation in Rhodesia, thanks to the successes achieved in the search for unity, will force the racist aggressors in the Salisbury regime to diminish their effective support to the Portuguese colonial war. The expansion of the fighting will create better conditions for our own people's struggle.

Development, under ANC leadership, of the challenge and mobilization of the people in South Africa is gradually creating conditions for higher forms of struggle at the very heart of the racist empire. In this context too, the legitimate armed fight by the Namibian people under SWAPO's leadership against racist annexation and for national liberation has diminished the Pretoria regime's aggressive capabilities and presented more favourable conditions for our peoples' struggle and victory.

The heroic and magnificent fight by the peoples of Indochina, and their victory over the bloodiest and most brutal aggressor of our age, American imperialism, has not only won our deepest solidarity, but has also provided constant stimulus and inspiration to our own struggle.

The fight of the Palestinian people for their national rights, the liberation struggle of the Arab, Latin American and Asian peoples, as an integral part of the broad movement of peoples for national liberation, provide powerful support and stimulus for our own fight.

The anti-colonialist African countries are fundamental allies in our fight. Many of them, such as Tanzania, Zambia, Congo, Guinea, Zaire and Senegal, have made great sacrifices to support us. Their blood was often shed during the barbaric attacks carried out by the colonialists. Africa's fight to recover its national resources, for economic and social development and for democratic freedoms, is also a considerable spur to favourable conditions for our fight. Action by the African countries, and by the OAU in particular, has been crucial in isolating Portuguese colonialism and strengthening international solidarity with our struggle. It should be noted that OAU mobilization has encouraged the Afro-Asian and non-aligned countries to take our side more decisively. The outcome of the recent Algiers summits, of the non-aligned and of the Arab countries, reflects this.

The anti-colonial, anti-Fascist and anti-racist cause wins support from all sane forces of mankind. Our experience has shown that it is possible to establish a broad front throughout the peoples of the world for the isolation of Portuguese colonialism. Within countries committed to NATO, which support the colonial war economically and militarily, action from the people can make governments dissociate themselves from Portuguese colonialism, as has been shown by the positions taken by the governments of Holland, Denmark and Norway. The recent stand taken by the people in Italy and Belgium, among others, has had a positive effect on the governments. Other governments, such as those in Sweden and Finland, which traditionally had good relations with Portugal, are now, thanks to the people's sentiment, committing themselves to support our cause.

Progress by the representative movements of the European labouring masses, development in the trends that strive for unity of the progressive forces within capitalist society, are tending to weaken imperialism and so contribute to our common success.

Of particular importance to us is the development of the anti-war movement in Portugal. Increasingly heavy casualties for the colonial troops, the astronomic rise in the cost of living due to the war, along with campaigns by the Portuguese democratic forces, have led to increasing consciousness on the part of the broad masses. The labouring masses and the working class who bear the main brunt of the war in lives, taxes and worsening living standards, and students and intellectual circles, have played a relevant part in this. We must emphasize that the Portuguese Communist Party and other progressive and democratic forces have been crucial to this process. We find today that all social strata and non-Fascist sectors are committed to struggling against the colonial war, as was shown in the anti-war manifesto approved by the Congress of Portuguese Democrats at Aveiro in 1973.

We record with satisfaction the widespread movement of deserters and resisters which is reaching a quarter of the rate of annual recruitment. Here it should be noted that according to the figures of the colonial-Fascist army, the number of deserters and resisters since the start of the colonial war has already exceeded 250,000.

It was within this framework of growing Portuguese anti-colonialist political consciousness that we saw in 1970 a critical new phase in the fight against the colonial war: democratic organizations, such as the ARA and the Revolutionary Brigades, as part of their strategy for anti-Fascist struggle chose the colonial war machine as a target for their armed attacks. The new phase was hailed by us as the opening of a fourth front against the colonial-Fascist regime. The success won on this fourth front not only encouraged and supported our people in their struggle and demonstrated the friendship of the Portuguese people, but in turn activated the movement among the Portuguese people against the colonial war and encouraged new elements to campaign. The Democrats' Congress in Aveiro before the Fascist elections and the demonstrations held by the united democratic opposition during the electoral campaign, revealed the breadth of the Portuguese anti-colonialist movement and militated in favour of fraternal friendship and solidarity between our peoples.

In the socialist countries, where, with the example of the great October Socialist Revolution, the system of exploitation of man by man has been overthrown, the masses in power are building a new society and are establishing a liberated area of our planet, a strategic rear-base for our fight. The wealth of theoretical and practical experience they acquired in the fight for liberation from the old society and to build the new, is an inexhaustible source of inspiration for all of us. The moral, political, diplomatic and material support granted to our struggle is an important ingredient of the successes we have achieved. Those countries are our natural allies throughout the entire process of revolution, since their objective is to build a new society free of any human alienation. Their existence provides the crucial external objective factor for the current triumph of our people's democratic revolution.

From 1971 to date, there has been an extraordinary strengthening of the ties of friendship and solidarity between us, and of the exemplary fraternal support afforded by the socialist countries to our cause. We have established direct relations between FRELIMO and the parties leading the German Democratic Republic, Bulgaria, China, the People's Democratic Republic of Korea, Yugoslavia, Romania, the Soviet Union and the Democratic Republic of Vietnam, and this has been a profound inducement to a deeper knowledge of our mutual experience, to a better understanding of our needs and situation, with the consequence of more appropriate material aid.

Anti-imperialist world forces are tending to be strengthened by progress in the socialist countries, at home and abroad, by the ending of the atmosphere of cold war and hysterical anti-Communism the imperialists tried to impose, by a break in the isolation of the German Democratic Republic and of China, by the Vietnam victory and the start of a dialogue towards the reunification of Korea.

The anti-imperialist fight is inseparable from the fight for a just and lasting peace. As our own experience shows, the colonial war does not reflect any antagonism between our people and the Portuguese people. The cause of the war lies in imperialism, in colonialism and in the system of exploitation. The struggle against imperialism is a vital contribution to the cause of peace, just as the struggle for peace and the mobilization of all mankind against the causes of wars of aggression is a vital contribution to the anti-imperialist fight. The fight for a just and lasting peace through fraternal relations between peoples is a constant basis for FRELIMO's external policy.

FRELIMO therefore hails and supports the efforts for *détente* in Europe, and for the transformation of the Mediterranean Sea and the Indian Ocean, to which we are directly linked, into zones of peace.

Prospects

The heavy defeats suffered by the colonialist armed forces, combined with the increasing international isolation of Portugal and growing opposition to the war from sane elements of the Portuguese people, have led the colonialists to make certain concessions of a kind intended to deceive public opinion and maintain the essence of control. In this framework there is the so-called autonomous status about which the Portuguese Fascist government makes so much noise.

Over the past 20 years, Mozambique has been successively colony, overseas province and state. The change of name, reflecting a purported change in status, has meant no change in the content, form and method either of the colonial administration or of the system of exploitation it protects.

The better to fool public opinion and sustain the illusions of certain circles, Marcelo Caetano, while making the most solemn declarations on the unity and integrity of the 'metropole' and the colonies, allows others of his underlings to spread the idea that autonomy is a first step to independence.

So in Mozambique we see certain elements connected with the large Portuguese monopolies setting up a private army and puppet political organizations aimed at 'struggling' for independence and fighting the 'Communist threat' posed by FRELIMO. The same circles, along with some strata of the European population, nurse illusions as to the viability of a White independence on Rhodesian lines, with the eventual use of some African puppets to put a gloss on the manoeuvre.

Marcelo Caetano seeks to prolong the death-throes of his regime by playing on the ultra-colonialists who are nostalgic for empire and bene-ficiaries of the most blatant forms of exploitation, and on the ultra-racists who want to form a White empire in a southern Africa dependent on monopoly capitalism.

But the existing reality is stronger than all the illusions and hopes of the exploitative forces. FRELIMO is an increasingly powerful political and military force. In provinces where armed struggle has not yet been launched, FRELIMO's presence is strong and the waves of thousands of arrests that have been taking place attest to this presence.

In the areas of armed struggle, the Portuguese army has suffered such disastrous defeats that Portugal's racist allies are expressing increasing alarm and concern; this leads Marcelo Caetano to accuse them in public of inexperience and of 'playing the enemy's game'.

Seventy thousand Portuguese soldiers, plus another twenty or thirty thousand puppet soldiers, equipped and financed by the NATO countries and supported by the air and land forces of South Africa and Rhodesia, are so incapable of preventing the spread of the war, and their own withdrawal from increasingly large areas, that the Portuguese leadership is obliged to consider raising conscription to six years.

The expansion of the struggle to Tete and Manica e Sofala Provinces has touched the enemy's most sensitive economic and strategic inter-ests, and made him mobilize enormous forces to protect these places, with the result that the garrison has been withdrawn from new sectors and the colonial army is decisively weakened. The strategic hope the enemy has in air-power has been shown to be entirely vain. In fact, the essential is control of the land, which is where the men and the resources are found.

FRELIMO's line and action, which express the objective interests of our people and of our labouring masses, have through the practical process of fighting led to a deepening of the content of our struggle. From the moment this deepening process struck the roots of domination, the system of exploitation of man and the institutions that maintain the system, our struggle was transformed into revolution.

This revolution is democratic and national, because it aims at the liberation of the country from all forms of foreign domination, the elimination of the obsolete forces of feudal domination inherited from the past, and the effective winning of democratic freedoms by the masses. It is a people's revolution too, since it proposes to install a new social order based on the objective interests of the labouring masses, where power belongs to them and is exercised by them in all sectors of society. This process is taking shape day by day in the liberated areas through the institutions established, through social relations of production, through the new life that is being created.

It is this new life responsive to our people's aspirations that makes it possible for the broad masses to grasp the idea of revolution. The revolutionary concept taken up by the masses becomes an invincible material force that destroys the colonial-Fascist army and the bases of the system of exploitation of our country, and this force will destroy any new aggression that may perchance occur.

Our just war of liberation completes ten years in 1974. Perhaps the accomplices that Portuguese colonialism has, or even open aggression from imperialism, will further prolong the conflict. But our victory is inevitable, and as our President Mondlane declared shortly before he was assassinated, it does not really matter if we take 20 or 30 years to win the victory: what matters is complete independence for the country and victory for the people's interests. For us the choice is not between dying in battle or living under domination. Death is inevitable for man. The real choice is between living and fighting for victory or lying down under exploitation, domination and oppression. The reality we are experiencing shows that victory is possible, that victory is becoming a fact.

3. Make Beira the Starting-Point for an Organizational Offensive*

The Process of Infiltration

From the period of the Transitional Government, Sofala and the city of Beira particularly have been the centre for agents of opposition, faithful representatives and spiritual sons of colonialism. When we arrived in Beira, soon after the signing of the Lusaka Agreement, we were met by godsons of the administrators, godmothers of the National Feminine Movement, members of ANP, agents of PIDE. They were the ones who received FRELIMO here in Beira. They offered cars, houses, they set up parties and also set up a 'nice girl' for the FRELIMO commanders.

All this to curry favour with FRELIMO. One had to accommodate the commanders, 'poor things', who had been living in the bush, shower them with invitations, dinners, fine cars, lodge them in the best hotels, take them on the promenade.

That's how they took the lead and prepared the ground to manage the process in Mozambique. They were preparing conditions to manage the political option of the government of the People's Republic of Mozambique. Beira was a city of racial discrimination, but when they received the FRELIMO commanders they all presented themselves as genuine Mozambicans and consistent opponents of racism. They were the mentors of racism who offered their daughters to drive the FRELIMO commanders, seeking in this way to show just how far their anti-racism had reached.

The 'pretty girl' with a soft voice . . . like the buzzing of a bee in one's ear . . . the voice modulated to talk to the commander who was used to the sound of cannon, napalm bombs, bazookas and shelling. A beautiful voice asking the commander what he liked to drink, what music he wanted to hear. And the commander said: 'All the music.' As he didn't know any music, he had to say that he liked all music. And the lass played all the music. . . .

Next day when the population say: 'That one was PIDE', the commander replies: No, you don't know, I'm the one who knows.' Then the

*This speech was delivered in Beira on 11 January 1980.

73

population wonder: 'You weren't here; I know him, he killed my cousin, he tortured my husband, he arrested my brother, he raped my daughter, as a PIDE agent.'

That's Beira. And if we don't keep a wary eye on all aspects of Beira, we shall be aiming with our eyes shut and hit our friends.

Let us make a brief analysis.

The Dynamizing Groups began under the Transitional Government. They have great merit. But they found many difficulties in Beira, particularly because of the racism that was displayed in the hotels, in the buses, in the restaurants, in the boarding houses, on the beaches, everywhere.

The population saw their own initiative totally destroyed. Their resistance, their capacity for organization in strength were also destroyed. There was a lack of awareness of the situation, an inability to analyse the Beira phenomena and to find the right answers. So we had manifestations of populism, ultra-leftism, liberalism and indiscipline. For them this was freedom demonstrated in violent language, disorganization, failure in punctuality, failure of planning, failure to define tasks clearly. And then the enemy took advantage. The enemy moved in.

Beira was a centre for the training of criminals. Jardim's agents humiliated the population, brutalized the population, abused women. That was a particular speciality of the GEs.

We Have Not Yet Removed Them But We Shall Be Unrelenting

When we proclaimed independence, there was a flight by the settlers. Then these former enemy agents infiltrated government structures, enterprises, factories, infiltrated everywhere and took the reins. And up till now we have not removed them. They have been identified, they live among us.

With the precipitate departure of the settlers, the enemy agents occupied major responsibilities in the FRELIMO structures, in the Dynamizing Groups. Some of those who the day before had been murderers of the people managed to become our administrators. How can they be good administrators for FRELIMO?

So there is money being stolen from the co-operatives, from the People's Shops. And when we ask: 'Where are those 400,000 escudos you stole?', the reply comes: 'I've already spent them, go ahead and criticize me.' He stole the state's money, he stole the people's money which we could have used to build roads, schools, maternity centres and hospitals, and he wants us to criticize him. But when all's said and done, he never stole the settlers' money.

When we proclaimed independence we handed out responsibilities, but we did not hand out the responsibility of stealing. If an administrator, or a Dynamizing Group secretary, or a factory manager, or the members of an administrative commission steal, then they are not representatives of our power. A crime committed by a police inspector is never discovered, because he's the one who appoints the investigation team. He orders the dossier to be filed away and so the crimes, abuses, rapes, ideological, physical and moral attacks go on.

We all know the story of the animals meeting to choose their chief. They chose the leopard who began to use a big chair and to dress in clothes. At night the chief, with his court, went out to hunt other animals. Relatives of the victims came to complain to the chief, who would always answer: 'Did you notice the characteristics of the animal that ate your child?' The complainant would retort: 'The only characteristic we saw was that the animal has a tail.' But the chief had his tail inside his trousers and remained seated all the time. So it was impossible to identify him.

We see this in Beira. The former PIDEs, ANPs, Commandos, GEs, by occupying positions of responsibility, installed injustice in Beira and that created confusion among the population. They used our power to wreak violence on the people. Since they are used to corruption, they cannot live in our way, cannot behave as we do. And it's what we are seeing in the country, and most commonly in Beira.

Our school is the greenhouse of the new mentality, but there are parasites there too. And when there are shapers, there are also misshapers of the new mentality. The teachers themselves, distorting the essential aims of education, encourage corruption, and feed the indiscipline of the pupils in regard to their parents. The girl student, who knows the teacher well and agrees to go dancing with him, will be given high marks without studying. Meanwhile another one, who studies but does not agree to play the teacher's tune, has low marks. We witnessed this in Beira in 1976. We had to take a series of steps then against those corrupt teachers. Former FRELIMO deserters, traitors to the people's cause, had set themselves up in this city's secondary schools.

Along with them were potential enemy agents, insulting the People's Republic of Mozambique, running down state policy, slandering its leaders, and describing the Mozambican people as incapable. We shall be relentless with them. We overthrew colonialism. If their bosses did not win, how much less will these last-minute agents? All they are left with is a mania for imitation. They think they are civilized, knowledgeable about society, but all they can do is to copy the settlers' mannerisms.

We know the story of the monkey who saw his owner shaving with a razor. The monkey thought that was fine. So he prepared a long razor, found a mirror and you know what he did? He cut his throat and died, because he thought that was how to shave. These degenerates are like that monkey. And that is the situation in Beira.

Criminals Trained in Rhodesia

We applied sanctions in 1976 against Rhodesia and a wave of violence, criminality, disrespect, panic and general disorder was set off in the city of Beira. The former criminals found a place in Rhodesia and went over there. They found what they had been looking for during the Transitional Government. We wanted to re-educate them by sending them to Niassa, as we are generous and respect human life. Although they were criminals, we did not kill them. We arrested them and sent them to re-education camps. They ran away to the land of their uncle, Ian Smith.

Why uncle? Because he is cousin to the settlers who were here. Those settlers went but the uncle remained. So they ran away from the re-education camps and went to Rhodesia. Many of them are from Sofala, Manica and Tete, where the colonial war was most active and where repression created most criminals. We cannot forget the massacres of Inhaminga, Wiriyamu, Joao and Mucumbura. Who were the authors? Was it only the Portuguese troops? No, it was the Commandos as well and these Mozambican GEs.

I was talking about Mozambicans, White and Black, who were in the colonial army and who in the Transitional Government were found with skulls as ashtrays. They were found with flasks of alcohol holding human ears. They are madmen who live by slaughter. Some are in the administration, in enterprises, in schools, as agitators. They are the ones who are constantly putting the wind up the population by saying: 'Something's going to happen . . . Beira is going to be shelled . . . there were aircraft over last night . . . you hear shooting at night.' They are the former PIDEs, native police, chiefs, GEs, Commandos and Flechas who sow panic among the population.

The godmothers of the National Feminine Movement are also involved, the ones whose only part was in learning to make embroidery and cakes and who cooked only when there were ANP celebrations. That's why we say the proof of the pudding is in the eating. This kind is here in Beira, alienated and petty assimilated individuals who still regard the population as natives and look down on them.

So they went to Rhodesia to continue this sort of life. They were trained and issued with weapons – grenades, mortars, mines and rounds – to come hunting in Mozambique. And so we find that Beira is the scene of the shooting, that grenades are lobbed into public places, that economic targets, fuel depots and roads are attacked, with loss of human life and material damage.

Who Commits These Crimes?

Who are the perpetrators of these crimes? They live and talk with the population. They use tribalism as their social base. They use regionalism, family connection, local affiliation and often racism by attacking the white skin to provoke a state of panic. We are against racism but the struggle against racism needs daily practice, needs to be experienced by everyone. It is not enough to say that one is against racism. If we were racists we should have no justification in condemning the South Africans.

Tribalists and racists serve international imperialism; imperialism has no colour. Its colour is exploitation, it is oppression, its colour is the assassination and massacre of populations.

They do not even serve their own interests, these simple tools and pawns of imperialism. They were the ones who brought the Rhodesians to shell Dondo, Nhangau and the FPLM barracks. And it is among them that we find widespread indiscipline and sloth. These are characteristics of the enemy and not of the Mozambican people. They come to the People's Republic of Mozambique, a country born in the people's blood and sacrifice, and they want to set up their base for disorder in Beira, a city liberated by us with our blood and sweat, a city liberated by our sacrifice and determination, by our courage and heroism. We shall be relentless against them.

The terrorist actions in the city of Beira are backed by acts of economic sabotage and deliberate disorganization in industry. Sabotage of the Inhaminga quarry, for example, has a highly damaging effect on the production of cement and asbestos, both for domestic use and for export. These are the bandits who are destroying our economy so that we should remain poor.

The acts of sabotage are felt not only in the city of Beira but also in Sofala Province and other provinces in the centre and north of the country. Cement, gravel, asbestos go from here to other provinces and they destroy it.

They also destroy trade routes, and destroy our vehicles. They come here from Rhodesia, destroy lorries, kill carriers and drivers and so the population's products do not get out, are not shipped. They attack co-operatives, People's Shops, destroy the communications system as they did on the Gorongosa to Amaringue highway. So we do not ship out the population's products, maize, cotton and sunflower in particular.

There is illegal storing and hoarding of essential items too, as we saw in today's newspaper, *Noticias da Beira*: 15 tons of beans have rotted in the People's Shop warehouse. And they do this when there are long queues.

Our Struggle Killed the Tribe

We are infiltrated. And there are many who are aware of this and do nothing because the bandits call on tribal backing. But our struggle killed the tribe. It was the first thing we killed because the enemy's strength is tribalism. So we had no hesitation in acting against tribalists, racists and regionalists. We killed the tribe to give birth to the nation. This is not a nation of tribes, it is not a nation of races. So when the lice reach the underwear, one must boil some water and put all one's clothes into it.

We have already mentioned corruption in the secondary schools. They are also affected by drug-peddling and drug-taking. There are teachers of drug-taking who teach their charges how to smoke. Is that normal? Certainly it's normal in a colonial state, in a capitalist state. That's their character. But we are not capitalists. We seek socialism. Socialism means health and education, nourishing food in abundance for everyone, good-quality clothing, blankets, sheets, shoes, road, rail, air and sea transport. And bicycles as well. In such countries as Holland, China and Vietnam, the bicycle is the main mode of transport. But we are trying to get the aeroplane before we have the bicycle. We do not all have the same opportunities.

Good roads, clean water for all, housing for the entire people, for the 12 million, each with his own home, and sport for all as well. This is the socialism we want.

Socialism means an organized society: fighting disease; respect for the family, education for children, responsibility. We must have schools for everyone, hospitals for everyone. That's what we call socialism.

Now what do the bandits want? They destroy the few, meagre infrastructures we have in the country. Their aim is clear. They encourage indiscipline and disrespect in the schools. They address the teacher with intimate forms and as 'comrade teacher'. We don't want that. There is no 'comrade teacher'. There is no 'comrade chief'. The correct form is 'Mister', 'Mr Joao', 'Mr Antonio', 'Mrs Amelia', 'Mrs Deolinda'. Once there were ladies and women. The ladies were the Whites, the women were the Blacks. And so I say 'Dona Margarida', 'Dona Deolinda', 'Dona Gertrudes'. That's the respect we want. Sometimes when we are talking about bandits, criminals, many people say: 'This comrade stole . . . when the comrade burglar entered my house. . . .' A comrade stealing? Others say: 'That evil-living woman, that evil-living comrade, came to my house. . . . Is a prostitute a comrade? The term 'comrade' is used for anyone. We don't want that. We should say 'Mr' and 'Mrs': for the male nurse, the female nurse, the doctor, the midwife, the teacher, the administrator, the governor, the director. All have a category.

In Beira enemy pamphlets are in circulation; enemy watchwords scrawled on the walls, obscene, immoral words. And this goes on in the schools too. We shall not go on standing idly by.

This occurs in Beira because the values of the colonial epoch have not yet been eliminated. And what are these values? We say again: racism, tribalism, corruption, regionalism, banditry. Beira was already a city of bandits and we did not carry out an offensive against them to remove them. There is anti-social behaviour, drug-taking, rumour-mongering and slander running down the People's Republic of Mozambique.

Strong Leadership and the People's Participation Are Essential

So I want to say that our party and government structures must be strengthened. But our strength lies in the people. If the people do not participate, if they merely watch, our structures are unable to formulate and define the tasks for the people and explain how to act against the bandits.

A strong leadership is essential, and it is essential to involve the people since it was the people's participation that brought us victory in the war. If the people participate in the pursuit, location and arrest of the bandits, Beira will within six months be the most peaceful city in our country.

We have structures that don't function, don't work. We have OMM which is a strength since Mozambican women are brave and have a heroic spirit. The Mozambican woman is not afraid of sacrifices, is not afraid of difficulties. She showed this throughout the resistance to colonialism, in the armed struggle for national liberation, and today in support for Zimbabwe. The Mozambican woman wants clear tasks. If we tell our women 'wipe out the bandits', they will wipe them out. The Mozambican woman is strong and so OMM must have the task of restoring order, tranquillity and calm to the city of Beira. We want Beira to set the example to other cities. There is no place for riot and disturbance in the People's Republic of Mozambique.

The Mozambican Youth Organization has to be effective as well. We have some vigilance groups who do not watch over anything, perhaps they are compromised as well and so the infiltrators exploit their membership of the vigilance groups to do what the animals' chief did in the anecdote I told you. We have the militia, we have the production councils for workers. They must be more effective so that there is no indiscipline, no slacking and we can meet our targets.

All our instruments, the governor, administrators, courts, police, security service should go to the people. The people are unwittingly sheltering bandits. Sheltering them means receiving them and giving them food. We want to put a stop to intrigue, rumour, indiscipline and corruption, so as to advance the revolution. If we are to build a happy future we must end hunger.

This is the first time this year, 1980, that we are speaking to the people. A new decade has begun, the decade of the 1980s. What do we want to do in the next ten years? Are we going on as we are? To sow and reap a good harvest, one must first clear the ground. One must turn the soil, one must weed and water, and then we shall have a good harvest.

For our house to have a pleasant, homely and lively feel, we must clean it every day, clear out the dust that affects our lungs, that will affect our life if we have not provided healthy living conditions.

When we decided to speak in Beira we did so because it is a city with particular traits, where there is tribalism, racism and regionalism, and a population filled with complexes. That is why we did not leave yesterday when we concluded the Front Line states meeting, but decided to stay and talk to you here. Our fight must begin from here, from the centre of the country, a starting-point for us to remove the bandits.

4. Transform the State Apparatus into an Instrument of Victory*

The state, the state apparatus, is not an abstraction. The state apparatus is all of us meeting here, heads of well-defined structures. It is the ministers, provincial governors, secretaries of state, national or provincial directors, executive heads in cities, districts and localities.

We are here because we are the people with responsibilities. We are here because we merit the political confidence of the party. We have the task in our sectors of smashing the structures, working methods and mentality of colonial-capitalism. We have the task of building a new state apparatus that in character, content and working methods serves our interests.

But some people, with a certain nostalgia, the worshippers and admirers of the colonial system, cherish and nurse its structures instead of smashing them. This is typical of a mentality in bondage to decadent values, negative values – counter-revolutionary values. It is not by chance that we are discovering in the offensive we launched: a failure of management: the hammer-blow does not reach the factory, the warehouse, the docks, the shop, the school, the hospital; red tape established as a working method; routine as a way of life, routine that is conservative; promotion of incompetence; neglect, lack of interest, regarded as something normal; lack of a sense of organization; indiscipline, theft, drunkenness, a disregard for punctuality; waste, squandering, destructiveness; lack of hygiene and cleanliness, an absence of courtesy; corruption, bribery.

The widespread failures in management and discipline have reached such a pitch that in the face of the offensive that was launched, we have already witnessed signs of open challenge to the guidelines we laid down. This challenge is led and guided by a handful of infiltrators who find room for manoeuvre in the various sectors because our power is missing, our discipline is missing, and our interests are not defended.

*This speech was delivered in Maputo on 7 February 1980.

What Are the Reasons for This?

We issued guidelines and created the basis for smashing the colonial-capitalist state apparatus. We put forward measures, passed laws, established new institutions of state power, appointed officials in our confidence at least to the level, for example, of national directors.

However, there is no certainty of the influence of officials able to carry out the guidelines in departments and sectors. In other words at the rank-and-file level, the sectors are unaffected and, what is more serious, they constrain the decisions that the heads must be taking all the time.

We have not yet broken with colonial working methods: it is impossible for us to recognize reality and alert ourselves to the population's difficulties, if we stick to the red-tape machinery of documents alone; we are not in direct touch with reality – we don't go to the factories, the warehouses, the docks, the schools, the hospitals, the farms, or even to our offices; we often do not know the secretary in our private office; in settling problems, we do not heed public opinion, we do not seek the views of the sectors directly affected.

We think we can understand reality in our sectors merely by way of official documents, minutes, reports and memoranda. In other words, we stay immured in our offices in a sea of paper. So we lose a sense of urgency, we lose a sense of the important. We fall into the routine of petty issues. A chain of these petty issues becomes the pattern of our daily round. We lose initiative, we do not lead.

We are seeing again that the principle of constant co-ordination of the various structures has not been taken up. We all talk in meetings about co-ordination, interaction and interdependence, but we do not make the systematic effort required to co-ordinate. We said that ministers must meet to find a joint solution to common problems. But this is not done. The problems go on being settled in isolation, or remain unsettled. We said that national directors must travel in groups to the provinces to deal with specific problems there. But this is not done. We said that provincial directors must as a group travel regularly into the districts to understand the local reality and settle problems. But this is not done either.

The structures in the state apparatus are infiltrated and disorganized. We do not punish indiscipline, we tolerate it. We do not punish saboteurs, we coexist with them and still pay them salaries. We do not remove or combat those who hanker for colonial structures, hierarchies and methods. Quite the reverse, we use them as if they were good cadres.

Smartness, a good appearance, courtesy, delicacy are not yet norms, are not yet an integral part of the approach of workers in the state apparatus, of their approach either to work or to dealing with the public.

A keenness to study, an effort to make the best use of professionalism are not yet current or encouraged. We do not yet make general use of examinations as the criterion for selection, admission and promotion of workers in the state apparatus. Several of the state structures are still fertile ground for the sowing and nurturing of ultra-leftist concepts. The mistakes and deviations are not spotted until months or years later.

Our structures are infiltrated by elements who are irresponsible, negligent, incompetent, thieving, malicious, dishonest, and the faithful servants of colonialism. Our structures shelter opportunists and the power-seekers who, under the banner of racism, tribalism and regionalism, stir up confusion, division and chaos, to satisfy their own personal, selfish and petty secondary interests. They are the mud on our boots that we must take off and clean.

And it is those of us meeting here who have the task of creating the conditions for the mud to be cleaned off all sectors in the state apparatus and in the apparatus of economic management. Each of you here has management responsibilities at various levels in the state apparatus.

We do not wonder that businesses, factories, farms, service agencies, schools and hospitals are at the mercy of saboteurs, infiltrators, bandits, thieves, idlers, misfits, grubs and rodents, when this sort of thing goes on in the state structures that must lead these other bodies.

We must take the initiative, we must be permanently on the offensive. It is the battle of class struggle. We must keep the enemy always on the defensive.

State leadership over the economy, over the productive sectors (not excluding education, health, information), does not make itself felt merely through instructions, orders and regulations. It also comes through example and the daily effort of organization, discipline, efficiency and effectiveness, speed and energy in doing tasks, deep knowledge of and sensitivity to the people's problems, respect for work, devotion and enthusiasm for one's duties.

The state must be the first to be organized and totally committed to serving the interests of the people. We must always be clear that the example is set at the top. The example in the exercise of power must come from the top. If this has not yet been done fully, it is because we have not yet banged home the hammer we have in our hands. The nail has not gone in, has not reached the heart of the wood. So our structures are weak, they are not solid, they are susceptible, they do not form a unity with all their personnel on the same road shoulder to shoulder and marching in step towards the same goal, towards development and the consolidation of socialism.

Measures To Be Taken

At the close of our meeting, we feel there is general agreement that we should take steps, including some legislation, to ensure the following points:
1. Full establishments in management structures, at ministry level, and executive level in provinces, districts, localities and communal villages.

2. Organization of management in enterprises and organization of the actual enterprises by providing them with regulations, capital, budgets, etc. On this point since there are numerous instances, there will have to be an operational plan to deal with them all.

3. We want managements to manage and not act as firemen responding to an emergency but letting it stop them tackling underlying issues. The management must organize, plan and control, and insist on accountability.

4. The system of internal information and co-ordination must operate. We have to ensure the exchange of information. In this field there is an urgent need for: a) correct linkage between the national directorates in the ministries and between the ministries; b) regular functioning of the provincial, district, city and locality executives; c) correct linkage and chain of command between national and local directorates; d) correct linkage between state executive bodies and enterprises such as to ensure that on the one hand the state executive bodies supervise and control, and on the other hand the enterprises are managed by their own management; e) monthly and six-monthly accounting by each person in charge to his hierarchical superior.

5. It is essential that, on the model of what has already been provided for in the state apparatus, the law should ensure discipline in enterprises and empower their managements to penalize indiscipline, slackness, negligence, carelessness and bad workmanship, and to reward good work. Absenteeism should be grounds for dismissal.

6. Criminal activities, theft, misappropriation of goods, poor maintenance of the enterprise's equipment are common-law offences that should be controlled by the courts with greater severity.

7. It is essential to link enterprises on the basis of objective laws of a socialist economy and legal system. In this field, it is particularly pertinent to define the role of production units, wholesalers, retailers, carriers, importers and exporters. Interrelationship between enterprises must be stated in contracts that provide penalty clauses for a breach of their conditions.

8. Salaries and wages must reflect the reality of the enterprise's economic performance; deviations from the planned performance should be reflected in pay.

9. We must ensure competence and responsibility at work. Recruitment, promotion, pay rises should follow objective criteria, and appropriate qualifications must be demanded for each post. A worker's usefulness and behaviour should be studied before any promotion, and such promotion should normally be made on the basis of tests.

10. Personnel must not be recruited to one sector to the detriment of other sectors. Services and enterprises cannot compete with one another by poaching cadres, technicians and workers. It is imperative that our country should offer equal pay for equal work. It is equally imperative that we put a stop to the tradition of special privileges for workers in particular sectors. If a brewery worker can take beer home, if a worker at

Avicola can take chickens home, then the works driver will borrow the car for his personal use, the bus driver will do the same thing, and soon the cashier will be taking the money home. It is robbery, it damages the enterprise, and it damages the public.

11. Workers must come to work properly dressed at all services and firms. There are some sectors where uniform or a working dress is compulsory. The working dress must protect the worker, and in the food industry must also maintain health and hygiene requirements. Administrative personnel in government, services and enterprises must come to work in a suit and tie or tunic. Going to work in shirt-sleeves, sandals, T-shirts with slogans and advertisements, or jeans shows a lack of respect for the place of work, for colleagues, for superiors and above all for the public. As well as the poor taste it often reveals, it leads to disrepute, liberalism and indiscipline. As regards women, we must urge decency and good taste. It is unacceptable to come to work in a headscarf. Where the head needs to the covered for purposes of hygiene – in the food industry for example – then the workplace should provide a cap.

12. Ministries, services and enterprises must without fail organize an upgrading system for their staff, combining practice, study and theory, in-house training, secondments and training seminars, evening classes, etc.

13. We must make the fullest use of internationalist solidarity and technical co-operation to train cadres at home and abroad. We shall have to send tens of thousands of people for training abroad to meet the demands of development.

14. The quality of our products and their packaging and our advertising must be competitive.

5. We Are Declaring War on the Enemy Within*

Colonial Situation – Lourenço Marques

Today we shall have a conversation which will be disagreeable. When we have a jigger in our foot we must grab it and take it out. But that hurts and draws blood too.

We shall soon be celebrating our fifth independence anniversary. Many of us have already lost the real picture of our colonized country. Many of us have already forgotten what colonial oppression was. Many of us have forgotten what Lourenço Marques was: Lourenço Marques as the capital of colonialism in our country; Lourenço Marques as the disseminating centre for colonial oppression – boundless humiliation, degrading discrimination. Lourenço Marques was the laboratory and redoubt of all the evils of colonialism. Lourenço Marques was the organizational centre for interethnic and interracial conflicts: among Blacks there were conflicts between Changane and Ronga, conflicts between Changane and Ronga who despised the Vatswa, conflict between Changane, Ronga, Vatswa and Bitonga, who despised the Chope; but all the southerners joined in despising the northerners; northerners were looked upon and treated as foreigners in Lourenço Marques; and among Blacks too there was a handful of assimilated people who despised the natives.

That was your Lourenço Marques. That's what we found here. Lourenço Marques – a city of racial conflicts: suburbs – for Blacks and mulattos; and [at best] on the border between the cement city and the reed huts, Alto Mae, where some mulattos lived. There was also: an Indian neighbourhood; a neighbourhood for Indians from Goa; a neighbourhood for Pakistanis; a neighbourhood for poor Portuguese; a neighbourhood for middle-level Portuguese; a neighbourhood for rich Portuguese. Lourenço Marques was a centre for depersonalization and alienation – areas for Black prostitutes; areas for White prostitutes. Lourenço Marques, a centre for labour discrimination – people for

*A speech given in Maputo on 18 March 1980 which launched the internal Offensive.

86

clearing rubbish and yards: errand boys, cooks, houseboys, waiters in restaurants, cafés and hotels, grocer's boys, government messengers.

Who doesn't remember the fairs for the 'sale of lads'? There was a whole system established: recruiting agents went to the marketing centres of Manhiça, Moamba, Matutuine, Magude, Bilene, Macia, Canicado, Manjacaze, and to Gaza and Inhambane. They enticed young people with promises of jobs in the big city, promises of a future. They brought them here like cattle in trucks, rain or shine. When they got to Lourenço Marques they were kept in warehouses, in the cold and the heat. For food they had meal and pounded groundnuts cooked with salt. They stayed cooped up for months as sale goods waiting to be bought.

Along went the bosses, the rich settlers, the ladies with a dog on a leash, the wives of the upper bourgeoisie, and even some of the poor, to buy. To buy what? A hen, a chicken, a goat or what? They went to buy their lads. They bought them from the recruiting agents for 300 or 500 escudos, and paid them a monthly wage of 75 escudos. Which means they gave the agents 300 or 500 escudos to have a yard boy paid 75 escudos a month. With his 75 escudos a month, the lad had to repay the recruiting agent's expenses: pay for his transport and 'storage'. With his 75 escudos a month, the lad had to pay taxes and the usual expenses of a man who wants to marry and make his future. Then the lad wasn't used to handling plates and glassware! If he broke one piece in a set of crockery, his pay might be docked for a year to pay for the whole set. But the incomplete set of crockery stayed with the boss. It wasn't handed over to the lad who paid for it. The boss kept both sets: one complete and the other incomplete.

And how were they treated in the boss's house? The dog's food was better than that given to the boy. They had no medical treatment. While the dog went about in the boss's car, the boy went on foot in the sun. These lads were not from Lourenço Marques. They came from Gaza, Inhambane and other provinces. When the boss was transferred, as happened in the civil service, he would take his merchandise, who was the boy, since he was already used to him.

As for the Lourenço Marques boys, they were: the street scavengers; used as apprentices for the mechanic, the electrician, the panel-beater, the plumber, upholsterer or polisher at best. That was work for the Lourentine. There were women living on petty trade – the selling of bananas, tomatoes, cabbages, a few scraps of charcoal. People who lived on dealing in small shellfish or bean-cakes. People who were used as masons and carpenters. That was Lourenço Marques, the capital of social division which sapped our strength.

Lourenço Marques was a city fragmented by religion: Catholic, Protestant, Presbyterian, Nazarene, Episcopal Methodist, Wesleyan, Anglican, Muslim. When we took power, Lourenço Marques was the capital of crime, delinquency, banditry, robbery, rape, begging, licensed prostitution, a city of disquiet and murder (murders that reached their peak in the new year celebrations).

Lourenço Marques was the cement city, built to define clearly the difference between us and the settlers. Who does not remember the pass that was demanded of us after nine at night? Did you come here after nine in the evening? Lourenço Marques was also the city of reed and tin, relegated to the marshes, a storehouse for labour and suffering to provide the settler's luxury. Who does not remember his neighbourhood in the suburb patrolled by mounted police and the riot police dogs? Who does not remember his neighbourhood in the suburb? Don't the ministers remember? And the national directors who want to ride over the people, who are like crocodiles when they go to APIE, don't they remember their suburb?

That was Lourenço Marques: on one side, cement, opulence, the brightly-decked streets; on the other, insecurity, social injustice, discrimination, poverty and wretched darkness. This was Lourenço Marques built for the settlers by the blood and sweat of Mozambican workers.

When FRELIMO took power, we found our cities undermined by: PIDEs, OPVs, ANPs, Commandos, Flechas, GEs, GEPs, the National Feminine Movement, the Godmothers of War. Aren't they there among you? But you say: 'Oh, this Mozambican Government . . .' We are pure, you are the ones who are impure. We know you. You don't know yourselves. We did not coexist with PIDE. You did coexist with them. And you are afraid to drive them out. Because 'they'd be missed'? Missed? By whom? Who are they?

We even found some of the actual agents of the puppet organizations created by colonialism and imperialism – MOCONEMO, a party that came into existence after 25 April as a PIDE creation. They're there with you. They're in the factories too. Some even hold high positions; FICO; FRECOMO; GUMO; the Democratic Coalition; MONIPAMO; POPOMO; MIMO; the participants of 7 September and 21 October; those who took the Radio. They're there with you.

When FRELIMO took power, we found Lourenço Marques the model of all our country's cities: a city of patronage, orgies, bacchanalia, corruption, favours. It was the city where the Portuguese colonial soldier arrived and departed, bringing and leaving the seeds of vice, degradation, immorality, drunkenness, venereal disease and crime. The schools were the symbol of racial discrimination. They were workshops where young people were moulded to serve colonialism. The few Mozambican children who attended them were prevented from learning their people's history, their country's geography. We found the schools were authentic monuments to colonialism: Lycée Salazar; Antonio Barroso College; Lycée Antonio Enes. Who went to these schools? Who taught in these schools? What was taught in these schools?

The hospitals were centres of racial, social and economic discrimination. Who doesn't remember the Miguel Bombarda Hospital and the humiliation one suffered there? The consulting rooms were gold mines and a means of exploitation. The doctor grew rich at the patient's expense. Disease was an instrument to satisfy the capitalist ambitions of the hospital's masters. Death too was food to colonial-capitalism. The undertakers hunted for corpses like vultures. A funeral cost tens of thousands of escudos.

In administration and police stations, the highest position for Mozambicans was: as a native policeman; as a subordinate tool of colonialism; as the subordinate who wielded the whip and the *palmátoria* to oppress his own brother. The colonialists had their instruments: their laws, their lawyers' offices, the courts. For the natives there was forced labour, deportation to São Tomé e Principe, shackle law that bound our legs and made them bleed.

All this was Lourenço Marques. All this was a reality throughout the country. But there was more still: all industry was concentrated in the settlers' hands; large and small businesses concentrated in the settlers' hands. The Mozambican was the underling – a simple follower of instructions, a despised producer, a humble servant with no dignity, an unqualified driver, an unknown workman building wealth. Trade, supermarkets, shops, stalls, boutiques, barbers and hairdressers, all concentrated in the settlers' hands. The Mozambican did not even have a place to sell sticks. The Mozambican did not even have the right to an egg stall in the market. All buying, selling and dealing was carried on by the settlers.

The garages, workshops and civil engineering were concentrated in the settlers' hands. The qualified mechanic was a settler; the recognized metalworker was a settler; the foreman was a settler. The settler who came to our country as an apprentice became an expert. The settler who arrived as a peasant became a farmer, a landowner, a plantation owner. The settler who arrived unknown and ignorant was rapidly surrounded with wealth, assistants and runners.

As for the sale of reeds, the sale of zinc sheets, the sale of water tins, the sale of skirt-cloth, the sale of a needle, the sale of glasses, plates, knives and pans, the sale of cigarettes, the sale of paraffin and matches, the sale of soap, sugar and oil, the sale of charcoal, all this was in whose hands? It was in the hands of those who abandoned the country when we overthrew colonialism. It was in the hands of a clutch of settlers throughout the country – fewer than 100,000 settlers in the city of Lourenço Marques. They took themselves off. And that's what we found.

That's what colonialism means: exploitation, oppression, humiliation, social and economic discrimination, racism, tribalism and regionalism. That's what colonialism means: bribery, corruption and immorality; robbery; nepotism, favouritism and patronage; individualism and ambition; servility and subservience; prostitution; vagrancy; banditry; unemployment and delinquency; begging; orgies; bacchanalia and drunkenness; drugs; destruction of the family; social disruption, insecurity and fear – all synonymous with colonialism.

Destroying all this was the aim of the armed struggle for national liberation. Destroying all this was the aim of the class struggle, of the struggle against the internal enemy, of the struggle we are waging and will go on waging in our country.

Some of you ask: 'Why do you want socialism?' We say: 'We do not have a vocation to maintain and feed the colonialism we knew.' Some of you ask: 'What is socialism in Mozambique?' Socialism in Mozambique means happiness for us.

So for the world, Mozambique no longer exists. But it existed in the colonial time. All the Western press used to speak about the 'beautiful city of Lourenço Marques'. Great journeys, great tourism to come and see the prostitutes walking about. That was Mozambique. Then it existed for the whole world. And now Mozambique does not exist, it died on the day when we buried colonialism. We are here, and we say just that to these friends: here we are.

Whatever they do or want, nobody will change the geographical standpoint of the Mozambican people. Nobody will overthrow the independence of Mozambique. We have chosen socialism and we shall build socialism. Nobody will come from outside to build it for us.

It doesn't matter if they ignore us in the West. We do not exist because of them. They did not produce us. They did not give us independence. Whether they say anything or not, what does it matter? We are speaking, we have our own tongues.

They used to talk about it. It was fine for them. Western civilization was here, was what we characterize as colonialism. The spread of Christianity. That's what it was. That's what civilization was.

The Victories of Independence

After independence, we went on with our fight for liberation: the fight to restore dignity, identity and the Mozambican culture; the fight to build a new society, a new outlook, a New Man; the fight to destroy exploitation; the fight to build socialism.

We freed the land.

We nationalized the schools: education ceased to be a privilege; we abolished the private schools and private tutors.

We nationalized the health service: the hospitals were opened to all the people; we did away with private medical practice.

We abolished private legal practice: justice ceased to be a commodity.

We nationalized the funeral parlours: we ensured dignity for the burial of any citizen.

We nationalized rented property: the cities became the property of those who built them; the cement cities, for the first time in our history, took on a Mozambican face.

I believe that imperialism was happy before this. The West was happy. They want to stay where they are and have the money cross mountains, oceans and lakes to reach them. Whether they are in Switzerland,

Portugal, Federal Germany, Britain, the United States, Brazil, or wherever, the money would come to them from our city.

I know of no city in the world that belongs to foreigners. Bonn is the capital of Federal Germany, Berlin of the German Democratic Republic, Moscow of the Soviet Union, Sofia of Bulgaria, Bucharest of Romania, Peking of China. Brasilia belongs to the Brazilians. New York and Washington belong to the Americans. But they want us to have a Portuguese capital city.

And since we took the city and gave it a Mozambican face, they say that we are irresponsible, intransigent, unrealistic radicals. Are we unrealistic when we reap the benefit of our victories? We do not want them to have the benefit of our victories. They will be for us and no one else.

These are our people's revolutionary victories. They were the first steps towards the building of a new society, a socialist society. A socialist society means the welfare of all: the right to work; the right to education and health without discrimination; the right of every citizen to decent housing, to reasonable transport, to butter and eggs for our children and for all of us; the right to be decently dressed, to be able to eat chicken, rabbit, fish and meat, for all to have laundry soap to keep clothes clean, to have soap, blades, razors – that's what we want.

But our friends in the West say that if we go about well dressed, if we shave, if we have decent housing, we shall lose our African characteristics.

Do you know what African characteristics are? A skin, a loincloth, a wrap-around cloth, a stick in hand behind a flock, to be skinny with every rib sticking out, sores on the feet and legs, with a cashew leaf to cover the suppurating wound, jiggers in the toes – that is the African. That's what they see as African characteristics.

So when the tourists come, they are looking for an African dressed like that. Since that is the 'genuine African'. Now when they find us dressed in a tunic and trousers – we are no longer the Africans. They don't take photographs.

They need Africa to have no industry, so that it will continue to provide raw materials. Not to have a steel industry. Since this would be a luxury for the African.

They need Africa not to have dams, bridges, textile mills for men's, women's and children's clothing. A factory for luxury shoes? No, the African doesn't deserve it. A house with a swimming pool, a luxury hotel? No, that's not for the Africans.

For us a socialist society means: rest centres for workers; celebrations on holidays, a glass of beer, or wine, or orangeade, and good cakes; toy production for gifts to our children on their birthdays; flower-growing for tributes to our wives, the mothers of those who will carry on the revolution; clean streets in our cities; making parks and gardens for the recreation and delight of adults and children.

We have to advance to make these aims a reality. But we sense wounds in our body that are continually bleeding. We sense that our country's young body has diseases that hinder growth. We sense that enemy agents have taken advantage of our good nature and kindliness to worm their way in among us. All this is hindering progress. It is the mud that is weighing down our boots. We have decided to take off the boots and wipe off the mud.

The Internal Enemy

We spoke a little earlier about the colonial inheritance but now there is our own product. The product of the new phase. We cannot say it is a product of colonialism. We have allowed a minority to infiltrate our structures: a minority in the state apparatus; a minority in enterprises, factories, warehouses; a minority in ports, airports and DETA; a minority in the People's Shops, in APIE.

They are a minority of reactionaries, of enemy agents who have management and executive tasks. We have allowed enemy agents to hold key positions. This is the present state of affairs and we must search out its roots, identify its causes, discover and penalize those to blame. It is no accident that the problems arise in all sectors, in all provinces. It is no accident that they appear as a chain of interconnected problems. They are not isolated matters, passing difficulties, petty irregularities.

They are the outcome of a vast action, an action with precise aims: against the revolutionary process; against people's power; against our economic independence; against the building of socialism in Mozambique. It is no accident that the action reflects the propaganda on the 'Voice of the Hyena' radio.

It is deliberate, organized, co-ordinated action directed from abroad. The head is outside! Here we merely have the body, but the head is outside! The ones here are simply carrying out orders. They are mere tools. They are lackeys cut off from the exterior, abandoned children, bastard children.

But the enemy is operating in our country. He has infiltrated and established himself. He is found: at strategic points of our economy; in the ports; in road, rail, maritime and air transport; in enterprises, factories, hospitals, shops and various sectors of our society. The enemy has established himself in the most sensitive sectors of the state apparatus, in ministries and provincial governments. Why?

Because some officials have allowed themselves to be lulled by false reports, triumphalist reports, reports that juggle with reality. Because some officials are susceptible to flattery, to servility, to boot-licking, to sucking up.

They have lost their sensitivity to the people's problems, are deaf to the people's complaints, are compromised, lose the hammer, abandon the tiller, lose control. They do not lead, they do not exercise the power the people entrusted to them.

Since the FRELIMO Party's Third Congress mainly, the enemy has begun to operate at two levels: from abroad, particularly through criminal attacks by the racist Rhodesian regime and by infiltration of armed bandits; internally, through its agents and lackeys, with the aim of sabotaging from within the objectives laid down by the Third Congress, of destroying the people's victories, and furthermore of destroying the internationalist solidarity we enjoy from the socialist countries.

Their fundamental target internally is the state apparatus, the structures designed to ensure implementation of the Third Congress decisions. Their mission is to disorganize our party and our people's state. Their mission is to establish: indiscipline; liberalism; anarchy; corruption; tribalism; regionalism; and racism. Their mission is to encourage: inefficiency and lack of enthusiasm for solving problems; incompetence; negligence; systematic deviation from guidelines; contempt for the people; insensitivity to the people's problems; parasitism; and bureaucracy.

The enemy's physical agents have infiltrated the state apparatus. Who are they? They are PIDEs, ANPs, GEPs, GUMOs, FUMOs, FICOs, POPOMOs, MOCONEMOs, the Democratic Coalition, FRECOMOs, the participants of 7 September and 21 October, the patronesses of the National Feminine Movement, the Godmothers of War, those who were being prepared by colonialism to take over, who have remained here as long-range booby-traps.

The big fish fled, but the small fry remained. We were tolerant with them. And they have taken advantage. They took our goodwill for weakness. Now they are springing up as those charged with implementing our policy. They appear as the executors of state decisions, decked in our power, disguised by the use of our language, and they destroy the people's goods, state property, the revolution's victories – and we are still paying them salaries. We coexist with them.

They use the most diverse tactics to disorganize state structures: they spread indiscipline; try to isolate good workers through slander and rumour; use populism and paternalism to promote the incompetent and inefficient; use ultra-leftism to undermine the exercise of power; use favouritism and nepotism to build a network of compromise; introduce widespread bribery and corruption; use bureaucracy to slow down the solution of difficulties; use tribalism, racism and regionalism to foment division; rely on authoritarianism to conceal their incompetence and prevent debate on problems; preserve and defend colonial administrative working methods to prevent our structures being revolutionary.

The enemy's action has focused particularly on the state structures most closely linked to our economic development and to meeting our people's needs. His principal targets are: supplies to the people; housing; transport; health; production sectors. One of his essential aims is to hamper the state apparatus in its management of the economy. His methodology within the state apparatus is subtle. The agents do not act openly against our policy. They appear to carry it out, but in reality they corrupt it.

How We Are Going to Destroy the Enemy

We are going to destroy the enemy. The people are determined. They are the main strength. We have weapons, and we shall use them unhesitatingly. We shall not fight with toffees. We shall not fight with sugar-coated bullets or blanks. Let us use the same bullets with which we defeated Portuguese colonialism in Mozambique.

The enemy is the same! Black, yellow or white, the enemy is the enemy and deserves the same treatment. And in this case it will be bayonets. It is a shame that the head is abroad! We would like the head here, to smash it, pulverize and roll it! We shall use revolutionary violence against those to blame for the present situation. We shall take firm measures to smash counter-revolution. We shall cut off the limb infected with gangrene. We shall remove the enemy from within. We shall cut the umbilical cord that links him to the former master, with hatchet and axe if necessary. Usually you take a pair of scissors to cut the umbilical cord, don't you? In this case, it will be a hatchet or axe. We shall be ruthless with them. We shall insist on iron discipline in our midst – at once, without prevarication.

We are here solemnly declaring war on the enemy within.

On 25 September 1964 we declared war on the foreign enemy – Portuguese colonialism. Here today, 18 March 1980, we declare war on the enemy within. And we are going to flush him out by the end of this year. It will be a general clean-up. We are going to sweep him out.

There will be no quarter. Our weapons are prepared. The enemy has positioned himself in front of the muzzles of our guns. Let us fire.

This is a decisive battle. It is a battle in the class struggle. We will not share power with the enemy. Here there will be no complacency. There will be no accommodation or sentimentality. Those who tolerate, shield and accommodate are the enemy's accomplices. They are our enemies.

The revolution is irreversible. It is a steamroller, crushing every obstacle it meets as it opens and consolidates the broad road to socialism.

The revolution is the people on the march, building their future and determining their destiny. For that reason we have come here to say: our state apparatus is corrupted. It is sick, infested with parasites, some clinging to the skin and others in the gut. It is in the people that we find strength. It is in the people organized and led by the FRELIMO Party that we find the right solutions.

We want socialism. We want happiness, prosperity and well-being.

We are going to take measures, radical, thorough measures, to cut the ground from under the counter-revolution.

We are going to define tasks for everyone. We shall be ruthless with the undisciplined, the incompetent, the lazy, the negligent, the careless, those who go in for red tape, for inertia, those who fall into the trap of routine, those who despise the people, misappropriate state property or squander the property of the people.

In disciplinary hearings we shall take measures appropriate to the seriousness of the offence. In serious cases, severe measures. In the factories we shall use dismissal, unhesitatingly.

Other anomalies constitute crimes: theft is a crime; sabotage is a crime; negligence is a crime; lying and giving false information that leads to wrong solutions is a crime. They must be punished.

The person responsible for letting rice, maize, milk, batteries, beans, cloth and cashew nuts, intended for the population, lie rotting in the warehouse is a criminal. We call that criminal negligence. It is the action of the enemy. It must be punished.

The worker who damages machinery through carelessness commits a crime against our economy. He must be punished.

The driver who smashes up a lorry through bad driving or speeding commits a crime against our economy. He must be punished.

Crime is not merely stealing or murdering.

The machine, the lorry, the tractor, the generator, the welding torch and the saw were bought with money produced by the people. They represent sweat and sacrifice from the people. They are essential tools in the production battle. Destroying these tools through negligence or carelessness is a crime against the economy.

A crime against the economy is a crime against the people's interests. We have laws to penalize these crimes. We are going to apply them. We have SNASP, we have the FPLM, we have the police force, the revolutionary military tribunal and the people's tribunals and they are going to act.

Measures to Be Taken

We are going to take measures: in the state apparatus; in the factories; in firms; at all production sites.

We are going to implant iron discipline everywhere. We learned the value of discipline during the armed struggle. Our freedom fighters won because they were disciplined. Our people won because they learned to value discipline. It was through organization, discipline and struggle that we overcame colonialism. It was through unity, work and vigilance that we consolidated and built people's power. It is through work, discipline and organization that we shall win the battle against underdevelopment.

In the first place we shall purge our ranks, we shall clean up the state apparatus. We are going to sweep our house out. The broom will reach into every corner.

We are beginning with the state apparatus because it is the fundamental instrument of party policy. Our state apparatus must be rid of all the infiltrators, all the undisciplined, all the incompetent, all the idle and all the negligent.

Our state is a workers' and peasants' state. It is not a state of the useless, idle and reactionary.

We are going to give all ministers the task of cleaning up their respective ministries. Within three months, every minister must ensure that his ministry has a sound structure.

The people have the task of contributing to this purge. The people will once more be the filter, as in the elections for the People's Assemblies, as in the structuring of the party. The people must denounce the infiltrators, point out the undisciplined, unmask the incompetent, attack the arrogant, and drive out the villains. We shall create conditions for the people to play a part in this task.

An office for control and discipline, headed by the minister in person, will be created in each ministry. The population can contact this office directly or by letter. They must report cases of infiltration, indiscipline or incompetence of which they have been victim or of which they have knowledge. All cases will be carefully investigated. The results of the investigation will be announced either directly to the people who reported the incident or, where appropriate, in the media.

This is a permanent, continuous battle. Brigades will launch a similar process in the provincial governments of all the provinces. These brigades will be headed by members of the Council of Ministers.

The people are expected to give their views on personnel in the state apparatus. The people are our strength.

Only those with the necessary qualifications can be workers of the state. To be a worker of the state is above all to be a servant of the people. It is an honour and a great responsibility to work in the state apparatus. We must be demanding.

Only those who show patriotism, discipline, competence, honesty, a sense of responsibility, respect and courtesy in dealing with the public, dynamism and initiative, punctuality and a studious and creative attitude can work for the state. These are the qualities we must demand of any worker who intends to be a civil servant. The state cannot be a refuge for the useless and incompetent. The state cannot be a refuge for the in-disciplined and corrupt.

To be a civil servant it is necessary to sit a test. To be promoted within the civil service it is necessary to face a test. Every citizen must be conceded the right of appeal in these tests. The criteria for admission and promotion must be rigorous and objective. They must be laid down in rules and regulations.

The state apparatus is the basic instrument of our power, of the power of the workers and peasants. We cannot allow it to go on being infiltrated and corrupted.

It is the state apparatus that must direct the economy. It is the state apparatus that must ask enterprises to account for the execution of the plan, for reaching targets. It is the state apparatus that must demand efficiency, speed and quality of performance from all sectors. The state apparatus must itself be highly efficient, dynamic and operational.

For us to be able to demand discipline, we must be disciplined. For us to be able to demand punctuality, we must be punctual. For us to be able to demand honesty, we must be incorruptible. We shall transform the state apparatus into the basic weapon in the fight against underdevelopment.

Enterprises

In enterprises, we shall demand a high level of discipline, strict time-keeping and good-quality products and services. We want factories to reach their installed capacity. We want factories to be improved.

State and private enterprises must generate profits. Each worker must produce his wages – so justifying holding his job – and profits for the firm.

It is with the profits thus obtained that we shall carry out major projects and works to benefit the whole population – build new hospitals, schools, dams, roads and factories, improve our life.

The state is not going to continue to pay wages to staff who do not produce, to firms that produce only losses. The state's money comes from the people. It is produced by the people's sweat. The state's money cannot be used to pay the useless and the parasitic.

Another central issue we noted in enterprises is that of management. We found management diluted and power dispersed. Let us state clearly: in each firm, power is exercised by the manager. It is the manager who organizes, manages and controls production. It is the manager who makes decisions. It is the manager who has the authority to punish. He is responsible for discipline in the firm.

Power must be concentrated. It cannot be divided. We must be done with conflicts and confusion of tasks between the management and other structures in the firm. Each structure has its defined task, its sphere of operation. The central task of the management, of the other structures, and of all the workers, is to ensure that the firm's production plan is achieved. Everyone must be involved in creating conditions for the production targets to be reached, since the economic battle is our main fight. We shall ask the manager to account for the fulfilment of the plan.

The management in large firms must be properly structured, so that there is a clear definition of responsibilities in each sector, a correct exercise of authority in each specific area.

In firms where it is justified, there will be, in addition to the general manager, a production manager, a supplies manager, a personnel manager, sector managers, section chiefs and so on.

In the ports and airports and in transport in general, we found the same problem of dilution of power. We shall take steps to overcome this situation. In the port there must be a director with the confidence of the party, and all, I repeat all, structures operating in the port will be answerable to him. The same principle must be applied in the airports and all transport sectors.

The transport sector, and the ports especially, are currently of vital importance to our economy. With the liberation of Zimbabwe, our ports and transport system will serve many countries in our region. This is a great responsibility for our country and it will be a powerful lever for our development. For this reason our ports must be highly efficient and operational. In these sectors we shall demand a high standard of discipline. We shall expect our ports to be the most efficient, the most functional and the best organized.

Still in the realm of transport, I should like to mention the serious problem of road accidents. We have found incompetence, irresponsibility and a lack of professional pride. In the driving schools it is no longer necessary to be able to drive to have a driving licence. They no longer give instruction about the engine and car maintenance. Let's stop this.

Drivers today no longer know what it is to respect safety rules and speed regulations. Every day they destroy human lives. Criminally. They destroy the people's property. They drive at excessive speeds. They drive when under the influence of drink. They drive as if they were carrying cattle or firewood. They do not obey traffic signals.

Many drivers no longer bother to keep their vehicles clean and in good working order. They no longer bother with a daily check on the vehicle. They merely take the key, start the engine, and drive off and keep going until the vehicle breaks down. A monkey could do that.

We have found hundreds of wrecked cars on roads, in garages and on the scrap-heap. That is many millions of escudos in foreign exchange that our state loses. In the streets we saw walls and lamp-posts destroyed. In the city of Maputo, last year alone, we spent two million escudos on replacing electricity poles destroyed by vehicles.

It is no longer possible to walk quietly down the city streets, without the risk of being knocked down even on the pavement. There is a speed limit of 60 km an hour in the cities, but some people drive at speeds of 80 and 100 km an hour. Outside the cities, it is forbidden to drive at more than 80 km an hour, but some people drive at speeds of 120 and 150 km an hour. This is criminal negligence. It is crime that we are going to punish severely. The traffic police will be reinforced and they will have strict instructions to penalize criminal drivers. We shall demand strictness in issuing driving licences. We are going to begin at once by re-examining the drivers in the state apparatus.

The supply problems we are facing require radical measures. Our immediate aim is to create conditions in large cities for essential items to be distributed on a just and rational basis, and for most queues to be done away with. In order to achieve these major objectives, it is essential that all the people participate in controlling supply. Each worker and each family must receive a fair share of essential items without having to queue.

How are we going to achieve this? We have experience of organized consumer co-operatives – I stress the organized – where each member is supplied by means of a ration card. We shall create conditions in which each family has a card for a shop near home, and can buy rice, sugar, flour and laundry soap. Private shopkeepers will be included in this process. Other products will be for sale in any shop.

In this way we shall create conditions for every family to receive a fair share of all the available goods. We shall not yet be rid of all the queues, but we shall eliminate most of them. Everyone will benefit from this measure.

The enemy will try to obstruct this measure since it is going to benefit the people. The people must be vigilant. The people must play an enthusiastic part in this task. To implement the measure, we must be organized. We have to know how many people live in each neighbourhood, how many houses it has, how many shops and what their capacity is, how many people live in each house, and how many people in each household are employed.

Only in this way can we plan the right distribution of products to each area. First in Maputo, Beira and Nampula, we shall launch a major campaign to survey the situation, and this will later be extended to other towns. We shall form people's brigades in each neighbourhood to go from house to house finding out who lives there and registering them. Each neighbourhood must have a complete register of its residents. Any newcomers to the neighbourhood must report to the Dynamizing Group for registration.

This campaign will be a fundamental step in the process of organizing the cities and communal neighbourhoods. The campaign will also allow us to discover and neutralize criminals, vagrants, prostitutes and social misfits.

The party structures, the organs of people's power, the People's Assemblies, the democratic mass organizations (for women, youth, journalists, production councils), neighbourhood Dynamizing Groups, the FPLM and the defence and security forces, must all take part in this campaign, incorporating the people. The consumer co-operatives and private shopkeepers must play their part in the process of distributing goods.

The people, through their structures, must be vigilant in preventing deviations and abuses. For a start, let us put a stop to abuse and privilege in the queues. No one has priority in the queue. There is no priority for being in the Dynamizing Group. There is no priority for being a member of the militia. There is no priority for being in the vigilance group. There is no priority for being in the FPLM. There is no priority for being in the police.

The state cannot go on paying wages to thousands of workers in the People's Shop enterprise, many of whom produce nothing. The present People's Shops must be changed or handed over to the consumer co-operatives or private traders. Some will have to be closed because they have no customers or no one to rent them. Let us draw up a plan to transform the People's Shops.

Private enterprise has an important role to play in our country. This was stated in clear terms at the FRELIMO Third Congress. The state cannot go on being involved in hundreds and hundreds of People's Shops. The state cannot go on running small businesses.

The state must be concerned with directing the economy and reviving major development projects. The state must devote itself to dynamizing the communal village process, which will enable speedy development of the countryside. It must direct activity for agricultural development, for development of the main cash crops, crops that bring foreign exchange to the country (such as cashew, tea, cotton, copra, sisal, sunflower . . .). The state must devote itself to executing the key development projects in the Limpopo and Inkomati Valleys and in Angonia. They will produce food. They will produce employment. They will produce wealth.

The state must devote itself to bulding large dams and irrigation schemes, to the electrification of the country, to augmenting information on our agricultural, fisheries and mineral resources, to prospecting and taking stock of our wealth. The state must buld more factories to produce textiles, shoes and domestic appliances, factories to produce farm tools, tractors, lorries and vans. The state must create heavy industry for us to overcome underdevelopment. It must create a paper industry, an iron and steel industry, an aluminium industry. The state must devote itself to the main social sectors: education, health, housing and justice.

The state apparatus must ensure the conditions for increased production and improved quality of products, and must inspect factory output. It must ensure that there is no shortage of raw materials or spare parts in the factories essential for our development and for production of goods for the people.

For this reason, we repeat, the state cannot be absorbed with, and cannot waste its energies in, managing: a shop, a canteen, a bar, a boutique, a shoemender's, a small workshop, a garage, a hairdresser's, etc., etc.

The state will create conditions to support private traders, farmers and manufacturers whose activity lies within the framework of our objectives. The state will help them in organization and provide the means for them to work.

I have received many letters from Mozambicans living in South Africa, Swaziland and Rhodesia who want to know if they can come and invest in commerce, restaurants, farming and other activities. These are Mozambican patriots who want to contribute to their country's progress. They are waiting for the state to back them and create conditions for their return. And we say: welcome! Let them come back. We shall support them in investing their savings in agriculture, industry or commerce for the development of our country.

Green Belts
We have talked about what we found in the warehouses, about what was not distributed but stayed there rotting, about what was not sold while the

population endured queues. But now that these products are coming out of the warehouses, does it mean that the queues will disappear? Does it mean that the problem is solved? No, and you know it does not. We asked what the answer is – and the people replied: the answer is to produce. That's what you told me in the various meetings we had during the offensive.

Where are we going to produce?

In the green belts.

Here around Maputo there used to be an extensive green belt. It was the settlers who produced there. And when they abandoned their farms, production stopped. What must we do? We have land to cultivate. Here in Infulene, Marracuene, Manhiça, Matutuine, Boane, Moamba and Namaacha, where the settlers were formerly producing. We have the manpower. In the city of Maputo here only a minority of the population is working. The rest of the population is in queues, producing nothing.

When we proclaimed independence we occupied the settlers' positions – the positions and the pay. The majority of workers, particularly those from Gaza and Inhambane, particularly those from Manhiça, Moamba, Matutuine, Namaacha and Magude, left their wives at home. They left their children at home. They used to earn 500 escudos. How were they to keep children and a wife here?

They had a wage rise and went to bring their wife here to stay. They brought their children here. The children no longer go to school there, they came to study here. Not satisfied with wives and children, they went and fetched their brothers and brought them here. Still not satisfied, they fetched their mother – she is here in Maputo. Still not happy, they fetched their mother-in-law here. Still not happy, not satisfied, they fetched their brothers- and sisters-in-law to live here at the expense of one man alone. Some ministers did the same.

They fetched them from Cabo Delgado, from Nampula, from Beira. In the army and the police, it is enough to be a commander, and there you are. To show that he is a 'big man' he has to have this regiment at home. At least a platoon for him to order about. So he has his authority at work, where he is a chief, and when he comes home he is also a chief, and has a platoon there.

We are going to stop this. Everyone has done it. So Maputo is full. There is insufficient food.

It is those who grew the maize who came here, those who grew the cassava who came here. They were producing a whole series of such things as beans and fish. Now they produce nothing, they came here to stay. But you want to eat.

Independence meant moving to the city, so we have the labour force. First, there are those useless people in the state apparatus. We are going to reduce the staffing of all ministries, in all sectors. We shall have a precise establishment and the rest will go into production.

Then we will go to the enterprises: the lazy and the undisciplined will

101

go and produce. Nothing will stop us. That is why I asked here: is the army ready for a new battle? The battle is not only against those who went about sabotaging, it is also against the idlers, social misfits, criminals and vagrants. There are families of 20, where only one has a job. And they are adults. They eat a lot.

So what do we need then? We are going to give hoes and tractors to the unemployed and the underemployed for them to produce, in the Infulene Valley, in Manhiça, in Matutuine, in Moamba and in Namaacha.

All that the city consumes – tomatoes, cabbages, onions, potatoes, rice, maize, cassava, lettuces and bananas – used to come from all these areas. That is exactly what we shall produce. Meat, milk, chickens, rabbits and pork used to come from these areas. We are going to produce all that again. The state will help through the bank.

We shall grant loans for purchases of the means of production: tractors, hoes, seeds, fertilizer.

We are not abandoning them, but we do not want them to live like lice and locusts.

We shall review producer prices so that the producer benefits and has an incentive to greater production. Some farmers have come and said to me: 'Mr President, we are going to give up the farm. Pesticide is expensive, fertilizer is expensive, the work takes a long time and the prices don't compensate. It's better for us to quit production. For this reason we must review the price of produce.

In this way we shall stop the shortages of produce that was always grown in this region, produce that we are sometimes obliged to import.

Here on the city outskirts there are many farmsteads where the settlers used to grow vegetables and fruit, and keep small livestock. This means that there was investment in infrastructure: wells, rabbit hutches, pigsties, chicken coops, and water pumps. It's the case in Matola, Machava, Benfica, Mahotas and Catembe. With the flight of the settlers and the nationalization of rented housing, these farmsteads were rented out to Mozambicans.

Nowadays the infrastructures are neglected. Grass grows in the yards and the gardens. The tenant merely lives in the house. He doesn't use the well, the rabbit hutch, the water pump.

We are going to review this situation. Those who are occupying the houses must make full use of the existing facilities. If not, they must quit. We shall rent to those who can make use of them. This is also a way of making the most of our conquests.

But we do not want vegetable patches in the centre of the city. We do not want patches of beans, or cassava, or maize, or groundnuts. We don't want patches of sweet potato; we don't want any kind of vegetable patch. In the city centre, we want gardens and children's parks. We want flowers to lend beauty; we want beauty.

We want trees well cared for and well pruned. We are speaking here but the guidance applies to the whole country. We don't want the trees hacked about with hatchets and axes. We must prune the city's trees with special secateurs. The Governor of Maputo is here and the other governors are listening. The cities are being murdered, the trees are being murdered. Trees are a city's lungs, the city breathes through these trees.

In the current offensive, we identified three categories of people who must be integrated into production in the green belt.

The first category: the criminals who are now in detention. For them, hard labour. They are elements who stole from the state. They left the people's produce to rot. They committed various crimes. We don't want to keep these criminals in prison eating food produced by the people. They will be tried and if convicted sent to production camps. We shall send them to produce: first to produce their own sustenance, and second to compensate the people for what they stole.

They will not go to Niassa. They will be settled here in Maputo. They will be under military guard, for five, six years until they produce the money they stole, until they compensate for the produce they let rot. This is the first category for the green belt.

The second category: underemployed workers and unproductive workers. We saw during the offensive that many workers do not produce their own wages: we saw the People's Shop empty, but with 20 employees doing nothing; we saw the bakery that used to have ten workers and now has 20 to produce half as much as it used to; we saw firms with a labour surplus producing nothing (they draw their wages from the bank). We saw messengers in the state apparatus who have nothing to do. They just make tea for the boss. We are going to stop all this. The bank's money is the people's money. It cannot be used to pay the useless, the idle, the drunkards, the absentees, the negligent, the undisciplined and wastrels.

The third category: the unemployed and the social misfits. Only those who work have the right to eat in the new society that we are building. Anyone who does not produce has no right to a wage We cannot allow the parasites to go on sucking our blood.

We are going to create the conditions for all these people to produce. We shall supply them with land and a tractor. The Solidarity Bank will grant loans. We shall establish repayment terms. They are going to produce to repay. They will produce in order to have the right to eat.

In this way they will be able to organize their families, have decent housing, and education for their children, and they will take on their responsibilities as head of the family.

6. Every Revolution Is a Contribution to Marxism*

Dear comrades, with deep feeling we greet this august assembly where representatives of the forces of progress and socialism, from all continents and peoples, from all races and nations, are together celebrating the centenary of the death of one of mankind's most beloved sons, Karl Marx.

The men and women who accompanied Marx at his burial in a London cemetery were few. Today the lives of thousands of millions of men and women have been profoundly affected and changed by the enduring ideas of Marx. In four continents, workers, taking control of their destiny, are building a happy future, are building socialism, Communism.

Against Marxism, against Leninism, which is our epoch's Marxism, imperialism mobilizes incalculable human and material resources. The most sophisticated weapons, the threat of thermonuclear, bacteriological and chemical disaster, the ocean depths and cosmic space are deployed in an attempt to neutralize and destroy Marxism-Leninism.

The spectre that haunted the bourgeoisie in Europe a hundred years ago still haunts them, but now it is perceptible throughout the world.

For the oppressed peoples and classes, for the peoples and workers who have taken control of their destiny, Marxism is a shining path, a sun of hope and certainty that never sets, a sun that is always at its zenith.

Marxism, the science of revolution, is the fruit of practice, of mankind's struggle for a better future and so is renewed and developed through human practice. The experience of revolutionary struggle of the Mozambican people provides an illustration of this principle.

Dear comrades, our history validates the thesis that the motive force of history is class struggle. Class struggle was and is a reality on the African continent.

Our pre-colonial society was familiar with complex state formations, such as Monomatapa and Gaza. They were political and social systems of a feudal type, at differing stages of development. In some there survived elements of earlier slave systems. In others there were already emergent

*A speech given in Berlin on 11 April 1983, at the celebrations to mark the centenary of Marx's death.

mercantile strata which, in another phase of history, would come to shape a new evolution in society. In all of them there was a distinction between exploiters and exploited.

Colonial repression of these state formations and the integration of society into the capitalist and imperialist system, which was emerging in the era, brought new historical changes.

The antagonists within the society facilitated colonial occupation. Representatives of the exploiting strata betrayed the national cause and made an alliance with the foreigner to continue the domination and exploitation of their own people. Once the country was conquered the betrayers of the nation were also subjected to domination, since they in turn were betrayed by their erstwhile ally.

Colonial conquest, by introducing a system of large plantations and landholdings, exploitation of minerals, and the building of railways and roads, began the process of proletarianizing the countryside.

Our country's liberation struggle arose as a consequence of the contradiction between colonized and colonizers, between exploited and exploiters. Reformist patterns of nationalist pressure were precluded by the very nature of colonial-Fascism.

It was legally impossible to establish Mozambican social organizations and even less a nationalist party or a trade union. There was no earthly hope of dialogue with the colonial power to lead to self-determination, much less to independence.

The historical alternative for our people was recourse to revolutionary violence to put an end to Fascist violence. The Marxist thesis of making war on war to achieve peace reveals its correctness once again.

In the founding of the Mozambique Liberation Front it was essentially plantation workers, poor peasants subjected to forced labour, who provided the social base for the organization.

In the process of armed struggle for liberation, liberated areas were created. We had to determine in practice what power to establish in the areas. With the production of material goods, basic questions presented themselves in an acute form. It was a question of understanding whom the struggle served, since former feudal and new exploiters, aspirants for bourgeois status, wanted to establish their power over the people.

The conflicts experienced in the Liberation Front in the period 1967–70 were, above all, class conflicts.

Out of correct solution of the conflict a qualitative advance was made by the Mozambican revolution. Once again class struggle was revealed as the cause of advances in history.

The creation of liberated areas made viable and current the issues of property and power, and brought as an ingredient in the claim for independence the question of the social regime to be set up.

That is how in the process of class struggle, within the Front and in the liberated areas, the seed was sown of the Marxist-Leninist party, of the socialist revolution, of the people's democratic state.

There was an acceleration in the revolutionary process. An acceleration of the movement towards socialism, even though the working class was weak in size and in awareness of its class interest.

The war situation acted as a powerful catalyst which, thanks to political work, encouraged understanding of the real aims of the conflict. An awareness of the great sacrifices that were demanded stirred in the society a felt need for radical changes in its internal relations.

The accumulated experience of mankind in the struggle against exploitation, synthesized in Marxism, enabled the Mozambican revolutionary movement to benefit from and absorb that experience. In the process Marxism was enriched.

Under Mozambique's conditions, revolutionary practice led us to give pride of place to socialist revolution, and led us to launch the process of building socialism in a context of widespread illiteracy, a narrow working class and in the absence of an established Marxist-Leninist party. The struggle by Mozambican workers, under the leadership of the vanguard nucleus generated by the Liberation Front, enabled us to find correct responses to these problems.

In this sense, although each people's revolutionary experience is specific, it does not lie outside Marxist thinking.

Dear comrades, this description in synthesis of the main strands of our experience has led to some essential conclusions. A first conclusion indicates the universality of class struggle, of contradiction as the motive force of history. A second shows the leading and decisive role of working-class ideology in the correct solution of conflicts prevailing in present-day society.

Even in those countries with a weak industrial base, such as we have, the rule still holds that socialist revolution is possible.

It has triumphed in Mozambique with the victory of the people's war of liberation. It has triumphed in the sense shown by Lenin, as a correlation of forces, as a determination to build socialism, since with the people's support the interests and concepts of the proletariat have been placed in control.

Marx's thinking demonstrates that it is vitally important to settle the question of where power lies, who wields power.

The dictatorship of the proletariat is as alive today as at the time of the Commune. State action depends on it in the long and complex process of transforming social relations, in establishing a material and scientific base, in educating man. Such state action and the broad management of society require the organization of the workers' vanguard into a party equipped with the scientific ideology of the proletariat. So, at the Third Congress in 1977, our Marxist-Leninist Party was born from its embryo in the Front.

Dear comrades, internationalism, unity of the exploited of the earth, is one of the basic constants in Marx's thinking. In our own time, in the face of imperialism's mounting aggressiveness, it manifests itself in the need for closer and closer union between the components of the contemporary revolutionary movement.

Internationalism in our era acquires an extra dimension, with the need to struggle for peace and against nuclear catastrophe.

We are witnessing today an uncontrolled arms race, we see imperialism's insistent efforts to deploy its weapons of mass destruction in various parts of the world. We are witnessing today the growing support imperialism gives to the most retrograde forces of mankind, to Fascist and Nazi regimes that oppress, exploit and massacre the working classes.

These actions by imperialism are meeting growing resistance from peace- and progress-loving peoples, in the light of the unbreakable determination of the workers of the world to thwart such actions.

In the struggle for peace it is Marxist forces who must lead mankind's struggle for survival. The broadest front has been built around this struggle.

Leading figures in science, art, religion, institutions of every kind, youth, women's and church bodies, all honest people with respect for mankind join with the political forces that demand peace.

In this respect we salute the initiatives by the Warsaw Pact consultative committee, in expressing the desire of peoples for peace and in offering realistic and just answers to the problem of avoiding the spread of war or a nuclear catastrophe.

The struggle for peace must prevent the causes of war.

Imperialist exploitation and an unjust international economic order are a cause of war.

The imperialist policy of destabilization and aggression against states that refuse to submit to imperialism and that embark on the road of revolutionary change is a provocation to war. Economic, financial and military blackmail, provocations against socialist states in Europe, Asia, Latin America and Africa are factors for war.

The belligerent policy of Israel and of South Africa, cherished allies of imperialism in their regions, is a provocation to war. Racism, apartheid, Zionism, occupation of foreign territory, colonial expansionism are factors for war. Local wars, promoted by imperialism, may lead to all-out war.

The Pretoria regime in southern Africa is a cause of war that represents a threat to peace in the whole region. The Nazi-Fascist regime in Pretoria occupies some of the territory of the People's Republic of Angola, colonizes Namibia, encourages armed banditry in Mozambique, Angola, Zimbabwe, Zambia and Lesotho. The apartheid regime is responsible for the war situation that prevails in southern Africa and threatens to provoke an all-out war.

Mozambique's independence was the contribution made by the Mozambican people to the struggle for peace. Today, in association with other southern African countries for the purposes of regional economic co-operation, and in concerted action to prevent the real danger of war already posed by the apartheid regime, we have established a significant front in the struggle for peace.

In the struggle for peace, which of necessity entails a struggle against apartheid and against colonialism, the ANC and SWAPO are the favoured instruments of the peace movement in southern Africa.

This just struggle has the unfailing support of the socialist countries, of the Front Line states, of progressive and democratic forces, of all peoples who seek peace, freedom and progress.

The struggle for peace, as a people's movement, has to acquire this scale. It is precisely the scale that Marx made universal in his thinking and action.

Dear comrades, a century after the death of Marx, the cause of socialism and Communism has ceased to be a dream and has become a reality that changes the world. The vitality of revolutionary science, systematized by Marx, can have no better proof than the facts themselves.

The socialist countries assert themselves and advance. The overall record of socialism is one of great success. The experience of socialist revolution, of socialist construction, is overall an enrichment and constant broadening of Marx's original teachings. Each country and each revolution makes a new contribution to the development of our science, of our heritage.

We are celebrating this centenary in the German Democratic Republic, a Germany in which socialism has triumphed. A Germany where working man continually manifests the breadth of his intelligence, his energy, his ability, by creating prosperity, progress and happiness. A Germany in which militant internationalism makes the struggle by peoples against exploitation its own struggle.

We salute through Comrade Erich Honecker, General Secretary of the Central Committee of the Socialist Unity Party of Germany, the workers – labourers, peasants, revolutionary intellectuals – who have been able creatively to transform the genius of Marx into an invincible material force, for the triumph of socialism and peace. We salute the working classes in the GDR, who, led by their vanguard party, have so magnificently organized this assembly of representatives of workers of the world, as an affirmation that Marx's thinking, still alive and still young, is immortal.

With the concepts of Marx, the peoples of the world will triumph in their just struggle for peace, for progress, for socialism.

The struggle continues!

The revolution will win!

Socialism will triumph!

Part II:
National Reconstruction
Economy
Education
Health
Women
Youth
Defence and Security

7. Production Is an Act of Militancy*

Historic Responsibilities of the Working Class

The working class is the leading class of our country, it is the leading class of history, the only one capable of speaking for the whole society, able to conceive the process of transformation of the whole society, and to launch and direct this process.

So in our state, the People's Republic of Mozambique, power today is taken and wielded by the worker-peasant alliance. This power must be wielded against the bourgeois class whose aim is to exploit workers and peasants. Great responsibilities therefore lie on the working class, the class all of us represent. We all share the historic responsibility of the revolutionary vanguard for the transformation of society. We all share the immediate responsibility of making industry effectively the dynamizing factor in our economy it is stated to be in our Constitution.

Struggle for Economic Independence Entails an Increase in Production

We must ask: as the leading class, as the class that changes society and is responsible for it, how does the working class accomplish its historic duty to society?

We are at the stage of struggle for economic independence. But the struggle for economic independence entails more than anything else an increase in production.

By raising our country's production, we raise our capacity to fight against imperialism. By raising our country's production, we change the nature of the relations we inherited from colonialism. Without production it is useless to talk of transformation of the relations of production, or to talk of transformation in the economic basis of our society. We say therefore that the essential task in the current phase is the struggle for increased production: it is the generalized political and organizational offensive on the production front.

Many factors of production must be taken into account: machinery, raw materials, transport, etc. But we say that man is the essential factor.

*This speech was originally delivered in Maputo, on 13 October 1976.

Here too man and not the machine is the decisive element.

Now we ask: how do we, as workers in industrial enterprises, carry out our tasks? And the working class, the workers in industrial enterprises, must rise to the responsibility of providing an answer so that we and the country know how workers are carrying out their tasks, how we are meeting the responsibilities of the working class. Do we find that we are meeting our tasks correctly? We have made regular visits to the factories. I think we have already visited enterprises in all the industrial sectors here in Maputo Province.

On Worker-Peasant Power: Production Is an Act of Militancy

The enterprise, the workshop, is for us the incubator where class consciousness is nurtured. What we manufacture, the way we work, how we discuss and plan production, provides a window on our class consciousness. In our republic where power belongs to the worker-peasant alliance, production is an act of militancy. Now that we no longer have the whip, forced labour, the *palmátoria*, production is an act of militancy.

Productivity: A Thermometer for Political Consciousness

But production has one very special, very sensitive facet – productivity. This facet serves as a thermometer for political consciousness, for the reflex of class consciousness. Production means using material, technical and human resources to make a socially useful object. A workman who picks up a saw, timber, a plane, nails and a hammer, and makes a chair, produces a chair – this workman is producing, even if he takes the whole day to produce the chair.

Another workman, using the same materials, produces in the same time four chairs of the same kind. This workman has also produced, has also worked. But there is a basic difference between the work of these two workers. This difference is called productivity.

The first workman is a demobilizing agent, a saboteur of the national economy; he has no class consciousness, is a dead-weight in the work-shop, in short a layabout. And a lot of layabouts are seen in the factories. They are nothing but dead-weights in the factories. Any such person should be carted off to an appropriate place, as he is a crow waiting to pluck out our eyes as soon as we shut them.

The second workman has risen to his responsibility as a worker, knows what he is working for and knows that through his production he is contributing to national reconstruction. This workman who is concerned about productivity shows that he is politically conscious, class conscious.

Productivity is the factor that will improve our conditions, that will enable us to achieve progress and economic development.

Widespread Indiscipline and Corruption in Industry

We have been to your factories, seen how you work, seen what you produce. Now we ask again: what did we find in your factories? I am sure that those who were visited are aware; they know what we observed there and what we said about it. And now we are asking the working class, after we observed what happens in your factories: what shall we tell the country as a result of those factory visits? What must we say to the people about the workmen in our country's industrial enterprises, to the people whose clothing, shoes, food and survival depend on the product of your work?

We saw that you produce very little. So we then asked various technicians, workers and apprentices how we can increase productivity. The answer was always the same: it is impossible to raise productivity because in most enterprises there is poor time-keeping, absenteeism, liberalism, a lack of respect for institutions, confusion, power-seeking, rumour-mongering, stealing and racism. In short: widespread indiscipline and corruption.

And the result is low productivity!

Using the same machinery as you had in colonial times, in the same plants, with the same number of employees, and often the same technicians, you have reduced productivity!

Is this what the workers in these enterprises offer in return for the sacrifices of those who struggled to win independence? Is this the response we must give those who offered dear life for national independence? Is this the reply we must give our people and our children? Is this the tradition we must pass on to our children? And as for the population who day and night endured massacres but did not waver in the fight against colonialism, is this what they must hear? Is this what is owed to those who died carrying weapons, carrying medicines, ammunition and food supplies to encourage development of the struggle to smash and destroy colonialism and drive it from our country? Is this the reply we should give to those who were imprisoned and murdered in the prisons of Ibo, here in Jamanguane? Should all of them know that this is how these workmen esteem independence and the blood shed in the winning of our freedom? I am sure that some of you here were in Jamanguane and witnessed the brutality of PIDE and of colonialism, the violence of capitalism, and capitalism's loathing of workers.

We are seeing how complicated the situation is in your enterprises. So we ask: how are we going to deal with it? How can we go on with dead-weights, with feckless individuals, how can we go on with those who are establishing an enemy base in their factory or workshop, how can we go on with elements in the factory shouting for the return of capitalism, colonialism and exploitation to our country?

It seems to us that the best approach is to consider what are the causes of the current situation, how we reached this pitch.

Causes of the Current Situation: Neo-Colonial Manoeuvres

In the colonial period the enterprises were organized and operated with the sole aim of serving the interests of capitalism. All our strength, dedication, energy and sweat merely went to the interests of capitalism. But now we say power belongs to us. The colonial government, with its repressive laws, its administrators, its native police, was an instrument that capitalism used for the greater exploitation of Mozambican workers.

The structure and working methods of the enterprise in the colonial era were also repressive. They served the interests of an exploiting minority and not the interests of Mozambican workers. The Mozambican worker in the enterprise was directly subjected to racial and social segregation, to oppression and exploitation. His only right was to work day in day out. He was not permitted to know more than the immediate job in front of him. Nobody explained to him the enterprise's problems, the production schedule, or even the social value of his own labour. He was regarded as a worthless, unreliable and unthinking machine.

The Mozambican worker joined the enterprise as an apprentice and died as an apprentice. The highest he could aspire to was to be a third-class labourer after 20 years.

The heroic struggle of the Mozambican people led by FRELIMO, and the struggles of the brother peoples in Angola and Guinea-Bissau, led by the MPLA and the PAIGC, brought the collapse of the Portuguese colonial-Fascist regime. The 25 April movement was thus a product of our peoples' heroic struggles – we liberated the metropole. Without the struggle in the colonies, Fascism would not have fallen. It was not an act of charity but a sacrifice by our peoples. Portuguese colonialism in Mozambique crumbled in the face of FRELIMO's decisive victories.

Capitalism, in an effort to survive, is trying to devise new forms in which to carry on exploiting our people. Its first steps are to create economic chaos. This would increase our country's dependence on capitalism and imperialism. According to capitalism's calculation, it would then be possible to use such puppets as Kavandame, Simango, Gwengere and Joana Simeão, to divide the people and set up a neo-colonial government. But the ideological clarity of our line has thwarted the colonialist manoeuvre. That government would have the task of clouding the content of our independence and maintaining exploitation of our people. Capitalism, by taking advantage of the people's enthusiasm and feeling, has used the workers' frail political consciousness to promote agitation to its own benefit.

There Is No Political Struggle Without Political Consciousness

This is where the big manoeuvres begin against our independence. By encouraging widespread anarchy, indiscriminate sackings and wage disputes, the capitalists who have always exploited and humiliated our people want now to parade as their defenders. Have you ever seen colonialism defending the people's interests? The same capitalist, who in the old days would call the Fascist police and denounce to PIDE any worker who was disgruntled, tried to make a quick change into anti-colonialist, anti-Fascist and anti-racist dress, to pretend to be a good employer and a defender of the workers' interests. Do you trust him? But some say it's better to be eaten by a leopard than by a lion. Thus they want to open the front door and the back door, so that the leopard comes in at the back door while the lion leaves by the front.

But what do they really want? That's what our workers have been unable to spot because they have not sufficiently studied the intentions. First, they want to confuse the masses, by obscuring the correct definition of the enemy; second, they want to divide the workers; third, they want to disrupt the Mozambican economy; fourth, they want to aggravate the crisis, the crisis the enemy now talks about; fifth, they want to prevent the people who are taking political power from taking economic power as well. In sum, they want to erect a series of barriers to the transformation of our economy into an economy genuinely serving the people.

Anyone who fails to analyse these points correctly might think that the strikes, the indiscriminate sackings, the wage disputes, that were mostly instigated by the capitalist boss himself or by his agents, constitute correct forms of nationalist and anti-capitalist struggle. In fact the capitalist never has relinquished or would relinquish a jot of his interests out of regard for the worker. Let us have no illusions.

Many of you took part in strikes under the impression that this was a nationalist approach. But there is no political struggle, without political consciousness.

A stevedore might have said: 'I am not going to unload these crates because they pay me so little.' But the crates contained weapons, ammunition and bombs for the colonial army to use in fighting FRELIMO. So they went and paid the stevedore more and he did the unloading. Who was the winner? The Mozambican people because of the stevedore's pay rise, or our enemies who had more bombs in their hands with which to massacre the Mozambican people?

In order to split the working class, capitalism in the period of the provisional government of the 'learned doctor' Soares de Melo, a capitalist agent and puppet, invented the so-called workers' committees and councils whose uncoordinated activities merely served to sow anarchy.

The actions of these councils and committees accelerated the breakdown of authority in the workplace and paralysed our economy. Hence came the first wave of rumour-mongering. Indiscipline, corruption and theft became widespread. Capitalism had achieved the first objective of its plan: a dramatic drop in productivity.

Conclusions of the Analysis of Neo-colonial Action
We seem to have reached a significant conclusion: we have already discovered the roots of the problems we are trying to solve today. It is

capitalist strategy, in the wake of Portuguese colonialism's collapse, that provides the roots of the liberalism, indiscipline and corruption that are demobilizing the working class and bringing the consequence of low productivity. Capitalism has used the workers to split and disrupt the working class. It has used the workers to fight Mozambique's independence and the power of the worker-peasant alliance. Capitalism has taken advantage of the workers' low level of class consciousness.

Capitalism's Behaviour After the Lusaka Agreement
This was the atmosphere in which the Mozambican people's victory was put into effect with the signing of the Lusaka Agreement and the setting up of the Transitional Government, under the leadership of FRELIMO. Our victory brought despair to capitalism, which had to rethink its plans. It intensified sabotage of our economy. It contrived the massive flight of technicians, illegal transfer of foreign exchange, theft and destruction of machinery and equipment.

They dismantled whole factories and took the machinery over the border! Capitalism went on with false promises to the workers so that they would rise against FRELIMO. The workers were told: 'We should like to raise your wages, but FRELIMO won't let us!'

Who won independence, who liberated the people, who struggled, who made sacrifices? They wanted to 'help' the people struggle against the people's own victories – with FRELIMO and the people united from the Rovuma to the Maputo. So what FRELIMO is this that would not let them raise wages?

Many enterprises were abandoned, and others were at a standstill. Then in response to the watchword of spreading FRELIMO structures throughout the country, the Dynamizing Groups were formed. The Dynamizing Groups were and are our basic weapon in the struggle against all forms of economic sabotage practised by capitalism.

A Serious Weakness in Working-Class Organization
None the less, this fight was so costly in energy that we found it impossible to give due attention to organizing the working class. And that is a very serious weakness. We are now wasting time running after the enemy to discover and counter the sabotage it is doing to our economy, as we have not organized the working class. We did not give proper attention to organizing our principal strength.

We have been behind events. We have not yet taken an initiative. We have been working like firemen. This reflects a lack of structures, a lack of organization. And we say this is a bad thing. One of the key secrets is to hold the initiative. The initiative must always be with us and never with the enemy.

We shall not be able to take the initiative and go on the offensive until we organize the working class, until we have properly sorted out the structures within the enterprise, since the structures are our instruments and everyone knows his position in the structures. Then we shall have given tasks to every employee, to every worker from the smallest workshop to the largest industry.

But as we are not yet well organized at plant level, we are unable to study the causes of low productivity, spot the basic contradictions, and analyse the relations of production. We have already seen that the difficulties we are facing are not of today's making. Low productivity is not, as the enemy suggests, the result of workers' incapacity to wield power, to run their own country. The main drop in productivity occurred, as we saw, during the period of the puppet provisional government when the colonialists were still in charge of our country.

Current Situation

But we must go into the analysis more deeply. We have to see the symptoms clearly to diagnose the disease and we have to take the medicine to cure it. So let us look at the current situation. To summarize: what have we found in the enterprises?

Indiscipline

There is much absenteeism from work. Absences excused on the grounds of illness are often due to drinking; we might say the reason is a 'hangover'. When such a worker does go to work he uses his machine as a pillow.

There are some cases where people are absent for 20 days in one month. They virtually only go to work to collect their pay. They say they are independent, that FRELIMO brought independence, and as they were in prison, they want to drink now. There are a lot who go in to punch their card but not to work. The foreman comes along and tells them to work, and they answer back: 'You're a Fascist.' If someone is told he is damaging the factory and the economy, a shirker retorts: 'I shall make self-criticism.' Since when did self-criticism produce?

There is poor time-keeping. Late arrivals of 30 minutes, an hour, two hours. They abuse the leeway allowed them and when their attention is called to this, they say: 'Colonialism's finished, exploitation's over.' So who are the exploiters: isn't it the absentees, the latecomers who still want to draw their pay intact? We have already indicated some of the exploiters who are around now. They don't have to be factory owners.

Lots leave their post during working hours. They go off and hide in the warehouses to play cards or board games. Is someone like that a worker, does he belong to our class? Is he promoting proletarian ideology in the factory? Others even leave the factory to go and deal with personal matters and they have two time-cards so that the controller does not know they've slipped out.

There are some who turn up to work drunk. They sleep at the work-

117

bench, quarrel with their colleagues, provoke fistfights, destroy raw materials, stop the production line.

Another form of indiscipline is waste – not merely as a result of the drunken state in which some come to work, but as a result of negligence. There are individuals who destroy materials, misuse equipment, produce heaps of rejects. Negligence is shown even in their appearance: they go to work dirty, and some don't even wash, so their faces become stamping grounds for flies. They are bleary-eyed and instead of working they spend their time shaking off the flies. Their hair is dishevelled and full of blanket fluff. How can a worker like that look after a machine if he can't even look after himself? In factories where there are work clothes or other protective clothing, there are workers who don't bother to use it.

There is a lack of cleanliness in many workplaces. They are dirty, untidy, full of dust and cobwebs! Some enterprises we visited were so badly cleaned we could scarcely breathe. But those who work there for eight hours a day are people. This problem is particularly disgusting in the case of food-industry plants, such as we saw at 'Bonsuino' and other places.

But workers are not the only ones guilty of these kinds of indiscipline. We also observed indiscipline in management. We should say that in some instances the workers' indiscipline springs from and is encouraged by indiscipline in management. Managers too are absent, leave the workplace, neglect health and safety regulations that should be in force in a well-managed plant. We visited some enterprises and noticed in the offices of those in charge: papers scattered all over the place, a hat on the table, a coat badly hung up, etc.

At management level there is often material and sexual corruption. There are some management officials who do not respect women workers. We must eliminate from the People's Republic of Mozambique disregard for women's dignity. We said this at the swearing-in of the Transitional Government and we repeated it at Machava on the anniversary of independence. A bad example at leadership level is always echoed in the rank and file, in the working mass.

Disputes

There are workers who are still trying to settle their problems in the way they learned under the provisional government, in the days of the so-called workers' committees. These workers start a go-slow. They knowingly bring production down. We noted one case, that of a clothing factory, where the rate dropped from 700 shirts a day to 150. What they were looking for was a pay rise. And they told the management: 'We shall not raise production until you pay us better!' So where would the money come from? This is the wrong way to do it. What they had done in fact was to sabotage the factory and attack our economy.

In other places, that already have administrative commissions, the workers demand that profits be shared out among them. They fail to understand that the conquest of economic power is a conquest of the entire people, that the enterprises must serve the people and not one group of workers. A rise in production in this factory is the result of the entire country's efforts.

There are other cases where, after a technician has run away, the workers go to the management and say: 'Now you must divide his salary among us. We are still here and doing the work.' This is a confusion. We might call it ideological diarrhoea. They have gone soft in the head.

The confusion that reigns in the enterprises means that we should analyse this question of disputes. In the colonial time, power belonged to the colonialists. They had the army, the police and the government. The worker was not permitted any form of organization. So the workers, in order to find a solution to their problems, were obliged to devise their own forms of struggle. Hence they held demonstrations, strikes and other actions of dispute. Meanwhile the colonialist knew where his strength lay. If the demonstration was organized to demand independence, as in Mueda in 1960, he called the army in to carry out a massacre. If the strike had a mass content, as in Maputo, then called Lourenço Marques, with the dockers' strike in the 1960s, the riot police would arrest, beat and kill. If the demand was only for money, the colonialist would call in PIDE to arrest the ringleaders and later he would pay a small increment.

The small victories scored by our workers came after 1964, after the start of armed struggle. And why? Because the Mozambican people began to show organization and to demonstrate the first forms of power. Power today belongs to the people. The police belong to the working class, the army belongs to the working class, the government belongs to the working class.

Our police force engages in struggle against reactionaries and the enemies of independence. It oppresses the exploiters. In the old days it belonged to the exploiters and repressed the exploited. Our army defends our frontiers against the Fascists, racists, agents of imperialism. It fights capitalism. Our government restores the land, nationalizes medicine, schooling, legal practice, rented housing, and takes these sectors out of the hands of the capitalists to put them at the service of the people. Our government destroys the very basis of exploitation.

The worker of the colonial period could struggle only for his personal benefit. He tried to solve life's difficulties through pay. But his pay did not give him access to ownership of land, or to private medical clinics, or allow him to send his children to the university, or to live in a cement house. The worker today, with his power, can decide the destiny of his own country. So, in conjunction with colleagues and the political and administrative structures, he can seek better ways of solving his difficulties.

In the colonial period, when power belonged to the settler, the fruit of our labour served to enrich the capitalist. Our wealth was shipped abroad. Today, with our power, we have created the conditions for using the fruit of our labour for our own betterment. That is why we say we must produce more and better, since by producing more we increase our country's wealth, we shall build more schools and hospitals, and raise living standards for the whole people. In the colonial period we produced without knowing why and for what purpose. Today we are able to produce, to decide the pattern of production; that is, we know why we are producing and to what end. We are now in a position to control our economy and put production at the service of the people.

We see that the current situation is radically different from the past. And the forms of struggle must accordingly also be different.

Using the same forms of dispute as we did in the colonial period means that we have not yet fully understood the character of our struggle; we have not fully understood who our enemy is; we have not fully understood that power belongs to us.

In this phase of our struggle, the fight against exploitation moves into a fight against poverty, hunger and illiteracy, a fight for better living standards for our people. It is essential that we realize who now benefits in the first instance from production. That's why we say that in this phase the demand to make is: higher production, higher productivity. That must be our struggle, but no demonstrations have been organized for a rise in productivity.

The worker's trench is the factory; in the factory and the workshop, under the leadership of his revolutionary vanguard, he will raise his class consciousness, develop as a class. When he is armed with the scientific ideology of the proletariat, he will at each stage of the struggle be able to use the appropriate weapon to combat the enemy. The organized worker, incorporated into his structures, will be able to use the proper channels to solve his problems, will be able to subordinate individual interests to the interests of the majority.

Racism

For some there is the complex of racism. We are still encountering signs of racism at workplaces. Alongside the anti-Black racism typical of the colonial capitalist society, anti-White racism is now intensifying. For example: there are some individuals who do not accept the authority of their supervisors because they are Whites. That is an ideological confusion – mental untidiness, an imperfect understanding of our principles. There is a tendency to ask: 'So colonialism isn't over after all? The Whites are still giving us orders.' Others use unequal forms of address at work. The Blacks are 'comrade' and the Whites are 'sir'. They might be talking to a reactionary but they greet him as 'comrade' merely because he is Black. They are forgetting class struggle.

A disguised form of racism comes from those who refuse to learn from technicians merely because the latter are White foreigners. If it were a Black they would accept him. They say that this idea of learning from foreigners is not for someone already independent. In their view the technical, vocational and scientific skills of foreigners are of no use. Does science now have a colour? They are making a mistake that only harms our economy, delays the process of national reconstruction, and forces us into greater technological dependence.

Let us be clear in this regard. We are utterly against racism. Racism of any kind. Racism is a reactionary attitude that splits workers, by setting White workers against Black workers or Blacks against Whites and sapping their class consciousness. Racism impedes a correct definition of the enemy, by allowing enemy agents to infiltrate under a cloak of colour.

Let's give an example. The Black racist identifies his allies as Simango, Gwengere, and Joana Simeão, because they are Black like him. The White racist identifies his allies as Jorge Jardim, Kaulza and Spinola who are Whites like him. Where is our class sense, when we are saying that the principal feature of our struggle now is the sharpening of class struggle? We are saying that our enemy has no colour, no race, no country. Nor does our friend. We do not define friend or enemy in terms of skin colour.

There are Whites and Blacks who are our comrades. Including foreigners. And there are Whites and Blacks who are our enemies. Including foreigners. We are not struggling against a colour but against a system – the system of exploitation of man by man. The louse, the tick and the bug are not all of one colour, but none of them drinks water or milk – they live off blood.

Racism is a cancer still manifest in our society. A cancer that splits the workers and denies them unity and class consciousness. Racism is a cancer that feeds division and saps the common trench of anti-imperialism. It must be ended and eradicated to the last root.

Power-seeking

Power-seeking reveals itself as a struggle for power within the enterprise. The method of operation of the power-seeker is opportunism and his main characteristic is corruption. He is like a chameleon who is white on a white wall, and then turns red on a red wall. They are the ones among us who most obtrusively wave the FRELIMO flag. Corruption leads to vice and this in turn to crime. The power-seeker has a tendency to attack our line, and betray the working-class cause. A power-seeker has criminal intent.

As the power-seekers thought the Dynamizing Groups would take over management of the enterprises, they tried to infiltrate the Dynamizing Groups. There was a headlong rush for the Dynamizing Groups! There were instances of enterprises that formed three and four Dynamizing Groups, where there was electoral canvassing of the mass of the workers. We must study our mistakes. Each candidate made false promises to the workers and accused his rivals of the most terrible crimes. Each tried to outdo the other in obstreperousness with the management, and they claimed that they were the nationalists and in confronting management were defending us. All it really amounted to was opportunism. Individuals went so far as to pull strings, and to claim friendship or kinship with A, B or C. 'I'm the minister's cousin; I'm the national director's brother-in-law.' In Mozambique there should be no string-pulling. Such activities only serve to confuse and split the working class and to distort the aims of our class struggle.

Later they realized that the Dynamizing Groups were not an administrative structure. Administrative commissions were appointed even for abandoned businesses, and members of the Dynamizing Groups were ineligible for the commissions. Then there was a wave of resignations by members of the Dynamizing Groups.

Why did they resign? Some because they saw their personal ambitions thwarted, and now had no reason to go on saying: 'Viva FRELIMO.' Others because they had decided to achieve their personal ambitions by another route: they left the enterprise where, as members of the Dynamizing Group, they could not take senior administrative positions, and went to other enterprises where their past as a militant could be a springboard to promotion as head.

Others again left the Dynamizing Group to join the administrative commission in the same enterprise. We know of one case where a member of a Dynamizing Group, who wanted to join the administrative commission where he was but had no other pretext for leaving the Dynamizing Group, renounced his nationality. But he lost his nationality and his place on the administrative commission. Look how far the power-seeker will go!

There was the case of the Hazis bakery, here in the city of Maputo, where four members of the Dynamizing Group went into partnership with the boss. So what then of our labouring class, the working class?

All this demonstrates, as we have said, the tendency of the power-seeker to betray, split and demobilize the working class. There must be redoubled vigilance to detect, denounce and deal administratively with the power-seekers.

Enemy Action

Enemy action in the enterprises takes various shapes. The most significant is economic sabotage. Other examples of such action are: rumour-mongering, intrigue, infiltration by former PIDEs, OPVs, GEs, Flechas and ANPs, and attempts to bribe members of the Dynamizing Groups. Yesterday they were shouting long live Marcelo Caetano, and today they are saying long live FRELIMO. They are agents of confusion. Bogus promises to workers and destruction of cadres. It is a very subtle form of activity.

The enemy, in the hope of lowering productivity or bringing production itself to a standstill, lures a technician away from one employment to another, even if he has to pay three or four times the original salary. In some cases the technician will be engaged on tasks outside his special field. That we say is destruction of cadres. That line of attack was used particularly against government-controlled enterprises.

There are other forms of enemy action: a partnership is offered to Mozambicans, with unissued or phoney shares. The effect is to shift the contradiction between international capitalism and the Mozambican working masses to the Mozambican environment, with a consequent reinforcement of the internal bourgeoisie.

Lack of Class Consciousness

The fundamental cause of all these evils is that we have not yet really acquired consciousness of our class. Without consciousness, there can be no organization. And without organization, there will be no consciousness. The lack of class consciousness is also shown in the apathy about improving one's technical skill. Training courses are organized and then are almost empty. The candidates who are enrolled abandon the course before it is over, on the most varied pretexts, but the basic explanation is one of money. Unless the worker is organized, he can have no sense of structure, cannot be a good workman, cannot have a class consciousness, much less be a militant. And in this condition he cannot rise to his task and play an effective role in national reconstruction.

8. Organize Our Resources to Resolve the People's Problems*

We must understand what leadership is.

We are not a federated state. There is no province outside the nation. There is no nation without every single province. The nation is not the sum of the provinces, nor are the provinces fractions of the nation. It is a unity that cannot be fragmented. It exists in the communal village and in the country's capital. The nation exists in the communal village, in the district, in the capital.

Power cannot be fragmented. Power is single, it is power of the working class and its ally, the peasantry. There are levels of authority in the exercise of power, but it is the same power.

There are no provincial delegations. There are delegations of the nation, of the state. The governor is not the province's representative. Nor even is the Assembly deputy for a locality the mandatory of that locality. He is the people's deputy, he has a mandate from the entire people, but he exercises it at a defined level, in a geographically defined area.

The point of stressing this is to demand that at all levels we retain a vision of the whole. So no report is made to the nation; so in my locality – mine in the sense that I live and work there – I do not deal with problems regardless of those affecting another locality, another province. This is the very reason why bodies at lower echelons are subordinate to higher-echelon bodies, because it is the higher echelon that determines and ranks priorities within its sphere of command.

The higher echelon is not there to receive requests and provide resources.

The governor leads the province. In order to lead, he has the provincial government as instrument. No one can hope to be at one and the same time geologist and peasant, doctor and miner, agriculturist and driver, civil engineer and fisherman. No one knows everything. On a hand none of the fingers is more or less important, it is the combination; and the combination linked to the body, obeying the brain, supplied by the heart's blood, fed by the stomach, moved by the legs, guided by the senses. Each organ, each finger has its specific task.

*This speech was delivered in Maputo on 6 July 1979.

124

The governor in the province cannot lead without public works and health facilities, without the agriculture department and the bank, without each of the components of the hand that the government forms. Likewise no particular sector is a bantustan or an autonomous area. How can one plan a farm without taking heed of the road that leads there, the trade that will provide the worker with trousers and matches? This means that someone in charge of a particular sector has to know about other sectors, so that his work can be integrated in the whole, contribute to the progress of the whole and benefit from the support of the whole.

Leadership is not giving orders as a foreman. Leadership is not running all over the place all the time like an ambulance driver. Leadership is not papering over the cracks, allowing the emergency to put off the basic work.

Leadership means: first, study the problems, investigate, carry out a reconnaissance. I cannot arrive at a school and say 'Your target must be to raise 50 goats.' Why 50 and not 100? Why goats and not pigs? Why livestock and not vegetables? Why livestock breeding and not carpentry? This means: investigate the human and material resources to define the principal task. Investigate what the principal task should be in a particular place, at a particular unit. Do not let the secondary smother the essential. But likewise do not overlook the secondary.

After investigating, that is deciding on the tasks to be done and the means available, we must plan and organize. This means organizing the various resources on schedule. You do not leave the pan on the fire to run and fetch from the shop the salt you have forgotten. The stew will burn, since you planned the stew forgetting the salt.

Leadership means training cadres. Not having a complex about learning from a subordinate or colleague. Not being afraid of delegating responsibilities. Not being apprehensive of putting staff in at the practical deep end.

So we can decide and distribute tasks to everyone, holding them answerable for carrying out the tasks and insisting on accountability. So we shall gain the confidence of our cadres and they will gain confidence in themselves, and we shall be shaping a new generation of leaders.

Provincial directors are not post-boxes. Provincial directors, provincial officials in the various sectors, are leaders, members of the provincial government, immediate colleagues of the governor, his main instrument of leadership. Likewise they are the leaders at provincial level of their sectors, they are personally answerable to their ministry, to their national directors, to the secretaries-general, to the ministers.

We say again they are not post-boxes, they are leaders. As provincial leaders they are responsible for the entire province, which means that if one is the provincial leader for public works one has also to bear in mind and respond to agriculture's task. If one is in fisheries, one must also be aware of the bank. One cannot have a departmentalist or technicist approach and attitude.

A leader must not be satisfied merely to pass on problems, to make requests. As a leader, he plays a part in finding solutions to the difficulty. He is not a liaison officer, he studies means and resources, puts them together so as to solve the problem. If the solution of the problem exceeds his powers, then in the proposal he makes, we stress that he makes, to the higher level, he puts forward suggestions as to how the problem can be solved with the support of the higher level. What we have said about a provincial director applies equally to someone with national or district or local responsibilities. Having a responsibility is not a mere title.

A final point on this question of leadership is knowing how to spare our energies and concentrate on the essential. The decisions of the party's Permanent Political Committee on the organization of meetings are obligatory. We cannot have a profusion of meetings. We cannot have long meetings. People cannot do their work properly if they are constantly running between two meetings. People cannot do their work properly if as soon as they begin a job they have to interrupt it to go to a meeting. People cannot do their work properly if they are forever handling visits or escorting visitors. And for people to do their work well they must also have time to rest.

The Meaning of Reliance on Our Own Strength

In many of the speeches we heard at the same time demands for an increase in quotas and a statement that production targets had not been achieved. Raising or lowering quotas is not an arbitrary matter. State revenues, our state's foreign exchange, are not a piece of elastic that can be stretched indefinitely.

If I want more sugar for my province, the country will sell less sugar abroad. As a consequence I shall have less money with which to buy the lorry I'm asking for. If I produce less cotton, where will I find more money to provide a higher textiles quota? The state, the Council of Ministers, are not some kind of super-store distributing goods. The Bank is not a printing press that prints money to be shared out.

An individual works and receives his pay. Since his pay is not elastic, he knows that this month he will have to eat less meat if he wants to buy a new pair of trousers.

The provinces must be organized to achieve the plan's targets. The state's resources, especially foreign exchange reserves, must go as a matter of priority to the productive sectors, to create the conditions for the plan's targets to be reached.

Foreign exchange reserves must provide, for example, Textafrica with spare parts for machinery and textile dyes, and not go on imported textiles and finished pieces to the detriment of our industry. They must be used for industry to reach its maximum production level. The reserves must ensure that fertilizers arrive at the farms on schedule, that there are enough lorries to transport the cashew nuts instead of us wasting foreign exchange in buying maize abroad because we have not fulfilled our quota of maize production.

In our particular province there are human and material resources that we do not use properly. That is the case at all levels. For example, without roads or all-weather tracks, we want lorries. We want lorries although within six months or a year they will be off the road. Meanwhile we spurn the skiff or boat we can use on the river, the lake or at the coast. We want a mill with a diesel motor – then we shall have no diesel or mechanic. But a span of oxen, without diesel or mechanic, can turn a mill. We want a tractor before we have used the ox and the plough to accumulate the means to buy the tractor. We want a complex irrigation system with cement and pumps, and we reject the small earth dam and the water wheel turned by the wind.

We have heard reports of airstrips that are not operational, that are not mown and maintained by the local administration as its responsibility. The mowing of tracks was once a local responsibility, but nowadays it only means a request to the Public Works Ministry. There are delays in house building because of a shortage of cement and iron; in all the socialist countries, at the initial stage, houses were built of brick, without cement and with very little iron.

We have used the example of Nachingwea many times, and we are forgetting how at Nachingwea we began to use adobe to solve the housing problem. We are not forgetting how we began to use tanks and pools to solve the water problem.

We must make each province capable of being self-sufficient in the essentials, and supplying a growing surplus for domestic and foreign trade. It is the surpluses that solve the problem of quotas. Reliance on our own strength does not mean that every patch of our country is an island to itself, that our country is an island to itself. It means that we derive the highest possible value from our work and our resources, so as to have the right share in the national and international division of labour.

The family farmers must be given an incentive to increase production and to move to the stage of co-operative organization. Encouraging family farming requires the trade network to supply the farmer and his family with essential goods, and to purchase his surplus crop. This in turn requires of the trade network a clear understanding of local tastes. Mention has already been made of the absurdity of the People's Shop in the heart of a peasant area having its shelves loaded with tinned beans but devoid of skirt-cloths.

That is symptomatic of a failure in fact-finding, and of bureaucratic working methods. The People's Shop and the consumer co-operative will not play the leading role in domestic trade by closing down the private shop. The leading role is won by supplying more quickly, cheaply, attractively and courteously than the private supplier.

The co-operative triumphs by demonstrating its superiority in action and not in words. A co-operative really comes into being when the combined efforts of men and women produce more quantity and quality more cheaply than the separate effort of each of them. When we pool our oxen and cattle, and see that we have more milk, more meat and more money than when each owner was working on his own, then we know that the co-operative is better. When we have a co-operative and can benefit from the advice of an agricultural extension worker, a veterinary specialist, then we see that our living standard improves as we earn a better return on our work. The state, the central state bodies, must give technical and scientific support to the co-operatives, and this applies to internationalist solidarity. We cannot provide support to all the co-operatives at the same time, but in each province, and then in each district, we could choose one or two co-operatives, support them and make them models offering learning experience to the new co-operatives.

The communal villages are founded in the form of socialist property. The co-operative administers the communal village. The state agricultural enterprise administers the communal village. Gathering people together without production is to create consumer parasites.

The state agricultural enterprises must not cause deficits to the state. They must make profits. The state enterprises should become the main source of state revenue. In the provinces, we must put our best cadres at the head of these enterprises. Good cadres must not be lost in the provincial capitals behind desks loaded with papers.

Generally we must undertake the necessary steps to ensure: a) establishment of provincial planning commissions with skilled and experienced technical staff; b) support for export efforts of agricultural enterprises to make sure of selection, product quality and proper packaging for shipment; c) a solution to the shortages of raw materials, spare parts, equipment, fertilizers, pesticides, seeds and transport, all needed to achieve the plan; d) balanced preparation of large-scale projects; e) preparatory work for the 1981–85 Plan and the prospects to 1990.

The Third Congress decided that the former liberated ares should have priority in our work. The Permanent Political Committee of the party's Central Committee at the beginning of the year made an appeal for reconstruction and support in the areas suffering aggression from racist mercenary invaders from Southern Rhodesia.

There is nothing to justify the provincial and district directorates and the various sectors giving up their work in the areas under aggression, on the grounds of danger or difficulty of transport and communications. The people go on living and producing there, despite the aggression, and they resist the enemy, despite his crimes.

We fought and won the war against colonialism without having lorries or Land Rovers. Without these, we travelled to the south of the Zambezi, to Manica, to Sofala, and we created the conditions for putting arms caches in Gaza.

No official has the right to fail to go to an area because it is dangerous. The people are there. We are not suggesting being adventurers, but we are saying that it is a basic patriotic duty to accept risks. If we give up, then the enemy will occupy. If we do not supply, then the enemy will supply. We feel it should be more dangerous for the enemy to penetrate our land, to come and supply our people in order to entice and corrupt them, than it is for us to travel to supply our people. We insist therefore on unreserved compliance with the decisions of the party's leadership bodies.

9. Organizing Society to Conquer Underdevelopment*

Cultural Values and the School

Underdevelopment is not generally due to a lack of material resources. Poverty and underdevelopment reflect man's ignorance in using existing resources and man's passive acceptance of his situation of wretchedness. Peasant societies essentially are underdeveloped because they are fatalist. Mozambican society, even in the urban sector, carries the dead weight of the fatalist, resigned, passive legacy of the peasant society.

Time has a different meaning in the peasant society. What we don't do today can be done tomorrow. So there is no sense of time-keeping. In peasant society time has a different value. Life moves on in rhythm with the sun, in relation to sunrise and sunset. The peasant does not ask himself: how long did I take for this task? The peasant does not measure time in set targets. So he does not ration his time strictly.

There is no saving of energy, with the minimum effort used for the maximum return, no planning or rationalizing of labour. The peasants use a short-handled hoe, although it is inconvenient and inefficient, because they are accustomed to it. The family is not regarded as a household. To the man it is an economic unit that he governs for his advantage, and where increasing the number of wives means increasing the labour force at his disposal. Woman's way of existence in that society is to belong to someone, father or husband. The duty of educating the children is reduced to fulfilling certain ritual obligations. In a large feudal family, it is common for a father not to know all his children, and common for him to have wives of the same age as his granddaughters.

In the peasant society it is not the family's concern that the children should bath regularly, that the children's hair be combed, their teeth cleaned, that they have a handkerchief to wipe their nose, that their clothes be clean and in good repair, and that their eating times and amount of sleep be regulated. This is not the custom, even though it is within the family's power. Such attitudes have been carried over to the city and have been introduced into schools.

*A speech given at the start of the school year in Maputo, 13 February 1982.

A transposition of peasant ways to the city has meant the city being changed to the rural way of living. The father eats at the table and has the better food. His children and wife, or wives, eat in the kitchen or the yard, seated on a mat, with a stick in one hand to chase away the chickens and a mug of water in the other. The father is well dressed and shod, and the children ragged and barefoot. There may be a shortage of cash for the child's milk, but never for father's beer.

The assimilated man will replace traditional polygamy with promiscuity, eventually marrying one woman, the most polished, but not giving up the others. Traditional superstition will be supplemented by cinematic myths from karate films and the models of the foreign bourgeoisie.

The education given by our schools seeks among other things to break with this outlook, to bring man into a culture, to relate to the mode of production and to economic development. The scientific knowledge instilled there plus the ideology and class sentiment provide the irresistible force that will sweep away the old world and implant a new world. Our schools are a mirror to society and to the contradictions, including those of culture, that we are facing.

When we talk about student apathy, failure in punctuality, lack of inquisitiveness and eagerness to learn, ignorance of and indifference to the value of things that leads to vandalism and the smashing of installations and equipment, dirtiness and lack of pride in one's appearance, etc., all these things begin at home, reflect family life, are legacies of the old society.

Our educational effort cannot be limited to the student, but must also influence parents. Sometimes we have to address parents at their place of work. It makes no sense for a father to let his child go to school in tatters.

A particularly serious problem is the sexual abuse of girls of about the age of 12 and 13. They become pregnant, and some are married off. They are children even if they are given in marriage. It is sexual abuse, a direct attack on human dignity. What does it mean from the intellectual, cultural, social, moral and even physical standpoint for a child of 12 or 13 years to be the mother of another child? What level of moral and social responsibility can she have? None. Is the child she bears the fruit of a firm, emotional relationship? No. It is the outcome of a seduction, of inexperience and naïvety. We must severely penalize the seducers.

Unhappily we don't yet have a family law. The law does not yet provide for severe penalties for premature marriage or the impregnation of children. In our present society it is often the victims who, as a consequence as a bad interpretation of our principles, face punishment, denunciation and disgrace.

A young girl who becomes pregnant is taken out of school, and loses her scholarship, at the age, say, of 15 or 16. But the one who made her pregnant, who is grown up, who is supposed to be a cadre or an official, goes scot-free. It is a legacy of the principle that the man makes children and woman passively allows herself to become pregnant.

131

But there is also the legacy of bourgeois hypocrisy that shows up in the practice of abortion for minors. This practice, sometimes carried out with the consent or even the active encouragement of the parents, is intended to hush up the scandal, to pretend that the girl is still a virgin, to seek to protect 'family honour'. In other instances, the pregnant girls themselves seek abortion secretly. They want to go on with their loose living. Such situations sap the foundations of the family, destroy the parents' moral authority. The state will soon put forward for public discussion a draft family law.

In raising these issues at the start of the school year and in addressing pupils' parents, we are saying that the education battle is the responsibility of everyone and primarily of parents. We are saying that the battle can be won only if first of all we ensure that in our homes correct attitudes and behaviour are to the fore, and if we free ourselves from the old society.

We want to say also that our homes must be homes and not merely lodging places where there is one or more wife and children – places where there is one all-powerful father who insults and beats the mother, brings women to the house, and where scenes of immorality and drunkenness are witnessed by the children.

We know that often the only way to learn is from our mistakes. We know that in our minds and hearts there is generosity and determination capable of transforming the old world into a new world. We have already been able to overcome colonialism, to defeat Smith, and reinvigorate our country, and we are equally capable of building a better future.

Tasks for Party and State in the Education Battle

The educational battle demands organized and co-ordinated action by various party bodies, by the mass democratic organizations, and by the state, with particular effect in the locality, district and city. We feel that in the light of what was said earlier, we in the party must wage a battle over mental outlooks and attitudes. We have to wage a battle for society to take on its responsibility for education.

The party bodies at local, district and city level, the secretariats and the committees, must keep themselves informed about the life of schools and educational establishments. They must know the curriculum and see if it is being observed. They must inspect the quality of training given to the pupils, and the attitude and behaviour of teachers. They must know how the school is getting on, and press for it to progress, know if it is clean, if there are benches and desks and how they are used, if there are playgrounds, sports, cultural activities. They must encourage decoration of the schools, preservation of the building and school equipment.

The party bodies must above all promote a link between the community and the school, a link with parents, with pupils, a link between the school and production units, military stations, administrative structures.

They should bring artists, singers, dancers, writers, painters and sculptors to the school. They should bring as visiting speakers veterans of the liberation struggle, patriots, qualified production cadres, exemplary workers. In short, individuals who will educate the new generation in the spirit of heroism, patriotism, love of labour and socialism.

This is not a task that the party can do on its own. It is a task that the party guides through the OJM, the OMM, the production councils, local, district and city assemblies.

The party locally must indicate to each of these structures what its specific task is. The OMM, for example, in conjunction with mothers, must support the school's action in ensuring that the children come appropriately dressed, that they do not come to school tattered and dirty, that their face and teeth are clean and their hair combed. The OMM must contact families whose children come to school tattered, unkempt and dishevelled, and explain that these children are a disturbing element in the school and a sorry sight.

The OJM has a task in organizing the children's leisure time, encouraging sport, trips, cultural activities, debate and constructive exchange of ideas.

The people's deputies must keep a constant eye on the school, the distribution of textbooks and exercise books, the maintenance of equipment, the condition of lavatories, the local manufacture of desks and benches through voluntary labour. The deputies should act to avoid drop-outs. They should talk to parents whose children are absent from school, or are taken away for initiation rites. They must take part in parents' meetings, and at the People's Assembly sessions debate the situation of education at their territorial level, ask for reports from school directors, teachers, pupils' parents and sponsors.

The National Teachers Organization has an important task in this process, of mobilizing parents, of jogging the People's Assemblies, of controlling the standard and performance of teachers. It should participate in professional assessment, in selecting teachers for refresher courses, in designating teachers who merit special awards and also in the purging of their ranks.

The ONP, in collaboration with the People's Assemblies and the population in general, must contribute to ensuring respect for the teaching profession and be in the vanguard of raising their conditions.

This is not an exhaustive list, just a few examples. The party bodies at local level must study their specific circumstances, direct and co-ordinate action by the mass democratic organizations and the People's Assemblies, encourage concrete work schedules, and apply the watchword 'Education is the task of all of us'.

The Pupils and the School

We have had occasion to observe the our state is making an enormous effort to ensure education for the new generations. We should like education up to the seventh year to be available for all young people by the end of this decade. The rise in knowledge should not merely serve the individual. The effort and sacrifice of the entire people do not have the aim of ensuring that so-and-so should earn more because he has had more schooling. Obviously he will earn more because he does work of a higher quality. But the real purpose of our making the sacrifice, and investing in education, is to improve the people's standard of living, to develop the country.

Since the sacrifice is made by the whole society, it is natural that the party, representing the people, should mobilize the people to accept the sacrifice and should decide how best to use the new talents we are shaping. This means that priorities will go on being laid down, and students will be placed according to their aptitude, the priorities of national development, and the criteria of class.

No sensible man will sow rice in the sand on the beach. It would be wasted effort. The state and the people do not want to waste their efforts, to invest in misfits, the idle and the feckless. A student who fails because of poor attendance means a wasted effort for our people and our state, like rice seed sown on a sandy beach. Should we allow him to go on occupying a school place when he has failed the year for poor attendance?

A student who makes no effort to study, but sits passively in lessons, takes no notes when the teacher is explaining, does no homework, never reads a book, such a student is causing the people and the state to make useless sacrifices. Should we invest in students who consistently score low marks?

If a student throughout his primary and secondary schooling was mediocre, with marks ranging between 9 and 11 out of 20, what good will he do at an intermediate institution or university?

Do our people want to be attended by a mediocre nurse? Are we going to entrust a machine or a factory, which has cost millions of meticais, to an engineer who can only rate half marks in his exams?

We must invest in fertile soil, in those who want to serve the people, who are willing to learn and have the capacity to do so. We shall invest in students who in their school conduct show that they have appreciated the value of independence, of the conquests in the nationalization of schools, who can make the most of the sacrifice by their parents and the people and of the efforts of the people's state. This means that we shall invest in the disciplined student, who does his preparation, his exercises, and rates high marks, who is not satisfied with mediocrity, but works to show his best.

The match burns only when there is oxygen. Parents have a fundamental role in the student's behaviour at school, and what he makes of school.

The more demanding the parents are at home, the better their child will do in school.

Student youth have particular problems that differ from those of young peasants and workers. It is not by chance that the youth organizations of all countries include sections that devote themselves entirely to the incorporation of young pupils and students.

The Teachers and the School

The teacher is the decisive factor in the triumph of our education programme, for the school's proper functioning. The school is the main centre of activity during a citizen's childhood, adolescence and youth, and the teacher, the master, is the main modeller of the student's personality, and the inspirer of his view of the world. The country's future is born in the schools.

The school is the student's place of work, just as the factory and the farm are the workplace for the worker and peasant. A student has tasks and responsibilities at school. He has standards and targets to achieve. Just as we offer distinction to the best enterprises and production units, so we should also give distinction to the best schools. We have to commend those that do best in results, discipline, conservation and the maintenance of equipment, in the link with the community, in cleanliness and in sports. The school is where we prepare the good worker of the future, the conscious person, the New Man.

It is the school that shows the true scale of the integrated man or woman, conscious of mankind's conquests and victories. it is the school that awakens talent, intellectual curiosity, inventiveness, a clear approach to research and debate.

The school is the unifying centre for the nation. It is there that patriotic sensibility and national unity are forged and tempered. There is no place in the school for tribalism, regionalism or racism. Education is not merely teaching the curriculum, however important that it; it is also moulding the citizen's personality and worth.

To educate, the teacher must study, study the science he teaches, study the student's environment, study the character, potential and limits of each pupil. He will then know how to give expression to the personality of each pupil, how to make the most of the talent of every child, adolescent and youth.

The student must not be anonymous, a mere number. Each student has a family, lives in a particular house, in particular material circumstances, has or has not gone through initiation rites, has a particular mother tongue, has various entrenched habits.

The student from the city differs from one from the countryside. Someone who lives in a reed hut is different from someone who lives in a cement building, just as someone who lives with his parents is different

135

from someone living with an uncle and aunt, a brother- or sister-in-law, or cousins. Students whose parents can speak Portuguese are different from those whose parents cannot, just as the children of literate parents are different from the students whose parents are illiterate. The teacher must be aware of this reality and reflect on the circumstances so that his work should be guided appropriately to produce effective results.

A teacher who knows his students can decide the support they need, the demands that can be made on them, the changes that must be made. The teacher who gives the right support to the student must know the parents, and work with the parents or education sponsors, so that the efforts at school and at home are complementary.

Often where there is an organized school and a disorganized home background, the school's efforts are wasted, as the organized period in school is just an interval in an otherwise disorganized life.

As our society is still going through a transition from the hut, the village and the reed house to the cement building and the school, the teacher has a greater task. The transition requires sensitivity on day-to-day matters. The teacher may have to show someone used to a mat how to sit on a chair. A teacher may have to show someone used to easing himself in the bush how to use a latrine or a closet. The teacher will have to teach a child who has never learned to wash his hands and plays only on the ground how to play without getting dirty, and that he should come into the classroom with clean hands and face.

The teacher must press the students to observe the rules of personal tidiness, be concerned that they come to school clean, in clean clothes, with teeth cleaned, and hair combed. The teacher should teach the pupils not to sit around on the ground or the school walls and not to use the school yards and stairways for combing or plaiting their hair.

We ask giant qualities of our teachers, but they do not all have them. A teacher is more often than not as young as his students. So he sometimes does not have the necessary maturity and knowledge to guide and direct the process of instruction and training for the students. He does not recognize the students' mistakes as mistakes. For example, he is unable to see the need for teaching the students order and cleanliness, whether in regard to exercise books and textbooks, or at the level of clothing, room or dining room.

The teacher still does not pay sufficient attention to freeing the child's initiative and guiding this initiative. He doesn't care if the child is following the lesson passively, or is sitting on the ground or slouching. The teacher is often satisfied with making children repeat a phrase parrot-fashion, without ensuring that it is being understood. He does not use proper teaching or assessment methods.

He sometimes does not realize that he is a model for the pupils. He may in fact be a bad model, by his authoritarianism, or by being inconsistent in what he says, or contradictory in what he says and does, or in what he demands of the students and how he works, or in his own appearance, beliefs and values.

Such a teacher – for reasons that are sometimes beyond him – is not doing his job. He does not realize his power as an educator, and often works without enthusiasm. He sees the pupils more as numbers than as human beings. He automatically follows a syllabus and guidelines that he may not even have bothered to read and interpret.

He is not concerned as the leader of a teaching–learning process with knowing his pupils' origin, history and social circumstances in order to think out how to work with them and educate them.

Teacher-training centres must look at these issues. Teacher-training is not merely a technical question. It is a matter of training an agent of social change.

The teacher must educate the student to have pride in his class origin. So he himself must be able to relate to his own origin, and respect it by way of example, since the teacher is the lamp that leads us out of the darkness, obscurantism, prejudices and complexes of social origin.

The problem arises because teachers often feel impermanent. They feel that the profession is undervalued. So there are teachers who abandon it for better paid and less demanding jobs. There are some who skip classes to do outside work that pays better. They go so far as to make an advance payment for the penalty they are going to incur for absence. Others take turns to be absent, and leave their students with another teacher who will be absent for the next session.

Young, newly trained teachers sometimes resist being posted outside Maputo, and above all in the rural areas. When bad teachers are dismissed from teaching they should not be financially better off, and they should not be admitted to civil service posts.

We must, however, recognize that the majority of teachers behave heroically and worthily, making an effort to overcome failings and giving their energy, with the limited means at their disposal, to the training of new generations. The ONP, the People's Assemblies and the Ministry of Education and Culture must back these exemplary teachers, award them prestige and improve their conditions. These cadres should have priority in the award of scholarships and other means of improving their skills.

Parents and the School

The school is a fundamental battlefield. Youth offer fertile ground where any seed will flourish. At the outset they are neither revolutionary nor reactionary. So the youth are a perpetual bone of contention between us and the enemy. Whether right or wrong ideas triumph in each generation will depend on what that generation's education was. Since we have the right ideas, we are certain that the youth are on our side.

School is the essential element of education. But it is not the only one.

The home is the second basic element. School and home have to join together to ensure the correct education of each generation.

Parents are the first educators and lay the groundwork for the personality their children will have. The latter, even in adult life, reflect whether for good or bad the education they received at home. That's why we say 'he hasn't drunk tea', when we want to refer to a badly brought-up person.

We note in the schools the difficulties caused by the children of divorced parents. They are children with psychological trauma, with emotional upsets. And there are many such cases.

There are men who have children by several wives, and don't bother about any of their children. There are women with children by different fathers. These children pour into school and bring to other children the problems and immoralities they have witnessed.

The pattern of the family, understanding between parents, separations, polygamous marriages, the sending away of children to be brought up by other relatives are factors influencing a child's sociability, his psychological balance, dynamism, readiness to learn, and initiative. These are the elements that affect his behaviour with regard to study, school and society.

Some parents think their responsibility for the child's education ends on the day he first goes to school. This is a mark of ignorance, obscurantism, blindness, thoughtlessness, in short a denial of the educator's responsibility. Some parents have difficulty in monitoring their child's behaviour at school. They never went to school, don't know how the school functions, and think that they are incapable of guiding their children, because it is the latter who know how to read, write, calculate, speak Portuguese, understand geography, talk about history.

Others think they are too busy with their own routine to consider their children's life. We notice that even at FRELIMO schools, attended by the children of militants, cadres and leaders, very few go to parents' meetings, or keep in touch with the teachers who are effectively taking on the responsibility as educators.

Many parents take notice of their children's situation only when there are dramatic failures, cases of delinquency and anti-social behaviour, but they do not realize that these situations are the result of the apathy they have shown in regard to their children's education. Some parents contact the school only on the day their son or daughter fails the year for misbehaviour or truancy, or for being pregnant. Some parents only then put in written explanations seeking to excuse their children's absences from school.

Parents are still suffering the pernicious influence of traditional or colonial education, of the myths and customs of religion and superstition. So there is always a tendency towards a conservative influence on education.

This complex of factors demands close co-ordination between home and school, between parents and teachers. The parents must understand how the school operates. They have to understand such elementary matters as the marking system, failing the year, the need for regular attendance at class, how to use and take care of uniform, exercise books and textbooks.

They have to accompany the school, live the school, learn to link up with the teacher, the form teacher. They must know what their child's curriculum is and if it is being taught. They must check if their child does homework and exercises. they must organize and monitor their child's leisure time, know what he does when he's away from home, where he was, in whose company.

So the parents must combine home and school influence in ensuring their children's education. This means being concerned that their children go to school clean and brushed, with teeth cleaned, nails clipped, that their uniform or clothes are not tattered, and that they take the books and exercise books needed for the class.

A child who learns at school to use a latrine will go on using a latrine when he's at home. A child who learns to sit at a desk in school will not sit on the ground at home. A child who learns punctuality at school should have set times at home for meals, and going to bed and getting up. A child who at school is taught to ask questions and has his curiosity aroused and his initiative encouraged should not be crushed at home to make him passive.

The school–home, teacher–parent link should be gradually institutionalized. In the first phase we must form associations of the parents of children at each school, under the guidance of the party's local bodies and with the support and active involvement of the mass democratic organizations and the People's Assembly of the area. The people win power in the schools in an orderly way, to make the schools serve the people. Parents are the principal instrument for winning this power.

That requires parents rising to their responsibilities and in the first instance being sensitive to the task of educating their children and keeping in touch with school life. Being responsible entails accounting for one's actions and being penalized for one's mistakes.

Some parents withdraw their children from school without obeying the legal requirements. Girls particularly are taken away at the age of puberty. Some parents let their children fail through truancy and in the face of their children's indiscipline or even vandalism think it good enough to say it is a matter for the school or the teacher, as if their children were no longer their own. Taking children out of school and truancy failures should be subject to penalties. It is not enough to lose the right to a school place.

As the people have made an effort, and been put to needless expense, the expense and effort need to be reimbursed. In other words, taking a child out of school or allowing a child to fail through truancy should not only mean loss of a place but also incur a fine paid to the state corresponding to the unnecessary expense.

We cannot allow our boarding schools to be a dumping ground for bad or indisciplined students. The boarding schools and hostels should be for the good students, the disciplined students, for the children of workers, peasants and militants, who pledge by their conduct and capabilities service to the people. The Ministry of Education and Culture will consider these problems and put forward proposals to solve them.

Conclusion

Every society has its foundations in moral values, in ideological principles that form the groundwork of its power. Our revolution profoundly shook the foundations of the colonial society. Nationalization of schooling, legal practice and health, and the recuperation of the land brought a moment of rupture with the most sacred precepts of the colonialist and colonized mentality.

This shake-up in the superstructure is not only a transformation of ideological and political values. It is also a shake-up in behaviour, attitudes, personal relationships and social customs. Our society is changing.

Today it is characterized by confrontation between the vestiges of colonial society and the new society of free men and women that we are building. The issues we have been talking about, our school life and the role of parents in their children's education, reflect the problems we face in our changing society. They are issues that arise out of peasant customs that even in the city are still predominant in family relations.

Hence it is in the family that we must make the organizational effort to assert the values of our revolution. The family is our society's cell. The society cannot be orderly if the family is not orderly. The school cannot be orderly if the family is not orderly.

The child who at home is brushed and combed, who washes his hands before going to the table to eat, who asks permission to leave the table or to go out to play, who knows the time he must leave for school, the time when he should eat his meals, when he should study, when he may play, and when he should go to bed – that is a child with an orderly life, that is a child who contributes to making his school an orderly place.

That child is an important element in letting the teacher do his task properly, because the latter can give his attention to his main task of teaching. So we say that school is the continuation in society of the educative influence of parents and family. The school gives man a global dimension. It is in the school that he becomes conscious of his place in the world.

The family and the school are two aspects of the same process: the process of shaping the man or woman who will build and consolidate the Mozambican nation.

Nation entails organized society. To organize society, we need to establish a common attitude, so that we have the same aims and aspirations, so that we establish behaviour and attitudes that are consistent with our revolutionary values.

Organizing home life is a battle for each of us. It is a practical and daily expression of the struggle between the old and the new – a struggle in which the new must triumph over the old.

This is not a dream. It is a battle that has gone on since mankind began to organize society, since mankind has existed. It is in human nature to want to do better, to establish more organized ways of living.

Organizing society and consolidating the nation means strengthening our unity, means making every citizen a true patriot ever ready to struggle to build and defend his socialist country. And our patriotism begins with our children. They are the foundations of the Mozambican nation. They are the generation that should shine like the sun.

So we appeal to all men, women and young people, and to all parents, that by making education a task of us all, we should emerge victorious from this battle. In addressing parents, we are making a patriotic appeal, an appeal for mankind, let's say, that we must ensure a brilliant future for the children, we must ensure a brilliant future for our socialist country.

We urge them to create in their children pride in being good students, pride in being well-behaved students at school, at home, in the street. We want the parents likewise to have pride in their children's school performance and personal behaviour.

We want to create conditions such that in this generation disease, hunger, poverty, illiteracy and ignorance should begin to vanish for ever from our country. Just as we emerged victorious from the struggle against colonialism, just as we smashed the racist aggression of the illegal Smith-Muzorewa regime, so we shall also emerge victorious from this battle, because once again we shall be able to bring together the energy and intelligence of the entire people for peace, progress, prosperity and plenty. It is the task of us all to organize society so that we can conquer underdevelopment.

10. Transform the Central Hospital into a People's Hospital*

We are going to talk about health – health at the service of the people. If we say that we are going to politicize the health service, many will say: 'Politicize medicine? Politicize the instruments?' But we are going to try to explain why we want to politicize medicine. Medicine is intimately linked with the community, intimately linked with society, intimately linked with the people's life. So it is necessary to politicize medicine. Unless we do politicize medicine, it will become an instrument that is a danger to the people and one that operates against policy. There can be technical development only if there is political development. Without political development, scientific development is impossible, technical development is impossible. Politics maps out the path we should follow; the kind of development we should follow; the kind of science we should develop; the kind of society that science must serve. So we feel that we should rightly be concerned with politicizing medicine. Medicine does not exist in the abstract. For there to be medicine, there must be individuals, personnel such as those here. Our politicization of the personnel who are here means that we are politicizing medicine.

Comrades, members of the Council of Ministers of the People's Republic of Mozambique; comrades, militants and fighters of FRELIMO; comrades, internationalist comrades, workers and friends in the health service: we have come here with the clear purpose that in this short meeting we should have a positive exchange of views, and we should map out the correct path that we want to follow.

We have come here to discuss our people's problems, our revolution's problems, our life's problems. We think it important to make clear at the outset that we have come to discuss these problems – of our revolution, our people and our life. We have come here to study collectively and jointly, and to find answers to the questions concerning our people's health.

Health is indispensable for the accomplishment of our revolutionary tasks. Without health we are in no condition to carry out our task, our body does not answer the needs of the struggle and the community is put

*This speech was delivered at the Central Hospital in Maputo on 6 October 1976.

at risk. Without health the peasant is in no condition to involve himself in creating communal villages or to increase the agricultural production that provides the basis for our country's development. The unhealthy workman cannot make his contribution to the development of the industry that is the dynamizing factor in our economy. Without health the soldier cannot do his duty, cannot ensure the defence of the revolution's victories, territorial defence and consolidation of people's democratic power. Without health the student will be unable to study and to gather the knowledge that will allow him to give better service to our people.

Hence we say health is revolutionary capital that must be maintained to serve the struggle. Struggling for the health of the masses is one of FRELIMO's central concerns, and comes within the framework of serving the masses on the battlefront of health.

We are meeting here today to study a particular facet of the health problematic: the Maputo Central Hospital. And some of you will then ask: 'Why the Maputo Central Hospital and not some other hospital?'

We might answer that the Health Minister's introductory statement put the Maputo Central Hospital in its rightful place, in its historic dimension, in its appropriate form in regard to our people, in relation to all who work in the Maputo Central Hospital. And we say further to those workers: because the Maputo Central Hospital is our national hospital, the only hospital structured and organized to serve the entire people from the Rovuma to the Maputo. The Central Hospital is daily flooded by thousands of patients from all regions of the country. So its functioning has a direct effect on all our people.

Secondly, the Maputo Central Hospital is the main preparation and training centre for health cadres – whether medical or paramedical cadres. All medical students and about half the students on our country's paramedical courses study here. This is where they must acquire a sense of serving the people. They are producers. They have no off-season. While the peasants wait for the coming of the rains, the health workers are permanent producers, they are peasants with no off-season.

On the functioning of the Central Hospital depends the political and technical training of these cadres who will later be posted throughout the country. And so we regard the Maputo Central Hospital as the reservoir for cadres. Thus as well as being a hospital, it is a laboratory where new ideas of serving the people are distilled.

It is in the Central Hospital that we must acquire good habits, scientific rules, more developed rules. So if we neglect the training of these cadres it means that instead of sending cadres round the country, we are sending parasites that will destroy our people. We therefore believe that the Central Hospital's task of training cadres is an exciting one, albeit difficult and tough. Through the training of these cadres we shall destroy parasites and disease in our country. Through the training of these cadres we shall restore life and health to our people, cut down infant mortality and child death. It is therefore essential that the cadres trained at the

Central Hospital should be promoters of clean, scientific and advanced habits. And that is why we have such concern for the Central Hospital.

Again it is because of the decisive impact the Central Hospital has now, and will have in the future, on our battle on the health front that the FRELIMO leadership has followed its evolution so closely, and we have called today's meeting. We might summarize the aims of this meeting by saying that it is intended to study how to transform the Maputo Central Hospital into a hospital genuinely at the service of the people. If you, my friends, have other concerns, these are ours.

The Central Hospital: What It Was; What It Is; What It Will Be in the Future

To be able to determine the right way to transform the Maputo Central Hospital into a new kind of hospital, a hospital entirely devoted to the service of the broad labouring masses, we must study its evolution to date. The Maputo Central Hospital is the result of a merger in October 1974 of the Miguel Bombarda Central Hospital and the University Hospital.

The Miguel Bombarda Hospital, founded decades ago, was an instrument conceived to serve the system of colonial-Fascist domination over our people. The so-called Miguel Bombarda Hospital was in fact at heart a centre for racial and social discrimination. In the hospital were various categories or classes reflecting the social and racial structure of colonial capitalism, ranging from the White settler to the assimilated Black and even to the native. This is the context that gave us first- and second-class wards; private rooms; a native maternity clinic; subtly differentiated out-patients departments, etc. This racial discrimination was felt not only by the patients, but also among the workers themselves.

A centre for maltreatment and humiliation of our people – in the hospital there was a total lack of concern for the poor patient, which was manifested in the way the doctor or nurse looked at him, in the absence of hygiene in the wards, in licence and indiscipline among the workers. Our people were used in the hospital as guinea-pigs for new drugs and certain operations, which if successful could later be applied to the bourgeoisie in the private clinics and consultancies.

A centre of unbridled capitalist exploitation – apart from some very cursory examination, the patient was treated in accordance with his economic means. In the capitalist hospital treatment did not depend on the seriousness of the illness.

'Mr So-and-so, what have you got?' – 'I don't have anything.'

'What do you have in the way of goods?' – 'I don't have anything except the illness I'm reporting now.'

'Well wait a while.'

This was not the doctor or the nurse, it was the system. That's why we talk about serving the people. It is not a question of race or colour. It is the system that guides attitudes. The hospital was a centre of theft, immorality, licence, confusion, anarchy, indiscipline, in short a centre of political, ideological and material corruption.

The Hospital's Structure and Functioning

How was the structure of the Miguel Bombarda Hospital reflected in its functioning? The structures of the Miguel Bombarda Hospital were like all structures of the colonial apparatus: first: they were rigid, individualist and bureaucratic; second: they blocked initiative and prevented the participation of workers in hospital life – power was absolute and centralized; third: they alienated the workers, making them irresponsible, and where there is irresponsibility there is also childishness, with disastrous consequences; fourth: they gave favourable openings for dishonest and corrupt elements who used the sickness of others as a gold mine to enrich themselves.

These were the structures that allowed the hospital staff to work at the same time in private consultancies and clinics, where they picked up a mercenary attitude (a weakness for money) and the bourgeois mentality that was even more deeply ingrained in them.

Health services anywhere in the world are complicated. Anywhere in the world they are the most stick-in-the-mud institutions, deeply stick-in-the-mud. I recall that wherever there has been a revolution, the last place it reached was the hospital. We want to start in this hospital and we shall triumph. If we triumphed against colonialism, a more organized enemy, won't we triumph at this hospital? What could cause our failure at this hospital?

The Miguel Bombarda Hospital was geared up to make things totally impossible for honest workers. The way tasks and duties were distributed, the working methods employed, all this alienated the worker from his duty towards the patients and gradually gave him a bourgeois mentality and an increasingly overt desire to copy the colonizer.

The pattern was set by the colonizer. In order to be regarded as more civilized and more evolved, one had to copy mechanically everything the colonizer did. The ability to copy was what being evolved was all about.

In brief: the Miguel Bombarda Hospital was a façade of a hospital, one that never served our people and was a centre for the spread of a bourgeois ideology and outlook, a centre for the alienation of health workers.

The University Hospital was an élite hospital, whose founding about a decade ago only had the effect of sharpening divisions, whether among patients or among health workers. Why?

Because the University Hospital was for the more 'evolved' patients, while the Miguel Bombarda Hospital was for the 'barefooted', who could only be admitted to the University Hospital when they had some 'rare' or 'curious' illness that seemed of interest to the gentlemen doctors there; because the University Hospital staff had higher salaries than those at the Miguel Bombarda Hospital, which led to an élitist spirit among the former.

This was the situation we found in September 1974 when the Transitional Government was sworn in. And what did we do to correct the situation?

In the first instance we decided to merge the two hospitals into a single Central Hospital, as a means of struggle against divisionism, against discrimination by which one was for the 'monkeys', the other was for 'people'.

Where there is division there will be an enemy base or bulwark. When the health workers are divided, it means that an enemy base has been established. Division among us is the essential strength of the enemy. When we are divided we are easily gobbled up by natural disasters. So our main concern is to create real unity here: in thought, behaviour and attitude.

In the second place, we launched a battle to stop the maltreatment and the social and racial humiliation to which our working people had been subjected. We put an end to first- and second-class wards. We put a stop to the 'native' maternity clinic.

These changes were victories, but how to consolidate them? There was a series of battles to gain these victories. There were failures along the way. There were sacrifices. We should like you, comrades and friends, ladies and gentlemen, to see these changes as conquests by the Mozambican people in their just struggle against foreign domination. The conquests did not come out of the sky; there were no miracles. Our people had to accept sacrifices; make the greatest sacrifices, including life itself. So we achieved the transformation. Now we must consolidate these victories. How does one consolidate a victory? It will depend on the commitment of health personnel.

So it is essential for the health personnel to recognize as a victory what has already been done: merger into one hospital, elimination of the discriminatory system of wards, and native and European maternity clinics, and so on. Recognize all this as conquests and victories. Now we have to take on board the fact that we shall have to wage a new combat for consolidation. Without a battle there will be no consolidation; without sacrifice there will be no victory. So we must gird ourselves for the new combat. And combat demands complete relinquishment of the easy life. In war there is no easy life. And our people are now waging war to consolidate their victories. So this is not the time for luxury. It is essential that all health personnel accept and consciously commit themselves to this combat that our people continue to wage to consolidate their victory. No combat, no victory; no sacrifices, no combat or victory. We shall always be dominated and trampled upon.

In the third place, we began political mobilization of the workers so that they could make an organized contribution to transforming structures and outlooks in the hospital. But, we must admit, it was not done with conscious commitment, but with emotionalism. There was no study. A combat that is not planned is liable to fail; a struggle that is undirected, unorganized, aimless, targetless, is doomed to failure and total destruction. And that's why we have not been successful in the hospitals. Our successes have been sporadic. They do not spring from an organized combat. So we do not know where to begin consolidating the victories.

We were aware that what was done would be insufficient to transform the Central Hospital into a FRELIMO hospital, a hospital at the service of the people. The hospital was a cornerstone, certainly, but of a health system created by colonial-capitalism.

And so we studied the issue and we decided: to change this and other hospitals it will be necessary to attack and smash the whole health system created by the colonialists. And that's why some were caught on the hop and as they were unaware of the need for nationalization they reacted negatively to the measures. There was no complete, deep study and debate on the meaning of the nationalizations. They are conquests by the people, putting the health system at their service. But they may turn into failure and defeat as there has been no debate to foster a greater commitment.

Nationalizations in the Health Sector and the Central Hospital

After the proclamation of independence, the government decided to nationalize the health sector. Why nationalize the health sector?

First: to put health at the service of the masses.

Second: to spread health provision, putting rich and poor on the same footing; there is no question of one life being more valuable and another less valuable, all are human lives.

Third: to democratize medical care.

Fourth: to eliminate the mercenary attitude that was prevalent among health workers.

Fifth: to end exploitation of human suffering.

Sixth: to stop the ill health of some being a necessary concomitant of others earning a living.

Seventh: to deal a blow to profiteering over health and the abusive privileges reaped from this profiteering.

Eighth: to attack the individualist and easy-going attitude of health personnel, who lose the status as so-called freelance workers – of a liberal profession.

What was the people's reaction to the nationalizations? The people are our thermometer. This thermometer tells us whether we are right or wrong. It is not done by a clique. So in the first instance we study how the people reacted to the nationalizations. And according to their reactions, we shall know if we were right or wrong. So what was the people's reaction? What was your reaction? We are an integral part of the people.

We observed spontaneous and general enthusiasm; we saw adherence to and active support for the nationalizations, amply demonstrated by an influx of patients to the hospitals, only after the nationalizations. So, health personnel: what was done then to cope with this great influx into the hospitals? What answer can we give? Which of you did not support the nationalizations? We are not saying he is an enemy. We are simply asking who did not support the nationalizations?

How the Enemy Reacted to the Nationalizations

The enemy had long been acting subversively in the Central Hospital. What he did after the nationalizations was to step up this activity. And what form did the activity take?

Running down and twisting the nationalizations – that was the enemy's first reaction. There was and is dissatisfaction among workers who came from the sectors that were nationalized (the private consultancies and clinics) because they thought that as a result of the nationalizations they would have to work more and earn less. I believe that the real concern of a physician is to treat the patient. A physician is a scientist. His pride, the secret of his profession, is constantly to develop his skills. The enemy took advantage of these dissatisfied individuals to mobilize them against FRELIMO, against the government and against the people. The enemy is in a way helping us.

We saw that the nationalizations were actively supported by the people. So the enemy now wants to mobilize the people to attack their own conquests. Does that make sense? Moblize my arms to attack my eyes; mobilize my legs to go against my head – is that possible? But unfortunately there was a dissatisfied group. And what has happened to this group?

The dissatisfied are a recruiting ground for reaction. When reaction want to recruit it goes to the dissatisfied. They form a steady, permanent base for recruitment by reaction. If there are dissatisfied individuals among health workers this means that there is a recruiting ground for reaction. Are there some dissatisfied? If there are they'll be recruited by the enemy. A dissatisfied man is a base for the enemy; a dissatisfied man is a nucleus. The enemy has already scored a victory with him. So reaction exploited a base, a nucleus that was already formed and had only to be recruited. Reaction took advantage of inequalities between workers, above all pay differentials, to sow division and confusion among them; took advantage of the survival of colonial structures, of retrograde mental habits, of our political structures' shortcomings, in order to encourage indiscipline, disorganization, liberalism and theft. Reaction exploited the corruption that already existed, rumour-mongering and intrigue already rife in the hospital, against FRELIMO, and against the government.

Why did the enemy do that?

He was the one who shaped us. All of us here were trained by the enemy. So he knows our strong points and our weak ones. He knows what nerve he must touch in each of us. He was the one who trained us. So what did he do?

As we know, he touched the cornerstone: pay differentials; the material issue. The enemy simply came along and whetted our appetites and there he did his recruitment. Recruitment is very easy. It is enough to know the frailties, the weak points and from there to move into action. That's what the enemy did.

Reaction to the Nationalizations Began in the Central Hospital

What were the consequences of enemy action in the Central Hospital? First: the hospital was transformed into a centre for rumour-mongering and intrigue – a centre of reaction; second: the hospital was transformed into a centre for demobilizing our people.

Why? Why did the enemy choose the hospital? Since the people are victims of unconcern on the staff's part, since there is maltreatment, since there are deliberate delays, since there is a lack of cleanliness, since there is sabotage of equipment. The hospital was transformed into a centre of slander against foreign comrades.

Aims of the Enemy Action

It was an attempt to prove in the first place that nationalization is bad and that private medicine is good, and secondly to demobilize and demoralize the masses by stirring up discontents on the basis of legitimate anger at the malfunctioning of a service that is essential to life and society, and thirdly to generate hostility to the nationalizations in general and FRELIMO and the government in particular.

Current Situation

At a time therefore when it would have been natural for things to be going well for our people in the Central Hospital, we began to hear complaints from the masses. What are the complaints?

Some hospital staff deliberately make the people uncomfortable whether in queues for a consultation, or the outpatients', or on the wards; there is a widespread lack of concern in the hospital for the patient as a person – the patient is regarded and treated as a thing and not as a human being with feelings; there is a lack of cleanliness and order in the hospital; patients in the hospital often call for hours for assistance from the staff without being attended to.

The Mass Criticisms Are Right and Justified

After we were alerted by the complaints from the masses, we made a further visit to the hospital. And what did we find? What did we observe during our inspection? We observed the following: the absence of cleanliness is a fact in respect of the buildings and some members of staff. We saw workers with crumpled and dirty uniforms, long, tangled hair and beards, and they purport to be revolutionaries. We found a lack of order on some wards, incredible, everything scattered about. Sheets mixed up with basins, plates in the bathrooms, and the faces of some staff greasy and dirty as pigs. And they are like that in front of patients when they are treating them and handing out medicines. We observed indiscipline, liberalism and too much muddle. We had no sense of being in a hospital.

When we observed all that, we instructed the competent bodies in the party and government to study the situation in the hospital. What reports did we have back?

We found that the people's complaints are right and justified. We asked why the health personnel are like this. We felt there was a crisis of authority. Some elements called in question authority in the hospital. Who are they?

They are the ones resorting to racism. They think that with the departure of the colonialists they should be appointed to replace them. If a White person in charge ticks off some Blacks (who were in PIDE) they rush about and shout 'you colonialist'. To such a man colonialist is a matter of colour. Or he shouts 'you Fascist'. Does he know what Fascism is? Yesterday he was faithfully serving Fascism, was one of the informers in the hospital, used to denounce the most active opponents of colonialism. Today he is a great 'revolutionary'. And we shall say what they really are. Great opportunists and reactionaries – that's what they are. But they are unmasking themselves at the same time by their behaviour. We have to be a little attentive, watch their day-to-day conduct. So we found these aspects of liberalism and indiscipline, corruption, negligence and muddle; then we called in the competent party and government bodies. And the reports we received are that the complaints made by the people about the Maputo Central Hospital are right and justified.

Racism, Opportunism and Resistance to Revolutionary Change

A spirit of recalcitrance and conservatism reigns in the hospital, a spirit of routine and bureaucracy that makes change difficult. Revolution means radically transforming society. It is not a simple substitution. Are we going to put a Black director where there was a White director? Is this revolution? Are we going to put a Black in the place of a White charge-nurse? Is this the revolution we want? That's racism; that's apartheid. So the hospital is dominated by a spirit of resistance to structures and to changes. Many people are looking for the easy way out. An easy way out means mental laziness; they refuse to advance; they refuse to make their minds work. We call this mental laziness.

The hospital workers show little sensitivity to human suffering and often display a fatalistic attitude to patient death. They do not have the habit of collective discussion over the death of a patient to find out if the death is in any way due to inadequacies on the part of the hospital.

Causes of the Situation: A Failure to Fight Capitalist Structures

What are the causes of this situation? This is the answer: we have not been able to join battle to rid ourselves of the structures that were conceived to serve colonialism. We must realize that we can do nothing with what was bequeathed and conceived by colonialism as its instrument of oppression and exploitation, however brightly we paint it up.

Suppose we had two bottles, one clear and the other opaque, and there was wine in the clear bottle. Then we poured the wine into the opaque bottle. Could we say that there is no more wine simply because it is not visible? What matters is not the form of the bottle, but what it contains. Smashing structures means giving them a new content. The form is not important, but the content is.

So we say that the structures were conceived to oppress, to exploit. The structures were fundamental instruments for colonialism in carrying out its purpose. So we cannot say that some structures are good. They all had their aims. How can one adapt to the people's aims a structure that was conceived for exploitation? How can the two structures be reconciled? Reconciliation is impossible. What occurs is a conflict between them, a struggle between the old and the new. And the new must triumph.

Colonial structures persist, however. That's where our mistake lies. We did not deal a death blow to these structures. What we have now is merely a modification and a transfer of personnel. But they are still within structures conceived by colonialism. So we must start with the structure. The essence, the fundamental and antagonistic contradiction, is in the structure. Our structure exists to serve the broad masses, and the colonial structure existed to serve colonialism, to oppress and exploit. It therefore represented colonial power, whereas ours must represent people's power.

We are still finding conservative mentalities that resist the transformation. They refuse change. And here we must step in. The administrative structure must step in. The administrative structure is an instrument of the political structure.

Wrong Working Methods

We also found wrong working methods – wrong in relation to our structures. And we say that the working methods are wrong in relation to our structures, because they were right in relation to colonial structures. This is a difficulty we must obviate.

Furthermore we found enemy agents infiltrated among us – a physical presence of the enemy in the hospital. Aren't there 'PIDEs' in the hospital? Why didn't we expose them? They are the ones making trouble and representing the enemy in the hospital. How is this enemy or infiltrated presence felt?

It is felt through rumours. These agents have a specific task: to encourage rumour; to encourage intrigues; to encourage slander; to encourage the growth of racism. Racism is an instrument of the opportunists. Their precious weapon is racism. As they cannot exploit tribalism and regionalism in a national hospital, they use racism. Are you going to say there is no racism either?

We are going to struggle against this; we are going to smash all this. It is a matter of working out the right way to combat racism. To a comrade and friend, we offer criticism. But what do you do to an enemy? Do you offer criticism to an enemy as well? No! Against the enemy we use force – a revolutionary characteristic. Against the enemy we use force; for a friend or comrade, we offer criticism. We speak the same language. By the same token the enemy is deaf to our appeal.

Some staff maltreat the people. We are not saying all of you, but some. But we don't expose them. And there are some staff whose negligence causes damage to equipment. And they take advantage of our structure's ineffectiveness in the hospital. And to be quite frank we might say there is no structure. It is the colonial structure that guides the hospital.

We have heard the complaints from the masses about the Maputo Central Hospital, we visited the hospital and received reports from the party about the situation in the hospital. What conclusions can we draw?

The people do not yet see the Maputo Central Hospital as their hospital, a hospital made to serve them.

We have not yet been able to make the most of the nationalizations as they affect the Central Hospital.

We have not been able to smash the hospital's colonial structures, which persist and act as a barrier to transformation, nor have we been able to create new structures that would allow for a new kind of discipline, especially in human relations. There are antagonisms among hospital staff. And as there are no structures of a new kind to incorporate relations of a new kind, the latter do not exist. The hospital is just as it was left by colonialism. You have not broken down the barriers that divide you.

We have not done the groundwork to shake the sense of privilege and élite or to destroy the capitalist bent of health workers.

We have not done the groundwork to mobilize, organize and unify politically the various categories of hospital staff.

We have not succeeded in giving the people their role in the hospital which is theirs and is intended to serve them. I think there is still snobbery among you. 'What category is he? And that one? He's such and such.' We cannot all be equal. There are high-ups, middle-level, low-down. But that is no justification for contempt. A doctor can work because he has a nurse; a nurse can work because he has a cleaner; a cleaner works because we have the ward and the kitchen. Why should we despise the cook? Who feeds the hospital? Suppose we merely handed out medicines, could we cure our patients without a diet? So why should we despise the cook? They are all interconnected. Like a guitar. If a piece is missing, the guitar is useless. So why should we despise what plays the deepest note? 'Ah, that's not a string.'

The Question of Foreign Workers in the Maputo Central Hospital

There are several dozen foreigners of various nationalities currently working at the Central Hospital. Many other foreign technicians are to be found throughout the country. It is important to give some thought to this. Our own nationals do not have corporate structures, still less the foreigners. The latter live in Mozambique, but are not of Mozambique, as there are no structures for them.

The presence of these doctors, nurses and other technicians in our country is a clear manifestation of the militant solidarity of the world revolutionary movement with the struggle of the Mozambican people led by FRELIMO.

Solidarity is an assertion that no people is alone, no people is isolated in the struggle for progress. Solidarity is the conscious alliance of the progressive and peace-loving revolutionary forces in the common struggle against colonialism, capitalism and imperialism. In short, against exploitation of man by man. And this struggle may be in Asia, in Europe, or in America, or the struggle may be in Africa, but it is the same struggle. It has common enemies and its enemies are always principal.

Solidarity has no race and no colour, and its country has no frontiers. There is no solidarity just among Africans, no exclusively Asian solidarity, since the enemy of the people also has no country or race.

There is a tendency to try to make solidarity out to be an act of charity, a paternalist gesture. But in truth, solidarity is an expression of internationalist duty, brotherhood and friendship between peoples.

The Mozambican people's victory is based on the unity and sacrifice of its sons and daughters, especially during the armed struggle for national liberation. What we are today is the oucome of some of us giving our life; what we are today is also the outcome of our receiving international solidarity. We are what we are because we go on being backed by international solidarity.

International help, international solidarity of other peoples with our struggle, had and still has an important role in the advance of the revolution in our country and in the world in general. In the phase of national reconstruction on which we are engaged, the People's Republic of Mozambique receives help from African countries, from our natural allies the socialist countries, and from the governments and democratic organizations of other countries. The fact that this solidarity is an extension of the solidarity forged and developed during the armed struggle has still not been sufficiently understood, still less appreciated, by most health workers.

We know, for example, that the hospital management and the rest of the workers have not made the necessary effort to integrate foreign comrades in the various aspects of hospital life, and even less into the life of the Mozambican people. We know that the foreigners do not take part in the hospital's political meetings. We know that in the Central Hospital we are not involving the foreign workers as progressive militants, here to make their contribution to our revolution's advance, but merely as technicians – mercenaries contracted to treat so many patients and to whom we pay an agreed salary.

In brief, we are not fully responding to the meaning of international solidarity. And the enemy is taking advantage of our shortcomings. In what way? The enemy is trying basically to create contradictions between Mozambican workers and foreign workers.

Some of you say, and many believe: 'All these foreigners come for is to earn money. Isn't there any money in their country?' Or: 'Ah, these foreigners who come here don't know a thing, they come along to kill you.' Or: 'Ah, these foreigners who come here and say they're doctors aren't doctors at all.' And so the enemy finds fertile ground. Why does he find fertile ground?

The enemy, by playing on the low level of political consciousness of many of our workers, tries to project the foreign workers not as a factor of solidarity helping in the hard task of national reconstruction, but as a rival who will deprive us of some benefits and privileges. The enemy tries to make comparisons between the foreign workers currently in our country and the colonialists who left Mozambique after the taking of political power by FRELIMO. They are comparisons on technical grounds that deliberately ignore the essential, namely the political aspects and those of militancy and solidarity.

The enemy concocts all kinds of arguments intended to show that the presence of foreign technicians in the People's Republic of Mozambique is damaging to our people in general and to health workers in particular, and that we should have been better off sticking with the colonialists who have already run away from Mozambique. And why did they run away?

We say that to confuse the distinction between the colonialist doctor who is an exploiter, and the militant technician who is progressive is to walk hand in glove with the reactionaries and to contribute to a frontal assault on FRELIMO's political line. The foreign technicians who are in our country, and in this particular instance working at the Maputo Central Hospital, are our companions in arms, militants in the same cause as our own. They put aside their personal concerns and came all this way to give us support in the task of national reconstruction. They did not come merely as technicians, but above all as militants, as political beings, because it is politics that guides technical skill. And so we always say that politics must be put in the commanding position.

We must therefore learn from these comrades the lesson of militant solidarity, and work side by side with them, and share experiences at the political and technical level. We must march and suffer jointly with them in the tough but exciting battle of defending, preserving and improving our people's health.

Steps to Be Taken

We have just examined a range of issues. Perhaps we were not aware of these issues, some of you unwittingly, some wittingly, and some because of their low political level. But something we must always be aware of as we go about our tasks, and the question we must all face and face in ourselves is how the hospital can genuinely become a conquest of the Mozambican people.

We must smash the structures that keep a colonial face on the Maputo Central Hospital. It is not a matter of replacements, but of destruction. So our central task is to dismantle the colonial structures that exist in the Central Hospital and put in their place a new kind of structure, of a collective and democratic nature. These structures should allow each of us to play a part; allow each of us to know our place in the hospital. We can then broaden this experience to hospitals throughout the country.

We believe therefore that this is the pole on which turns the revolution's advance in the hospital. We must be prepared to smash the structure that keeps us enslaved, the structure that makes us dependent. Whenever we want to evaluate our health services, we look for an external model. This time, no. Let us make our hospital a pilot centre; a model pilot hospital, not just for Maputo. If we organize the Maputo Hospital politically, we shall be able to organize the provincial hospitals. And once we have the provincial hospitals organized and FRELIMO installed, then it will be easy for us to organize the district hospitals. But for that we shall have to kill the idea of the bush. That comes from colonialist influence, from an alien mentality, since the Portuguese colonialists in Mozambique came to Africa on service contracts. They had the right to six months' leave, to restore their nerves shattered by the heat of Africa, accursed Africa. And you, today, what is your curse? Where do you want to spend your holidays? In the metropole? Where is your metropole? Mozambique, since 25 June 1975, is our metropole.

As long as colonial structures persist that are opposed to the workers' collective responsibility, and subject them to enforced passivity, then it will be impossible properly to organize the health workers. Without organization of the hospital workers in collective and democratic moulds, it will be Utopian to talk of revolutionary transformation of the hospital.

11. We Must Strengthen People's Power in Our Hospitals*

I had the opportunity to make personal visits: to the Cabo Delgado hospital in 1976; to the provincial hospitals of Nampula, Sofala and Zambezia in 1977; to the provincial hospital of Niassa and the Maputo Central Hospital several times in 1979. In addition I visited several district hospitals, including those of Macia, Mocimba da Praia, Mueda and Cuamba. The situations I observed led me to conclude that there are problems common to these health centres, and to identify and categorize the procedures encountered.

The anomalies we saw, whether of a political or technical and organizational kind, are largely indicative of breaches of the political and organizational principles of the FRELIMO party, and of the universal ground rules of health care delivery. So we propose to offer some reflections on this issue, and to analyse the causes and characteristics of each situation.

The Question of Power in the Hospitals

The whole gamut of situations uncovered arose from one principal strategic deviation: the provincial director – who is often the hospital director – did not have authority over all the staff. This absence of authority arises from the notable absence of a hierarchy, from the absence of a clear definition of the powers and place each worker has in carrying out his main task.

Power is diluted, divided, dispersed. There is no decision-making centre. Anyone indiscriminately grabs the handle of the hammer: there is the cleaner who does not want to sweep up, because he says it is everyone's task; there is the doctor who orders treatment for a patient and the staff responsible do not carry it out; there is the doctor who prescribes, and the cleaner who wants to know what was prescribed; there is the nurse who wants the syringes sterilized, but did not order fuel for the oven; there is the patient suffering, with no one paying any attention;

*A speech made in Maputo on 4 December 1979.

there is the child in discomfort and treated as if he were in a store-room; there is the memorandum that arrives from the ministry or the provincial government, and the nurse wants to know its contents; there is no professional secrecy, no professional code of conduct. Professional ethics are not duly respected, ethics are not duly observed.

As a consequence of the prime cause – absence of power – situations arise in an endless chain of anomalies, in such a purposeful way as to lead one to suppose counter-revolutionary activity, ideological and physical infiltration among us by the class enemy.

Let us give some examples. The director's lack of authority particularly affects co-operants. They do not know from whom to receive orders. They feel isolated and marginalized from the body of the staff. A co-operant doctor is left like a foreign body, like an occupying expeditionary force, like somebody who has come to disturb the comfortable routine of our work.

On the other hand, the minimum conditions are lacking to allow technically qualified co-operants to pass on their scientific skills to Mozambican personnel. The hospitals' organization and working methods do not allow this. The co-operant doctor, when his contract in the People's Republic of Mozambique expires, feels professionally frustrated; since he goes back to his country without having totally accomplished the mission that brought him to Mozambique.

A foreign doctor working with us does not merely have the task of treating or operating on patients. The doctor comes mainly to train cadres for the new health system we are setting up.

The teacher comes mainly to train skilled cadres, which means training future teachers. The engineer comes to train skilled workers in the factories. The agriculturist comes mainly to train agricultural cadres. The economist who comes to a ministry or an enterprise comes mainly to train cadres for the economy, for finance, for accounting and for other special fields.

When a co-operant arrives, he is full of enthusiasm and eagerness to work. But he faces a series of problems as soon as he arrives. The first is the excessive bureaucracy that usually surrounds him as he sorts out his situation. Then there is the process of his integration into our country's political, social, economic and cultural reality. The co-operant is not introduced at the place where he will work. There is no process of outlining conditions of service, customary working methods, treatments practised.

The co-operant is often marginalized. He has no part in discussions, in hospital life, no place to air his difficulties. At the first – and understandable – slip, he is destructively criticized. The mistake is not used for the enlightenment of all. The mistake is used in reactionary campaigns that generalize from the particular, that aim to attack co-operants from the socialist countries, the most progressive workers.

This is a device to encourage a split between Mozambican and foreign workers. This is a device to encourage a split between co-operants of different nationalities. This is a device to encourage rivalry between professionals in the same field of activity.

Who has not heard of the virulent anti-Communist campaign waged mainly in the hospitals against doctors from socialist countries on the malicious argument of 'incompetence' and 'ignorance of tropical diseases'. Who are the 'sneaking' promoters of these criminal campaigns, who with impunity go on living alongside us and drawing pay from us?

Nowadays no one gives orders in the hospital. Or rather everyone gives orders, everyone is 'chief'. Which means there is no chief at all!

Anyone is a 'comrade chief', when no one has made him head of anything. He enjoys the worship, and the worshippers hope for some blessing out of a possible promotion for their 'comrade chief'. But for anyone nowadays to become head of a sector, he must meet certain political and professional criteria. The head of any echelon represents power at the level and in the field of his responsibility. Not every odd bod can be a head, and headship is not an automatic consequence of long service. Headship is a political responsibility that demands of the leader a leadership role that brings implementation of party policy, puts into effect state decisions in the area for which the leader is responsible, and ensures appropriate supervision of their execution. A leader commands. And only someone competent can command.

It is unacceptable that these so-called 'comrade chiefs' can go on exercising their functions with utter impunity. At bottom these so-called 'comrade chiefs' are concealing incapacity, hypocrisy, irresponsibility, lack of respect, lack of professional pride. In short, they are power-seekers – opportunist power-seekers. Opportunism runs hand in hand with power-seeking. I noted also, in the various visits I made, that when the workers introduce themselves, they are all in a bunch, in a jumble of categories and hierarchies that are difficult to make out.

We don't know who is the analyst and who the orderly in the mortuary or the laboratory; who the doctor and who the orderly in the pharmacy; who is the laboratory technician and who the kitchen help. Sometimes we don't even know who is the director and who are his subordinates. There are no grades, no ladder, no pyramid, no hierarchy.

We said during the war, in tribute to nature's impeccable order, that waters do not run up mountains. We said that the waters are born in the mountains and feed the ground, supply the base. In turn the base provides the nourishment, and inspires and develops the top. That was how it was during the war, how our struggle was organized, how we grew, how we developed, and drove out the enemy.

Not in the hospital. It's all a muddle. We don't know where the waters spring from, we don't know where the base is, and where the top.

The doctor is no longer respected as the most qualified professional in the hospital.

The doctor has the same status as a technician handing out pills or preventive medicines. Some nurses, particularly the older ones with a complex about seniority and a know-all attitude, have the cheek to declare that they know better than the doctor. It's enough for them to work with a stethoscope – no matter whether well or badly – and they soon think they are the equal or superior of the doctor.

The doctor incarnates health policy through science, the relationships he establishes, his conduct, his actions. He is the symbol of competence, the symbol of scientific and technical skill in the hospital. The doctor is responsible for the lives of all the hospital patients. The doctor is responsible for the lives of all the population in the area he covers. When he is absent his stand-in on the ward or at out-patients is the nurse, his stand-in in the maternity ward is the midwife.

When a doctor comes into the hospital today, he seems like any ordinary, anonymous citizen. No one pays attention. When a nurse comes in, a cleaner remains comfortably seated. Even when the director comes in, it's as if nobody has come in. It makes no difference!

If the doctor arrives at the children's ward before the nurses, if the nurse arrives before his colleagues, it doesn't matter whether the preparations are made or not. Let the doctor wait, let the doctor deal with it.

The doctor when he goes to the ward should find his collaborators already there with all the preliminary work done. When the doctor sees patients, he should find everything already prepared so that he can do his round most efficiently. When a doctor visits a ward, he should not be the one to take the patient's temperature. The doctor should receive a detailed report on the progress of each patient. The doctor should not be kept waiting! On the contrary, he should be waited upon. It is the same in school: the teacher should be the last to enter and the first to leave.

Demagogy in the Abolition of Categories

There is no longer a category of cleaner. It was purely and simply abolished. Today we are seeing the absurd and incomprehensible situation in which a cleaner is not called by his category. There is a fear that he will object. There is a fear of being called a reactionary, or a colonialist. So now cleaners are called service auxiliaries. A real linguistic euphemism, whose façade purports to express something it is not. It's like saying the minister's driver is the minister's auxiliary. It's like saying the waiter at a restaurant table is the customer's auxiliary. It's like saying the school cleaner is the teacher's auxiliary. It's like saying the bus conductor is the passenger's auxiliary. I should like to know where in the world, in what service or institution, are there no cleaners!

This is demagogy and paternalism.

The task of a hospital cleaner is to sweep up, wash floors and walls, clean the ablutions. The orderly or porter may move the patient from the ward to the physiotherapy centre, to the X-ray room, to the operating theatre, to the consultancy. He takes dirty clothes to the laundry and brings clean linen to the wards.

The cleaner serves. He serves the doctor, serves the nurse, and receives orders from them to obey, in carrying out all his stipulated tasks. He serves the patients and the public. The cleaner is a cleaner. Not an auxiliary. The nurse is a nurse. The doctor is a doctor.

Those who clean are cleaners, those who launder are launderers, those who cook are cooks, those who carry are porters, those who drive are drivers.

The cleaner does not face a competitive test to join the hospital staff. This means that we do not demand a vocation of the cleaner, that he does not need to be particularly drawn to being a cleaner. It's the same for domestics in schools, hotels, boarding houses, hostels, crèches, services, civil engineering, laundries. That's how it is for a hospital cleaner. Cleaners must accept their designation without complexes. The demagogic myth of 'service auxiliary' must disappear, must cease immediately. All tasks are important and have their place. All tasks depend on each other. There is a close, reciprocal relationship. It is like the human body, where everything functions in co-ordination, where all organs work in harmony, otherwise man could not remain alive.

Playing with words to cover up complexes creates demagogy and encourages liberalism and anarchy. It is only by categorizing tasks that we can give respect to professions.

I want this point to be absolutely clear! There should be no confusion about this. From now on these so-called 'service auxiliaries' will again be called *serventes*.

The point I have just made is only a particular aspect of a more general issue that demands our attention: health workers no longer address each other by their real categories. Today they are all 'comrades'. The nurse is Comrade Antonio, the doctor is Comrade Zacarias, the cleaner is Comrade Timba, the midwife is Comrade Josefa, the analyst is Comrade Roberto. Where does all this 'camaraderie' come from?

No one knows who is the nurse and who is the analyst. No one knows who is the doctor and who is the orderly. This is once again demagogy, paternalism and anarchy. Addressing someone as comrade is a victory of the revolution. This form of address was not in use at the founding of FRELIMO. It was the outcome of the triumph of the revolution. The very term 'comrade' bears with it the history of the struggle between the revolutionaries and the reactionaries, between the old and the new, between the dialectic and a static conservatism, within FRELIMO. The designation of comrade is the outcome of the triumph of the revolutionary line. It is the outcome of a triumph of revolutionary ideals over reaction in the pay of imperialism that tried to take the leadership of FRELIMO by assault in order to obscure the true essence of national liberation struggle.

The designation 'comrade' is the outcome of the defeat of those who wanted to make independent Mozambique a puppet state, a preserve of the capitalist bourgeoisie and of international imperialism. For us to succeed in establishing 'comrade' as our form of address during the war, much sacrifice was needed. Many of our fighters had to offer up their lives. In the liberated areas 'comrade' meant FRELIMO.

In the transition period and after the proclamation of independence, FRELIMO brought its values to the areas hitherto occupied by colonialism. FRELIMO had to incorporate the whole population from the Rovuma to the Maputo. It could not marginalize the citizens, the overwhelming majority of whom identified with the struggle and FRELIMO's aims.

This form of address was really to give the people the chance of distinguishing themselves from colonialism. So the use of 'comrade' spread rapidly. It reflected a step in our revolution.

Now, when the FRELIMO party has been structured, with its membership committed to organizing society, we cannot go on with the generalized use of 'comrade'. The designation 'comrade' is now reserved for party members only, in the relationships and exercise of their party tasks. The minister is 'Comrade Minister' at a party meeting, and 'Mr Minister' on state duties. The hospital director is 'Comrade Director' when attending a party cell meeting as a militant, and 'Mr Director' when carrying out his tasks in the hospital.

That's what we mean when we say the form of address 'comrade' is a conquest. We must appreciate it and defend it as a conquest. We cannot allow its genuine meaning, the real essence of the term 'comrade' to be adulterated. So we must stop the form of address of 'comrade' in the hospital. The generalized use of the term 'comrade' must be ended in all sectors.

Lack of Cleanliness and Neatness

A shocking thing that contradicts the most basic and elementary rules of health organization is the almost total absence of moderately presentable gowns for the tasks that the health worker does. Cleaners' and nurses' uniforms, when they do exist, look more like those of a hotel cook, bakery staff, grocery assistant, or butcher. Another feature related to this is the almost total absence of white shoes, or white plimsolls. We should say that clackety wooden clogs and suede boots are the more general rule, and white shoes or plimsolls the exception.

We find some workers too with beards, and dirty, dingy white coats, and long, dirty and unkempt hair appropriate for 'hippies', drug addicts and misfits. We find some with 'ye-ye' or bell-bottom trousers, or platform shoes, all in various colours, sizes, patterns and lengths, in a tasteless, thoughtless mixture.

It is a carnival of gowns, trousers, shirts, clogs and long hair. a festival of bad taste! There is no uniformity, no regulation.

Some do not have the slightest professional consciousness of the task they are doing. They're only worrying about their pay.

I ask:

– Does someone who fails to comply with the minimum of ethical rules, someone who sees the patient as a sack to lug around, deserve his pay?

– Does someone who plays with patients' lives and works merely for the sake of working and treats the patient like an item in a supermarket deserve his pay?

– Does the health worker who behaves towards the patient with complete indifference or coldness, with no human feeling, deserve to call himself a health worker?

The Constitution of the People's Republic of Mozambique says that everyone receives 'according to his labour' and not 'according to his irresponsibility, negligence, idleness, incompetence and dirtiness'.

Our hospitals have already established a routine of lack of cleanliness, lack of smartness, lack of sensitivity, lack of respect and lack of courtesy. And incredible though it may seem, we find all this in the staff who should set an example of hygiene and cleanliness, smartness, respect, courtesy and sensitivity!

What we have seen is the antithesis of a health worker. Moreover I should like to point out that the question of uniform and shoes is not merely a question of dress, or of smartness – it is a professional requirement. It is a matter of the patient's very life. It is intolerable that a health worker should arrive with clothing sweat-soaked and dusty, and in these clothes come into contact with patients. It violates the most basic principles of health and hygiene. It is through courtesy, sensitivity, smartness and cleanliness that health staff inspire in patients a confidence that will often lead those patients to confide their personal problems, and so ease the doctor's task and the cure of the patients themselves.

In the same way when the army parades in a smart and disciplined way, the people respond enthusiastically, identify with it, and gain confidence. They react like this at seeing the soldiers on parade, organized and disciplined, with hair cut to the same length, wearing the same trousers, shirt-sleeves rolled in the same way, with the same weapons, same cap, with firm, measured tread, with a determined gaze – calm, confident, forceful and victorious. So when the army is on parade its appearance is imposing, impeccable, clean and uniform.

By contrast our hospitals, instead of being places of rest, tranquillity, silence, relaxation and recuperation, seem more like the Xipamanine market, with a jumble of shouts and noises that are inappropriate to a health centre. We don't know who is the buyer and who the seller, who is the doctor and who the orderly.

The situation is growing worse because there are no longer criteria for admission to the job. Anyone comes in, whether he has a vocation or not, whether capable or incapable, competent or incompetent. The admission tests are merely administrative. New recruits need only complete the necessary bureaucratic formalities, and they can consider themselves already at the peak of the required political and professional qualities. All you need do is apply and you are admitted.

The best and the mediocre are treated alike, and the bad and the good have the same category. The aim seems to be a production line of personnel to a standard model, without regard to quality. What matters is showing impressive-looking quantities. The incompetents and the best, the mediocre and the talented have the same chance of dealing with the patient's life. Skills are no longer demanded of a health worker. The values of competence, virtue, capability and skill are no longer cultivated. They are regarded as 'reactionary and bourgeois values'. Seniority has replaced competence and dedication as the criterion for promotion.

The Causes of This Situation

A detailed analysis of the hospital situation leads to the conclusion that the central issue once again is that of power. The dispersal of power in the hospitals provokes a dilution of responsibilities, and thus creates an environment of generalized irresponsibility.

As there is no power, there is no authority. As there is no hierarchy, there is no authority, there is no definition of remit. As there is no definition of remit, the principal task and the priorities remain unidentified. As we said at the beginning, anyone indiscriminately grabs the handle of the hammer.

The hospital has been readily taken over by liberalism, demagogy, ultra-democracy and the principle of absolute egalitarianism. Populism and ultra-leftism have set in.

Populism is the causal factor in this situation. Methods of the people have been deliberately muddled up with populism, and there has been a confusion between populism and people's power.

Populism clouds the revolution, is an enemy of revolution.

Populism is a current that historically has infiltrated the revolutionary movement, and is led by the petty bourgeoisie to destroy the revolution.

It's what we see in the hospitals. It is disorder deliberately provoked to challenge us. It is a petty-bourgeois radicalism behind a revolutionary façade, and it waves the revolutionary banner in order to destroy it. It is fine-sounding talk, but empty and devoid of revolutionary content. It is favourable ground for the sowing of ultra-leftism.

Ultra-leftism is the ideology behind all this activity.

Ultra-leftism is the radicalism of the petty bourgeoisie to scorch the revolution's steps.

Ultra-leftism raises the revolutionary flag in order to destroy it.

Ultra-leftism is the instrument for infiltration of actions by the bourgeoisie.

It is almost a rule that ultra-left tendencies make their appearance at all moments of revolutionary struggle, with the target not the bourgeoisie and the exploiters but rather the forces that struggle to install people's power.

Ultra-leftism always uses as its main instruments liberalism and absolute egalitarianism.

Liberalism affecting behaviour and attitudes has the mission of creating compromise with the enemy, and corrupting our revolutionary principles. It provokes indiscipline and a relaxation of vigilance. It thus has a broader field of action against the revolution. Liberalism is a virus that leads to epidemics. The treatment for liberalism when it is diagnosed is shock treatment that removes the underlying causes. If it is not diagnosed in time, the aims of the revolution may be gravely compromised.

Liberalism appears when the hammer blow is weak. It appears when power is divided, when the decision-making centres are dispersed and operating in parallel.

Liberalism appears when working methods are dominated by ideas that make democratic centralism a mere cloak, a mere formality. This infiltration into our revolution has not escaped the general rule, although it has been manifested in a more subtle and subversive guise. Since our power is strong, the enemy is using subtle and subversive means.

The manifestations of liberalism in our hospitals have a variety of impacts. Its activities lead to the conclusion that it is an organized component of ultra-leftism. Ultra-leftism in turn promotes and encourages absolute egalitarianism.

For the petty bourgeoisie, we are all equal. They think equality is absolute. There are no categories, no hierarchy, no levels of responsibility.

We as revolutionaries can define responsibilities. Our society is organized, with a defined structure and clear aims. Equality is not an abstract concept. For the bourgeoisie, equality is the theme of philosophical reflections that are alien to the reality of the changing world. Bourgeois conceptions of equality are formal, and merely seek to demonstrate that inequality is a normal situation. Their aim is to maintain exploitation of man by man, by doling out some crumbs from the profits of capitalism, and by operating under the metaphysical and reactionary cloak of egalitarianism.

In our view equality is built as we advance towards a new society. As we advance towards building socialism, inequality will lessen. Ours is an organized society. The structures have hierarchies. Those responsible for those structures have hierarchies.

In the party we have the Congress, the Central Committee, the Permanent Political Committee, the Central Committee Secretariat. And successively we reach down to the rank and file in the party cell.

In the state, we have the People's Assembly and its deputies, the Standing Committee of the People's Assembly, the Council of Ministers and its members; we have Secretaries of State and national directors. And successively we reach down to the rank and file, to the person responsible for the locality, the communal village, the communal neighbourhood.

Every leader has his specific responsibility. Every leader has his own place in the hierarchy. Every leader has to answer personally for the task he is carrying out.

So I pose this question: should a director be put in the same ward as one of his subordinates? Should the wife of a member of the Council of Ministers be put in the same ward as her cook's wife? Should a woman doctor be put in the same ward as her children's nanny?

Some will counter: how will the people react? How will the people view this distinction? And to them we say: they do not know the people, do not have the popular touch. The people, on the contrary, are surprised when they see a leader or official at their side in the ward – or behind them in the bread or meat queue. The people like to see their leaders well treated, because they know the power they represent is the power that reflects the people's aspirations, aims and interests. The people are proud of their leaders and identify with them.

The colonial scars are still deep. The élitism that went into the 'assimilation' idea has been replaced by false modesty, hypocrisy, dishonesty and paternalism. They are typical of the superiority complexes bequeathed by colonialism. They are also typical of populism.

A combination of historical circumstances affecting health personnel under the colonial-capitalist regime goes some way to explaining the heavy penetration of petty-bourgeois ideology and ultra-leftism that is apparent in the day-to-day hospital routine.

The hospital was one of the institutions where the Mozambican had job opportunity. Mozambican staff, thanks to the access the hospital gave to certain technical qualifications, rose easily to a privileged social position in comparison with the overwhelming majority of Mozambicans. But their status remained unchanged and manifestly inferior in comparison with the colonial bourgeoisie.

They did, however, rapidly assimilate and they tried to digest the values that colonial civilization was propagating. They then began to rely on petty-bourgeois ideology, betray their class origin, and renege on the people to whom they belonged. They adopted the values of the colonial bourgeoisie. By swallowing these they achieved the status of third-class Portuguese citizens.

The work routine they were subjected to gave them the highest regard for technical values and smothered their own creativity. After the nationalization process in medicine, they tried to escape from this oppressive situation by finding an escape hatch of a demagogic and egalitarian kind, and easily fell into ultra-leftist traps.

The task and very idea of a cleaner they regard as 'degrading'. The doctor is relegated to a limbo where his technical and scientific knowledge and skill are not heeded. The young doctor, on the other hand, who comes from the privileged social stratum, is unable on his own to remedy this situation. He is aware of the problem but cannot find the appropriate solution. He is afraid of confrontation.

Why? A high proportion of doctors are white-skinned or of Asian origin. Their social origin is petty bourgeois – that's how they had access to schooling in the colonial period. Now they are in charge of their sectors. But because of their skin colour they are afraid of being identified with the colonialists. So they do nothing, take no action, are afraid of insisting on discipline.

They are afraid of giving an order. They are unable to say: 'Cleaner, do this. Nurse, I want that.' They are unable to exert their authority as doctors, as those with responsibility. The same often happens with the nurse and the cleaner. So we have a chain, a chain of destruction of power. That is why we have been saying anyone indiscriminately grabs the handle of the hammer.

It is a situation we are seeing in the hospitals. And some Black opportunists take advantage of it. They turn their colour into an asset. As he is Black, he is already a power. Opportunism.

The same thing occurs in the health sector schools. Teachers are afraid to rebuke the students – incompetence and incapacity are allowed to pass, are promoted.

The students argue with the doctor, argue with the teacher. We cannot allow this in the People's Republic of Mozambique. But it's happening nowadays in health. The doctor comes in and the nurse remains seated. The nurse smokes in front of the doctor. The cleaner smokes in front of the nurse. It's a feast – a feast of indiscipline and liberalism, a feast for the ultra-leftists, the populists, the anarchists and the unruly. One where values and categories are muddled up. In conclusion, all that we have seen and witnessed in our hospitals is a lesson in what a hospital should not be in the People's Republic of Mozambique.

All such anomalies are normal where the bourgeois revolution triumphs. But in our country they have come into collision with the revolution.

Our revolution is not a bourgeois revolution; is not the triumph of the bourgeois conception of the world and society; is not the triumph of petty-bourgeois conceptions of health.

Our revolution is a proletarian revolution, a socialist revolution. It is power of the worker-peasant alliance, and its exercise through dictatorship of the proletariat; it is democratic exercise of workers' power and suppression of reactionaries.

The bourgeoisie do not share with us the machinery of worker-peasant power. There must be no doubts on this point: there is no peaceful coexistence with the enemy. So let us get rid of petty-bourgeois ideology, let us rid ourselves of the petty-bourgeois manifestations we have and of which the hospitals are still one of the most stubborn bastions.

As revolutionaries we are courageous! We are certain of the justness of our path. We are not afraid of confrontation. We do not let the petty bourgeoisie parade in front of us. We confront them and destroy the petty-bourgeois ideology.

Let us form the antibodies and take the antibiotics necessary to erect a strong barrier against the penetration by petty-bourgeois ideology of our revolution and, in this particular case, of our health centres.

In this phase of our revolution when the entire people are enthusiastically laying the foundations of socialism, the correlation of forces is unmistakably in favour of the working masses. We are not being adventurist in deciding to confront the enemy. Those who attack and provoke us are the adventurers.

In the daily struggle to make the hospital a socialist reality our watchword must be: eliminate all petty-bourgeois influence on us. Eliminating the influence of petty-bourgeois ideology means eliminating the demagogy, superficiality, paternalism, populism, liberalism, ultra-democracy and ultra-leftism that dominate organizational methods in our hospital.

Our hospital cannot be a broadcasting centre for bourgeois and counter-revolutionary values. Our hospital cannot be a broadcasting centre for disunity, division, regionalism, tribalism and racism. It cannot be a broadcasting centre for rumour, false tales, intrigue and slander, for inward struggles, discouragement, disqualification and disinclination.

Our hospitals must be transformed into development centres for the spirit of national unity and comradeship, for modesty and brotherhood, for courtesy, solidarity and sensitivity among health workers and between them and the patient. That will provide a basis to inspire the patient's confidence in his health services.

Our hospital must be: a symbol of national unity from the Rovuma to the Maputo; a trench of revolutionary warfare for the transformation of society; a cultivation centre for scientific and technical knowledge, competence and dynamism.

A patient from Tete must feel at home in Maputo; a patient from Cabo Delgado must feel he is among family in Sofala; a patient from Niassa must feel among close friends in Gaza; a patient from Inhambane must feel he is in his birthplace in Zambezia; a patient from Nampula must find the same reception in Manica.

How are we to eliminate the petty-bourgeois outlook that still prevails in many health workers? How are we to fight this evil and tear it out by the roots? How are we going to organize victory in our hospitals? That is the constant question!

Before a battle, the principle is to reconnoitre the ground and the enemy positions. We saw what the enemy is doing in the hospitals and what form of petty-bourgeois practice has emerged. We have studied the nature of his activity. We have also studied our own shortcomings.

What we regard as urgent is to establish people's power! This means: urgently establishing a strong management in the hospital that forms a united and cohesive block; establishing the authority and prestige of the director, as representative of people's power.

Then we shall demand individual responsibility in the first instance, and subsequently collective responsibility, within the principle of accountability. Where there is management, there is a work collective where all problems are discussed, and where all its members give their point of view. But it is not the work collective that makes the decision. It is the director who decides. He holds an absolute majority, and for the decisions he takes he answers to the structures to which he is subordinate.

We have to put a stop to the custom of 'I want to deal with my point with Comrade Director when he drops by here', of 'I want to talk about my transfer as soon as he comes into the hospital', of 'I want to talk about my pay when he comes out of the ward'. To speak to the director, one should make an appointment.

At a health post where there is no doctor, there should also be management with someone in charge, on the same principle as we have just indicated. The person who makes the decision, who should call the ambulance, who should refer the patient to another hospital, is the charge-nurse. For he too expresses power. At that moment he is exercising authority.

We must:

- urgently establish hierarchies and the respective categories, in line with the methods of democratic centralism;
- establish discipline, define clearly and precisely everyone's place in the hospital hierarchy, eliminate and pluck out by the root harmful agents, enemy agents among us;
- launch the fight to eliminate everything identified with penetration among us of petty-bourgeois ideology and practice;
- eliminate populism and all the anomalies it provokes: liberalism, abuse of power, failure of respect, absolute egalitarianism, ultra-leftism;
- establish a chasm between us and the class enemy, as a priority task for all health workers.

12. Defining Woman's Enemy*

One of FRELIMO's fundamental concerns is the Mozambican woman, the question of the Mozambican woman. One of the issues that most concerns our organization is Mozambican women's emancipation.

First, what kind of battle must be waged so that women can eliminate the evils that oppress them? We must define who are the basic enemies of women in general and the Mozambican woman in particular. We must define the enemy. Let us study our process of growth: are we growing equally, or is there an imbalance in the growth process? In Mozambique, is man more developed than woman, or are they all, men and women, at the same level?

It is a question of studying mental growth and not physical growth, growth in awareness, in our consciousness of national problems, problems of mankind, problems of our society. Whether we have the same grade or not. What factors enable man to be rather more developed than woman? What are the barriers that have prevented and continue to prevent the Mozambican woman's growing awareness of the situation?

Defining the Enemy

It looks as if we should begin with the division of tasks. There is a certain effort that drives the growth in our awareness, drives the development of the human mind. This effort is what allows a speedy understanding that we are victims of something. Generally speaking, we are all oppressed, we are all colonized, exploited. But the exploited often enjoys having his own exploited. The oppressed enjoys his own oppressed. This is the central question for us. A correct definition of the enemy.

What kind of battle must we wage to eliminate the enemy? We might ask at this point: who is the enemy of woman in general, and who is the enemy of the Mozambican woman? What is needed to free her? And thus we shall study the situation of women from the Rovuma to the Maputo.

*A speech delivered to a women's meeting in Maputo, on 3 April 1976.

To carry out any task we need tools. When we founded FRELIMO, we were creating the tool to eliminate colonialism, to struggle against colonialism. We defined the kind of organization FRELIMO must be. That seems to be the central point when one creates an organization: what kind of organization and what must its tasks be? To be a revolutionary organization it must have certain vital characteristics: where there is tribalism, there will be no progress; where there are conservative elements, conservatives, there will be no revolution; where there is tradition or traditionalists, there will be no progress. Just reactionaries. And we find that there is a great deal of conservatism in our country. Above all among women. There is a lot of tradition among women, a lot of division among women, a lot of contempt and discrimination between women. So the organization cannot be revolutionary. Discrimination, regionalism, we might even say localism, among women. Here and everywhere else in the country, a woman is valued in the light of her region, the region of her birth.

We grade them. We look over her head. The first thing to find out is: where's she from? Then we assign her a grade. Not for her consciousness but according to the region where she was born. Then we say: whose daughter is she? These are major obstacles to woman's development. Perhaps due to a lack of contact with reality, with the essential tasks.

These are the tasks of shaking up women's way of thinking.

When we know the father, then we show respect. The tendency among women, and among men too, is to respect the exploiters. The daughters of the great exploiters are admired. We admire the exploiters and despise those who produce the wealth.

How OMM Was Born

So this is what, perhaps belatedly, we want – first: investigation of the Mozambican woman. Our essential task: a review of activity since the Mozambican Women's Organization was formed; of why we should have statutes, programmes and designation of tasks for the Mozambican woman. We created the OMM as our longest arm, the arm that would organize those women farthest from our country, that would reach women in the most remote, most forgotten regions of our country. We formed the women's organization in total confidence that only with evolution, with development, with women's emancipation would we be victorious in carrying out our revolutionary tasks. We were conscious that woman is responsible for all generations. It is the woman who is in constant contact with children. It is the woman who imparts revolutionary concepts to children, through her contact and particular responsibility. The women's organization was not created in the spirit, or on the model of organizations of bourgeois women with corrupt ideas. It was not for one class. The Mozambican woman is the most living expression of our class, the class of the oppressed, the class of workers, the class of peasants. We founded the OMM to give a true picture of the Mozambican woman, of her personality, of her dignity. A struggle without quarter was necessary and is necessary against the evils created by colonial capitalism. Likewise it is necessary to eliminate the division that exists, to eliminate the contempt that exists among Mozambican women, so that we can handle our tasks correctly.

We should correctly define our enemy. Who is our enemy? Who is woman's enemy? We know the peculiarities of women and we know some of women's characteristics. But we also know their potential, their ability, which provide a strong, positive base from which to stand up and wage a firm struggle. We think that your Organization . . . . Your Organization . . . . I do not want to put any ideas forward. First I want to research. I came here to listen to you: what are your problems, the problems of women. I did not come here to give a lecture. I came to listen, to learn about women's problems . . . the difficulties women face.

The Conflict

Complexes are among woman's characteristics. Complexes that destroy her capacity for initiative. And we understand why. It is the effect of so many traumatic experiences of which woman was victim over many years. In that respect there is no White woman, no Black woman, no mulatto woman. Every woman has complexes. In Europe we find the same difficulties. Women's problems have a common point: a state of conflict, often a spirit of conflict. A heap of conflict. Inability at the same time to detect and distinguish between cases. There is a mixture of cases. And this will affect woman in her essential task. She stops being active and becomes passive. These situations of lack of tranquillity create a sense of dependence, a sense of insecurity. Conflict often diverts woman from the essential tasks. So there is an inability to define the priority for tasks, to define the essential tasks, because of 'personal problems', because of individual problems.

Women can very easily create conflicts between themselves. They find this easy. But they do not find it easy to rid themselves of the problem. The problem of making problems is very simple. Here we are today, but one of you may be ready to turn away her face because she is beside her 'enemy'. And suppose we were to ask: is it because your children have been squabbling there at home . . . is that it? Although the press are here, we are going to be frank. It is because of us men . . . is that it? . . . There you are fighting, biting, scrapping with the pounding stick. . . . Is that the priority task? What about national reconstruction? I do not want to make a speech, I shall do that later. First I want to hear the women's problems. Why there is a need. . . . In 1962 and 1963, our revolution had not yet shown that woman has a potential – inexhaustible energy of imagination, is a source.

I believe that in this meeting we shall have difficulty in reaching the essential problems. Ages of women, age can be a problem. True or not true?

Division on the Basis of Age
First, the old women; then the young brides; third, women who have a child or two ('ntiwulani') and who cannot yet join the group of 'massumgukati' (adults). Then the group of married women with six children – 'they are the ones who know it all; who understand life'. For a start these cannot debate with the other women. They are 60 or so, don't talk to women 'still child-bearing'.

So dividing up, we have: in first place the 'massungukati' (adults); then comes the group of 'wamamana' (the mothers); the 'wamamanhana' (young mothers); the group of 'ntiwulani' (mothers for the first time) and the group of 'wahnuanhana' (girls). These groups are all standards. For women they indicate wisdom.

And now I don't know if we are going to have a serious debate, because there are some girls among the women here, some of 18 or 20. I don't know if we can really have a serious debate because the 'massungukati' (adults) are ready to give the lesson of experience. But what experience? How to look after the house? Is it that experience? And how to be obedient, never to fight with your husband. But neither should the man fight with his wife. Why should the woman be fighting with her husband, and the man fighting with his wife?

We want here to review our activities. Is our Organization genuinely carrying out its tasks or not?

The Central Committee when it met from 11 to 27 February studied very carefully OMM matters; studied very carefully the question of the women's detachment. The women's detachment provides, as was decided in 1973, a source of cadres for OMM, it is the reservoir.

How will OMM and the women's detachment co-ordinate together? I believe that this year 1976, as we want to achieve the tasks of national reconstruction, is time to renew the call to OMM for these tasks of national reconstruction. And what are the tasks of national reconstruction?

The first essential task is to destroy the colonialist structures and the capitalist structures. But to destroy these structures, we need in the first place to conceptualize our task; to understand our task; and to rise to our task.

There is still a tendency to put a high value on foreign ideas. We still have among us some mentalities enslaved to the foreigner and attracted by foreign values.

Banditry still exists in our country. To destroy banditry in our country we must understand and take on the task of giving politics priority. There are still gangs of thieves in our country. There are still among us murderous criminals, who were formed by the colonialists. There are still among us ex-PIDEs, whom we have been unable to expose and neutralize, because we are still disorganized. And being disorganized we cannot achieve our tasks. In the factories we are not yet organized, because we do not have the appropriate structures of the Mozambican Women's Organization.

Being Organized

In the hospitals we are not organized. In the schools we are not organized. In the neighbourhoods we are not organized. And so we do not have the concept of collective work.

There is still drunkenness in our society. Where there is drunkenness, there will be crime. Where there is drunkenness, there will be depreciation of man, of personality. A person becomes a thing. Alcohol destroys the human brain. It is the brain that shapes ideas. Alcohol leads to idleness, laziness. Idleness implies a rusting of our ideas. We do not have new ideas. There is a rustiness, and rust implies ideological corruption.

On the other hand, we don't yet have the notion of the family. Family, the origin of the family, a sense of family. It is not yet there. So we see instances of polygamy, divorce, and we see what we call adultery.

And let's face it, there is in our society something more degrading, more humiliating: prostitution in our country. This brings dishonour to our country. And why does this occur in our society? And how are women attached to these ways going to advance? We have not found the woman able to launch a battle against these evils.

In the countryside there is still ignorance, illiteracy. To a great extent in our country there are the so-called initiation rites. It is enough for a child to be subjected to these initiation rites for her to regard herself as a grown woman, who is prepared. Not by virtue of age, but because she has had lessons on being an adult. Her central interest is not to study the society. It is to study life so as to find a man. She transfers herself from her father, to a new father.

There are still forced marriages. There are still marriages dictated by the parents. There is still no consciousness of a meeting of minds between the husband and wife. But we still face enormous tasks in our country. And we are still ashamed of demonstrating our culture, of putting a value on our culture, because we are assimilated. The assimilated are still widespread.

They are nostalgic for certification, they are nostalgic for the identity document that was granted by the colonialists. That distinguished them from the rest of the population. They are nostalgic for their old class, the intermediary class, between the capitalists, the exploiters, the oppressors, and the rest of the population. They did not feel at ease when they were with the capitalist because they felt inferior, they did not feel at ease when they were with the people because they felt superior. This still goes on in our country.

There is a confusion in women and in men about what modesty and naturalness are. People confuse them with licence and liberalism.

We see today men and women with long, dirty hair. They say this is being natural and modern. We see instances of people of means going about in flip-flops, with long, dirty nails, full of jiggers. They say they are doing it to be the same as the people. Does being the same as the people mean going about dirty?

First, we shall launch campaigns against those who go around with long hair, and beards that are dirty. We did not win the war in order to spread anti-hygiene in our country.

We see among pupils in the schools: the use of drugs, sexual misbehaviour, cigarettes in the school. And some teachers encourage it. 'Because it is a FRELIMO Government. And a characteristic of the FRELIMO Government is indiscipline.'

Furthermore we see women teachers who take their grown-up students as lovers. We see some men teachers who take their senior girl students as wives and girl-friends.

We see really shameful situations that humiliate and discredit FRELIMO. They discredit the Mozambican woman.

At the hospitals we see dances held at the weekends with lots of alcoholic drinks; people dance, turn off the lights, take off their clothes, dance and drink in the nude. What's that called? Bacchanalia? Such things exist in our country, left behind by the colonialists. And they enjoy it. In the hospitals. They enjoy it, they do it. This practice goes on. Have you ever seen it? No? But it happens in the hospitals. They bring drinks, meet up there. All the staff. They dance. They start drinking . . . and when it's one or two in the morning, they begin taking off their clothes, start turning down the lights, and in the end they are all naked, dancing and drinking. Are they civilized?

Orgies. We must fight this. But the women do not fight this. Cabarets, nightclubs here in Maputo, Beira, Nampula, where there were concentrations of colonial troops, the troops of oppression. And our Mozambican men, our Mozambican women, are still regretful because they went away, the ones who brought advanced civilization. One sees women with three or four men at the same time. Does it happen now or not? It happens. They like it.

How are we going to struggle against all of this?

What stops woman advancing? keeping up with the revolution? being a dynamic element, a promoter of ideas? being a person who applies and lives the Organization's line? being a person constantly concerned to defend the revolution, to transform society?

That's why we think it necessary, mandatory, an essential step, to hold the Mozambican women's second conference this year.

During the national liberation struggle, we had two areas: one area controlled by FRELIMO, and the other controlled by the enemy. In the FRELIMO zone, the essential task was to speed up the transformation of the Mozambican woman into an active agent, a revolutionary agent, a new element in society, an element responsible for the society. She was an educative element, a model. Because we have our method, genuine and profound criticism. We were born out of profound and genuine criticism.

Periodically we made a profound analysis of our situation, and defined our tasks. From time to time we purged our own ranks. We constantly brought in new elements, what we called oxygen, new blood to refresh the poisoned blood.

The gardener who tried to bring parasites into his own nursery was immediately expelled. Now you have to find new elements among you. New elements.

In the current context, the present phase, these elements are few, a very small number. They are a drop in the ocean.

During the national liberation struggle, there was a conflict of two systems: incorrect concepts and correct concepts. The correct concepts overcame the incorrect concepts. But these incorrect concepts live on in some people. Above all in the areas where the armed struggle, the armed struggle that provides the agent of change and acceleration in the revolutionary process, did not give a shake-up to the mental process.

So we have to know how to make a revolution. We have to purify the revolution. We struggled against the enemy, the physical enemy, and we struggled against the moral enemy, with moral agents. And we won. And conditions are favourable for a triumph over incorrect concepts. Conditions are favourable for a triumph of our political line, throughout the nation, from the Rovuma to the Maputo. We must commit ourselves to this battle without delay.

What We Are Today

What are we today? What do we have as a catalyst? The armed struggle gave rapid impetus to the process. And today what is the catalyst? What is our agent of change? What is it? There is no more armed struggle. But we are changing the armed struggle into revolution. What is revolution? Where there is revolution, there is reaction, isn't that so? Where there is exploitation and oppression, there is revolution.

We have chosen our path: the path of economic development in Mozambique. And we said: 'The participation of Mozambican women in all sectors of activity is a precondition for the triumph of our revolution. It is a precondition for the advance of the new society we want to establish.'

We cannot allow two societies to coexist, because these two societies are diametrically opposed.

Now we shall ask: why is it that your Organization does not advance? First, in Maputo: there was a time – let's admit it – during the Transitional Government, when there was a lot of agitation, a lot of rallies, a lot of meetings. Since we proclaimed independence, nothing more has happened, particularly here in Maputo. What's going on?

They say that some members of the OMM are witch-doctors. I've heard this said, it may be a slander, I don't know, but I've heard it said. They are witch-doctors and members of OMM. Superstition and revolution. But we should like some of them to be pointed out here, to see if they will go on with their superstition.

You go on being superstitious, you go on being tribalist, traditionalist, regionalist. This means you are muddled. Muddled people are dangerous. And dangerous people are reactionary.

You are not rising to the level of the revolution, the greatness of your tasks in the revolution, because of tribalism, because of tradition, superstition and regionalism. So if we are going to form tribal groups, there will be no Mozambican Women's Organization. Nowhere. What we shall have is tribal groups of Mozambican women. We shall have groups of assimilated women.

Furthermore there will be élite groups, of educated women. Then there will be groups of illiterate women, 'mamana'. There will be a particular group of women with some other calling. We shall start publishing their photographs. Black women's groups and mulatto women's groups of those, said to be many, who assert: 'We can't live here in Mozambique. How can we, how can we live? There are no dances now in Mozambique, nowadays you can't go dancing in Mozambique.' But we are saying: 'Now is the time you can dance in Mozambique.'

But there are groups who say there is no dancing now. I don't know what they mean. One hears that some Mozambican women when they are pregnant go to Portugal for the baby's delivery. Are there such women or not? We shall not build our new society like that.

The New Society

The new society is composed of women of all races and colours. What is the characteristic of Mozambique, the essential characteristic of this new society: women of all races and all colours. Those who die, suffer, live and share in national reconstruction, struggle to build a new society. It is not colour that decides who can be a Mozambican. No.

However, I should like to ask what are the current problems in Maputo Province. We have had reports from the other provinces, but around Maputo, what really are your problems, for us to debate and organize? So can we say or not? Over there is the women's detachment, who also have many problems, and they will detail them here.

To begin with, there is a series of problems. Women have never met nationally to assess the nationalization of schools. Have you studied the benefits of the nationalization of schools? They have not yet met to see the benefits – and the shake-up to the bourgeoisie – when we nationalized the hospitals.

We know there is sabotage. Sabotage in the hospitals to show that only private medicine is any good. And we have proposals for the training of doctors, training of nurses. There are no doctors. But the people do not study this, the victories of the revolution, the essential means to satisfy our people's most basic right.

Education: in education lies our personality. That is why the assimilated feel themselves tied to colonialism. Because of the education they received. It is education that gives us personality. A people's personality lies in education. The training of the New Man lies in education. The training of a new mentality lies in education. The formation of a new society lies in education. That is the reason why we cannot go on being dependent, being 'Balkanized' by the capitalists, by the bourgeois settlers, who made gold mines of our ignorance.

Education is not a privilege. Attendance at secondary school is not a privilege. Attendance at university is not a privilege. It is a necessity. It is a demand. So for us it is one of the victories of the revolution. The poor person must go to school. Schools are essentially for the poor.

Is the poor person barefoot today? Yes. Tomorrow he will wear shoes. To be precise, he must go to school to learn how to make his shoes. At school, he has no elevenses to eat during break, but this will help him to learn to produce. He will study to be able to produce. His studies will later on mean bread and shoes.

But this situation brought pleasure to the bourgeoisie. Knowing that some people do not have a snack at school, and go to school barefoot, they closed the doors saying you cannot come in without shoes.

We know that in the hospitals, since we nationalized private medicine, there are no blankets now to give to the patients. There are no sheets now, we have to bring them from home, we have to bring a blanket from home, which is meant to prove that when there were private hospitals there was cleanliness in the hospitals. We suggest there is a lack of organization, a lack of planning, incompetence by the hospital administrators.

In the war zones, our hospitals had no laundry soap. We did not have sheets, we didn't have anything, we kept our hospitals clean. There was cleanliness in our hospitals primarily because the nurse and the doctor had feelings and knew the value of human life. Those workers despised the value of money but not that of the life of a human being.

We said likewise that the land belongs to the people. Does anyone here have land? No? Well, that's why some people want to go to Portugal. Out of the money they stole from you over many years, they want to go and buy real estate in Portugal. Here in Mozambique we say: 'Flea and bug take your snout out of man's flesh.'

Now we are nationalizing blocks of flats. Who has been harmed by this? If anyone has been, put up your hand. Who had apartment buildings, who lived in the blocks of flats? Now you are going to live in the flats, aren't you? Do you want to go and live there or not? All right. But the city must be kept clean. We don't want skirts hung out on the verandas of the flats.

Women must organize the task of cleaning our cities. There must be hygiene in your homes, everywhere. Keeping the city clean is mainly a task for women. Are we going to take men out of the factories to come and sweep?

I shall stop here with a request to hear your comments because I came to learn too. I came to learn from you. Describe your problems however small. Right? Because if you do not speak I shall leave.

13. A Study of Mozambican Youth*

In our country recently freed from the colonial-Fascist yoke, the Mozambican people are laying, over the ruins of Portuguese colonialism, the material and ideological basis for a socialist society. We have in the first instance to consolidate our sovereignty in the face of more overt and frequent aggression from our standing enemy, imperialism.

We have to strengthen and encourage the worker-peasant alliance that provides the motive force for our revolution. We have to intensify mobilization of our working people with a view to their increasingly conscious commitment to the struggle to establish a new, independent, developed and stable economy. We have to give all the more vigorous and determined support to the struggle by peoples still subjected to the oppressive and exploitative order of colonialism, racism, Fascism and neo-colonialism. The tasks we face are manifold and complex. Their fulfilment in the right way demands a sense of sacrifice, meticulous organization and a huge number of cadres.

We have said that the essential role in achieving our aims, namely the establishment of the material and ideological basis for a socialist society, falls on the young. Why?

First, because the majority of our people are youngsters. In fact more than 70 per cent of our people are aged under 25. Young people provide the majority of workers in factories, schools, communal villages, collective farms, businesses, workshops, the civil service and hospitals.

If we turn to the composition of the Mozambican People's Liberation Forces and the paramilitary forces, we shall soon see that there as well young people are a majority. And within FRELIMO the influence of young people has been decisive right from the organization's earliest days.

Second, it is the young who, because of their youthfulness and their relative immunity from the alienating ideology and social customs of the colonial-capitalist system, are best equipped to respond critically to new values and to continue our country's revolutionary process.

*A speech given in Maputo on 15 December 1976.

Young people represent the greenhouse, the nursery, out of which will emerge the cadres of all kinds that are needed to build an advanced socialist society. Hence our concern to organize the young, and to provide the conditions for them to make the best showing in their historic responsibilities.

We have thus seen in outline the significance of youth for the triumph of the revolution. And two questions arise. First: what characteristics are necessary for the young person who accepts responsibility for creating a new society? Second: do our young people already have these characteristics? Let us try to answer these questions.

The youthful creator of the new society must be dynamic, desirous of change, of transformation, and endowed with a sense of initiative and creativity; he must be disciplined, not through outward signs, but principally because he knows and internalizes the structures in their political sense and is ready to respect them; he must be organized, with a clear plan of action for every month, every week, every day; he must have a great thirst for learning; he must be aware that the more knowledge he acquires, the better equipped he will be to serve the revolution.

He must be a young person with a profound love of the working-class cause, constantly concerned to link every step in his education and training to the practice of productive work, concerned to link all this thinking and activity to the struggle of the working classes against exploitation.

He must be concerned with enlightening other youngsters, and so winning over and uniting a growing number of young people to proletarian ideals. He must be deeply committed to the fight against the vices and the erroneous habits and concepts of the bourgeois society. He must be able to absorb in a critical spirit the experiences of progressive youth in other parts of the world, with the ability to distinguish these positive contributions from the manoeuvres set in train by imperialism to turn young people away from revolutionary ideals.

These are the essential characteristics of the youthful creator of the socialist society, the embryo of the New Man.

To answer the second question, we have to study the actions of our young people in recent years, from the start of the defeat of Portuguese colonialism in our country up to the present. There has never in the history of the Mozambican people been a youth organization, no specific tasks for youth have ever been laid down. However, young people, despite not being organized, have on many occasions shown their commitment to the process of national liberation.

Since the founding of FRELIMO, on 25 June 1962, we have seen young people carrying out tasks of crucial importance to our struggle. With the launching of revolutionary people's war, we saw young people engaged on the principal task: the armed struggle. With the development of the fight for liberation, young people responded perceptively to the popular element in the war and understood its characteristics and demands: young people fought the living forces of Portuguese colonialism, carried war material, played a part in the people's militias, in collective production, in literacy instruction and in health education. Young cadres of FRELIMO took part in organizing and mobilizing the mass of the people. They formed the base that impelled the vanguard force in the process of class struggle in the liberated areas.

Young people made a brave contribution to establishing and consolidating the liberated areas, nurseries of the revolution, where the model of the new society was created and is developing today. In this process young people distinguished themselves in their defence of the deepest interests of our people against Portuguese colonialism and against the tendencies and reactionary line of those aspirants to be new exploiters who arose within FRELIMO.

Abroad too, on the diplomatic front, we saw young people engaging in tasks of great importance in broadcasting the heroic resistance and fight for liberation of our people led by FRELIMO against Portuguese colonialism and imperialism.

But the foundation of FRELIMO, and above all the launching of armed struggle, did not merely mobilize those youngsters directly involved in the war. In fact in the very areas where the enemy felt himself master of the situation, in the areas where his machinery of occupation, oppression and pillage seemed unshakeable, youth performed an outstanding role in the national liberation struggle.

We saw young people in underground work mobilizing our people, distributing pamphlets, copying the broadcasts of 'The Voice of FRELIMO', organizing study and discussion groups, playing a role in all available forms of propaganda activity. Among the numberless martyrs of Mueda, Xinavane, Machava, Ibo, and the rail strikes were many youngsters. Many young Mozambicans in the criminal hands of PIDE gave their lives in defence of the people's interests. In the areas occupied by Portuguese colonialists, an increasing number of young people, who were aware of the justness of the people's war, managed to escape the shadowy mesh of the colonial security net and came to join FRELIMO.

After the defeat and surrender of Portuguese colonialism, with the signing of the Lusaka Agreement, Mozambican youth could more amply demonstrate adherence to FRELIMO's political line and commitment to the various fronts of national reconstruction. The battle by youth was basic to the annihilation of the puppet forces of neo-colonialism.

We have also seen the important role played by young recruits to the Mozambique People's Liberation Forces and to the paramilitary forces in defending sovereignty and consolidating national independence. We should not fail to mention the decisive share of youth in the FRELIMO structures, in the Dynamizing Groups especially, and their contribution to spreading people's democratic power throughout the country.

We saw how youth enthusiastically supported nationalizations and how quick they were to defend, consolidate and make effective use of the nationalizations. We were profoundly moved by the way in which young people took to the internationalist nature of our struggle, and undertook a whole series of activities to strengthen support for the struggle of our brother people in Zimbabwe.

We have seen too that the successes already gained in literacy campaigns, in health education and in the development of our revolutionary culture are highly dependent on youth activity. But this catalogue of tasks in which young people have proved their commitment to our revolution should not lead us to the conclusion that the youth are perfect, or that the young people are free of negative or even discreditable traits. Such a view would come from a superficial study of the issue, would show a lack of understanding of youth and of its characteristics.

In fact our youth are still suffering the effects of the negative side of traditional-feudal society, still suffering the effects of colonial-bourgeois ideology.

Mozambican youth, above all in the rural areas, are still living in subjection to influences whose roots must be sought in traditional-feudal society. This is the case with tribalism and regionalism, divisive factors among our people. It is the case too with obscurantism and superstition that prevent the young from gaining a scientific and materialist view of nature's and society's development.

The inertia and lack of creative energy that we find among some sectors of our youth, particularly in young peasants, are a legacy of the traditional-feudal society that Portuguese colonialism tried to preserve with the aim of facilitating its exploitation of our people. The young peasant is still a victim of certain negative customs, such as initiation rites and premature marriage. These retrograde practices, which have a traumatic psychological effect on youngsters, lead to a distorted mental outlook and to imitation of the old society's values.

In the urban areas, in cities and small towns, the pattern of colonial-capitalist life is stronger. It is precisely the urban youth, whether worker, civil servant or student, who is most harmed by the deleterious effects of the bourgeoisie's decadent ideology.

In our country, and particularly after the founding of FRELIMO, colonial-imperialism was forever trying to divert young people away from the ideas and deepest hopes of the people, and trying to isolate young people from the working-class struggle, and to alienate them from the historical process.

So the colonialists, taking advantage of young people's taste for amusement, made great efforts to spread entertainment based on drinking, drug-taking, sexual promiscuity, contempt for national culture, and blind imitation of the decadent values of the foreign bourgeoisie. Hence the parties or celebrations in high American or South African style, where drinking, drug-taking, promiscuity and sexual aberration were rife; the sessions of 'passing round the joint' or drug-addicts' gatherings where inexperienced youngsters were initiated into the drug culture;

so-called 'free love', imported directly from the bourgeois democracies and meaning no more than low sexual promiscuity with the most profound disregard for women; the so-called 'freak' talk, the slang of misfits, that rapidly spread among student youth – expressions such as 'Hi Joe! Hey chick! Let's go and make the scene, but keep it cool.'

There were the exaggerated style fads, from 'Beatle' shoes to trousers up to the chest, from shirts that didn't reach the navel to military jackets with the insignia of the criminal imperialist armies – US Army, US Air Force.

The colonialists, by encouraging élitism, arrogance, superiority complexes and contempt for manual work, tried to instil in young people contempt for the mass of the workers and so to isolate the young people from social reality. This explains why some young degenerates are ashamed of having a father who is a workman.

Banditry, corruption, immorality, pornography, 'machismo', individualism, a know-all attitude are constantly glorified in films, photonovels, magazines, records, books and other forms of bourgeois propaganda. And some youngsters took to and immediately imitated such values.

Racism and division on the basis of religion were instilled in young people in the schools themselves, the promotional centres for the settler's culture. The negative impact of bourgeois values, although it affected mainly the young in the cities, also had an influence on peasant youth. This is the explanation for the influx in recent years of young people from the countryside to the town under the magnet of the false glamour of the 'soft and sweet life' of the cities.

When Portuguese colonialism was defeated, imperialism's manoeuvres to corrupt youth away from revolutionary ideals did not come to a halt; quite the reverse, they were honed down and perfected. In recent times and particularly since the proclamation of independence, we have noted an intensification of activity by agents of the bourgeoisie in the schools. This explains the wave of indiscipline, disorganization, liberalism and corruption that is washing into some schools. It is the handiwork of small groups, for sure, but they are highly organized.

Why is the enemy concentrating his attention on the schools? Because it is the schools that forge the New Man. It is in the schools that the process of awakening the consciousness of new generations takes place, to prepare them for the responsibility of carrying on the revolution. The schools are the nurseries from which the cadres needed to build the socialist society will emerge. By attacking the schools, the class enemy tries to undermine at its roots our project of creating a new society, a New Man.

So we can see that, although our youth have clearly proved their deep commitment to the revolution, there are still some negative influences and traits among them that must be eliminated. So we now come to the central issue of our meeting: how can we strengthen and perfect the commitment of young people to our revolution? How can we create conditions for young people to overcome the prevailing negative traits within them and go forward more effectively to take up their historic responsibilities?

We have already seen that if the commitment of our youth was no greater than it was, this was essentially due to the fact that they were not organized. As we mentioned earlier, there has never in our people's history been a youth organization, no tasks for young people have ever been laid down. So we are confident that only by organizing youth, giving young people a structure, shall we win our battle to establish a new society; only by organizing youth, shall we triumph in our battles, consolidate our independence, and build on our victories.

We must, therefore, organize youth so that it can take pride of place alongside the working classes in the fight to establish the material and ideological basis for a socialist society. We must create structures that will allow the transformation of the eagerness and enthusiasm of young people into a potent material force at the service of the worker-peasant alliance.

14. We Must Remove the Enemy Within the Defence and Security Forces*

Mozambicans, men and women, we are here today to analyse an abnormal situation that has arisen in our country. In the People's Republic of Mozambique we have witnessed systematic violations of legality: violations of the Constitution, violations of laws and regulations, and violations of our principles.

A particularly serious aspect of this situation is that these violations are in many cases committed by members of the defence and security forces. They are committed by members of the Mozambique Armed Forces (FPLM), by members of the police force and militias, and by personnel of the Ministry of Security (SNASP). In other words, legality is in many cases violated by members of those very forces that were entrusted by the people and the party with the glorious task of defending the Constitution of the People's Republic of Mozambique.

The Constitution is the fundamental law of our independent country. It is a victory of the armed struggle for national liberation. It is a victory of the heroic battle fought by the whole Mozambican people against the foreign oppressor and against national reactionaries.

The Constitution defines the aims and principles of our state and is an essential instrument in achieving them. The Constitution of the People's Republic of Mozambique is a powerful weapon in the class struggle: in the fight against hunger, poverty, ignorance, misery and underdevelopment; in building a socialist society in our country.

The Constitution is the fruit of the blood, sacrifice and dedication of the best sons and daughters of the Mozambican people. For this reason we cannot allow our Constitution to be violated. We cannot permit the violation of our laws, laws that translate our constitutional principles into concrete terms. We cannot allow the political principles of our party to be attacked. Above all, we cannot allow such violations to be committed by members of the defence and security forces.

It must be made quite clear, here and now: anyone who violates our Constitution, our laws, our principles, is an infiltrator, is a reactionary, is a counter-revolutionary, is against the people. He may wear the glorious

*A speech given in Maputo on 5 November 1981.

uniform of the Mozambique Armed Forces (FPLM), but he is not a soldier: he is an infiltrator in our armed forces. He may wear the uniform of our People's Police, but he is an enemy infiltrated into our police. He may present a SNASP pass, but he is not the people's security: he is a reactionary infiltrated into SNASP to set up an enemy base. These people, wittingly or unwittingly, are at the service of reaction and counter-revolution.

We have come here today to make this quite clear to everyone. We should not hesitate in denouncing those who violate our Constitution, our laws, our principles, even if these people represent themselves as members of the defence and security forces. We repeat: these are not our soldiers; they are not our police; they are not our security.

It was the people who alerted us to this situation. Since it is the people who have been the victims of abuses, despotism and violations of legality by infiltrators into the defence and security forces. And our people will not, and cannot, accept this. Just as they did not accept colonialism. We have a heroic, courageous people, a generous and worthy people, a people who struggled and made sacrifice to win their freedom, their independence.

Our people defeated colonialism, defeated the Rhodesian racists and resolutely face racist South African aggression. Our people are fighting underdevelopment, building socialism. Our people cannot be intimidated. They will not accept the oppression and abuses carried out by a handful of infiltrators, by a minority of reactionaries. That is why the population denounced these anomalies.

The people went to their vanguard party, the Frelimo Party, and said: 'There are infiltrators in the defence and security forces who are robbing us, raping our wives and daughters.' *Khanimambo*, thank you, Mozambican people!

And they went on: 'Frelimo liberated us. You fought, you won and liberated us. But the government is fooling about. It is ill-treating us. We face arrest even when we do nothing wrong. Frelimo knows about fighting, but it does not govern well. It has handed government over to children. They arrest us even when we do nothing wrong.'

The people went to the Presidency of the Republic, to the People's Assemblies at various levels and denounced these events. We received information and reports from every province, from every district, and from many individual citizens. The Council of Ministers held an extended session to analyse this question. We saw that the situation demanded tough measures. As is our custom, we have come to the people to analyse the situation and determine what measures should be taken.

In the first place, we wish to thank the citizens of Mozambique for having alerted us. In this way they demonstrated their strong trust in their party and government. They showed that they can distinguish between our party line and deviations from or violations of that line. They showed that they can distinguish between our heroic defence and security forces,

forces that defend the people – and the reactionaries, the enemy agents who are infiltrated into our forces. So we say: thank you, Mozambican people.

We wish now to appeal to you to go on denouncing the enemy agents in our forces. We shall create the appropriate mechanisms for all these complaints to be investigated, so that the infiltrators can be neutralized, removed from our ranks, and severely punished. And woe betide anyone who dares to exact reprisals against a citizen who denounced his abuses! For him we shall have no mercy. Let that be quite clear.

In the People's Republic of Mozambique we want respect for people, respect for the freedom of the citizen, respect for people's lives and property. It was the people who bore the brunt and violence of colonial oppression, and who struggled and sacrificed their children to wipe out all forms of oppression. All this demands, in the first place, respect for the Constitution, respect for laws, a guarantee that our principles are followed, and respect for the things we struggled for. This is the meaning of the present offensive, the offensive on legality, the offensive in the defence and security forces.

We began the Political and Organizational Offensive in other sectors of the state apparatus and in businesses. Now the time has come to turn our attention to this highly sensitive sector: the sector that is the principal guarantee of our power; the sector we armed to defend people's power, our country, the socialist revolution. Under no circumstances can these arms be used to serve petty personal interests, revenge, spite or resentment.

By virtue of the special nature of the defence and security forces, as the vital sector for the defence of our country and the revolution, and because the sector constantly demands special attention, the offensive was not launched in the defence and security forces at the same time as in other sectors. But we were well aware of the need for the offensive that we are launching now.

Ever since national independence, we have discovered within the defence and security forces violations of legality that threatened our political line. The fourth meeting of the FRELIMO Defence Department, in July 1975, the prison visits in 1976, the inquiry into conditions in the re-education centres, were occasions when certain anomalies were uncovered and immediate short-term measures were taken to correct them. Throughout the various phases of the main offensive, instances of illegality and abuse of power were also detected and these were the subject of analysis and appropriate measures by the party and state leadership.

Today, in keeping with the spirit of the offensive, we want to go deeper into these issues. We want to take more far-reaching measures. The present offensive on legality will enable us to purge the ranks of our defence and security forces. It will remove the traitors, the kidnappers, the infiltrators, the corrupt, the despots, the authoritarians, the arrogant, the negligent, the incompetent, the abusers, the thieves, the rapists of women and minors, the murderers, and those who would ride roughshod over the people.

Once more the people will be the filter. This process will prevent our legitimate pride in our defence and security forces being besmirched by the acts of a handful of bandit infiltrators. It will allow the indestructible unity between the people and the armed forces to grow stronger and deeper. This process will enable our revolution to progress more quickly, because we shall clean the mud off our boots.

The Situation Today

The situation today has two main characteristics: crimes, abuses and arbitrary actions carried out by enemy agents infiltrated in the defence and security forces, which are a result of persistent values and practices from colonial-capitalist and tribal-feudal society; and mistakes and deviations that are the result of our own shortcomings.

With regard to the first aspect, the following kinds of circumstance have been discovered: elements infiltrated in the defence and security forces beat and torture people on a variety of pretexts. Aggression and torture are employed: as a means of punishing often imaginary faults; as a means of making people confess to crimes, whether committed or not; as a means of intimidation, to prevent the population denouncing the crimes committed by those same infiltrators; to extort goods from the population; and as a form of personal revenge.

Elements infiltrated in the defence and security forces make undue and arbitrary arrests in the following circumstances: as a means of settling personal quarrels; as revenge against people who lodge complaints about the abuses committed by these same infiltrators; to intimidate the population; to steal the belongings of detainees; to obtain the houses of detainees; to abuse the wives and daughters of prisoners; to abuse women prisoners.

Infiltrators in the defence and security forces also abuse women in other ways, for example: rape by physical force or by threats with a firearm; rape of minors, either by force or by exploiting the prestige of the uniform or of the structure they have infiltrated; seduction and impregnation of young girls after false promises of marriage (in many cases, as soon as a problem arises, the person implicated avoids his responsibility by arranging a transfer); seduction of married women, by exploiting the prestige of uniform and structure; offences against modesty, in forcing women to undress with threats or on false pretexts – this has even been done in public.

Infiltrators in the defence and security forces steal from the population, especially in the following circumstances: armed assault; theft at road and border control points, on the pretext of confiscating goods for the state; break-ins at houses around the barracks, with the thieves then hiding in the barracks itself.

In addition to the thefts already mentioned, the infiltrators in the defence and security forces, including the militias, when on duty at control points and border posts: show disrespect for the people; are authoritarian and arrogant; inflict beatings and torture.

Infiltrators in the defence and security forces use their uniform or staff pass to queue-jump and to obtain privileged treatment from shopkeepers.

Infiltrators in the defence and security forces misuse vehicles: by driving without a licence; speeding; systematically breaching the highway code; using state vehicles for private purposes; refusing to obey orders of the traffic police; illicitly requisitioning vehicles and fuel.

Infiltrators in the defence and security forces carry out the following abuses of housing: illegal occupation of houses, often by way of forced entry (when the inspection teams arrive, the intruders refuse to identify themselves); illegal and abusive eviction of tenants in order to occupy their houses; non-payment of rent, even in houses occupied legally; demands for luxury residences; the destruction of the houses they inhabit, with the result that these quickly take on an air of abandonment; illegal occupation of houses to accommodate prostitutes and lovers (when the appropriate authority evicts them, they are reinstalled by use of threats).

Infiltrators in the defence and security forces show a lack of respect for the party, the government, and for such symbols of the country as the flag and national anthem.

Infiltrators in the defence and security forces put to personal use goods confiscated by the state, especially money, vehicles, furniture, stereophonic equipment, domestic appliances, clothing and drinks.

Infiltrators in the defence and security forces, police and prison guards particularly, take bribes from jailed prisoners in their charge: the prisoner with money is allowed out to the local bar, or to spend the weekend at home; the same thing happens if the prisoner is a relative or friend of the guard. The prisoner with money pays the guard to let him escape. In some prisons, the prisoners leave at night to carry out burglaries and then return to jail – this is not a prison, it is a criminal barracks. In some places it has even reached a pitch where the longest-serving prisoners do the guard duty.

Infiltrators in the defence and security forces recruit their relatives and friends to these forces, on the basis of nepotism, thus creating a web of obligations that often entails complicity in the crimes and deviations committed.

Infiltrators in the defence and security forces, in SNASP in particular, reproduce the style and methods of work of the capitalist secret police, in an attempt to intimidate and terrorize the population.

Infiltrators in the judicial apparatus practise racism. They are arrogant and élitist in their dealings with the population.

Infiltrators in the judicial apparatus make a practice of nepotism and favouritism with detainees, holding up the files of friends and relatives and others to whom they have obligations, and hiding the files in desk drawers.

Infiltrators in the judicial apparatus, under cover of a narrow interpretation of the law, apply outstanding legislation against our class interests.

These are just some of the activities of agents infiltrated in our defence and security forces that have been discovered. This partial list shows that we must take speedy and firm measures to neutralize these elements and purge our ranks.

Apart from these cases due to the enemy's action, there are also those that are due to our own shortcomings.

We had barely ended the war against Portuguese colonialism, when we had to face another war, promoted by the racist, rebel and illegal regime in Rhodesia. We fought and won this war, side by side with our brother people in Zimbabwe. Today we can say with pride that we contributed to the birth of independent Zimbabwe.

The effort we had to make in the war, in our act of solidarity with the people of Zimbabwe, meant that in the first few years after independence we could not give all our attention to our own internal problems.

For this reason, at the beginning of last year we launched the Political and Organizational Offensive, to clear the ground and to create the conditions for our rapid advance in building socialism.

And today, as we said, the offensive reaches the defence and security sector, reaches the question of legality. Here too, in addition to neutralizing the internal enemy, we must overcome our own shortcomings, incapacity and disorganization.

As a result of these shortcomings, we find the following situations: citizens detained for months, awaiting trial, because the police are slow in preparing the case file, or because the courts are unable to clear the backlog of cases. Our courts are still slow and scarcely operational. We have few magistrates and the training of those we have is often inadequate.

Trials are successively postponed without justification and there is no sensitivity to the difficulties of people who travel long distances to attend court.

Crimes go unpunished, owing to the incapacity of the investigators or owing to the courts' mechanical application of existing legislation, that in many instances is now obsolete.

On the other hand, many districts do not yet have people's tribunals, a factor that delays and impedes the administration of justice. To a large extent this is due to the fact that many magistrates have not yet understood the political importance of setting up people's tribunals.

There are many logistical and organizational problems with compulsory military service. The young recruits often do not receive the necessary support and integration.

In the re-education centres, as has already been disclosed, many irregularities and instances of injustice have been discovered. These are already being corrected, so that we can strengthen and develop this important victory of our revolutionary process.

There is a lack of co-ordination between the various defence and security forces and between them and the judicial apparatus, so reducing their effectiveness.

Still persistent in the defence and security forces are: excessive red tape, negligence, slavery to routine, and a poor understanding of the nature and importance of the forces' task. The same is true of the judicial apparatus. Such factors often make these structures inoperative.

That is a broad outline of the characteristics of the present situation. We must now analyse the causes of the situation and how we have reached such a state of affairs today.

The Origins of This Situation

The first question we need to answer is: how was it possible for our defence and security forces to be infiltrated?

We must understand this situation in its historical context. The FPLM, during the armed struggle for national liberation, was a guerrilla force deeply rooted in the people. The war against Portuguese colonialism was victorious only because the army and the people forged a deep unity. The army mobilized, educated and defended the people. The people fed the fighters, transported war material, and provided information on enemy movements. The FPLM soldier – the FRELIMO soldier – lived among the people as the fish lives in water. This stemmed, in the first place, from the popular character of our war and our army.

However, the fact that our war was a people's war, that our armed forces were of the people, did not signify that all the contradictions between the army and the people were automatically resolved. These contradictions also existed during the armed struggle. This is nothing new.

Then, too, there existed those who, under cover of our uniform, tried to oppress, exploit and ride roughshod over the people. But we always managed to make it very clear to the people that these were not really our soldiers – they were enemy agents infiltrated into FRELIMO, into the FPLM.

We succeeded in this clear definition thanks to four basic factors. First, the care given to the political and military preparation of the fighters. This guaranteed that the vast majority behaved correctly. So it was easy to isolate and neutralize the infiltrators.

Second, constant political work with the fighters and the masses. This enabled us continually to raise the fighters' level of political consciousness. It also enabled the people to have a better knowledge of our political line. The people were themselves in a position to denounce behaviour characteristic of the enemy, even when manifested by those who wore our uniform.

The third factor was the permanent organizational work carried out within the FPLM. We drew up rules and regulations. We worked out guidelines for each specific situation that arose. We made constant visits and inspections in the centres and at the war fronts. These actions helped to discipline our work, to improve the structures of the FPLM and to eliminate organizational faults, through practice.

The fourth and final factor was the severe punishment of offenders. This punishment was particularly severe in cases of infractions against the people or their belongings. We were never afraid to go to the people and say: 'This soldier committed a crime, he violated our line and so he will receive this punishment.'

In this way we preserved and consolidated the prestige of FRELIMO and the Mozambique People's Liberation Forces in the eyes of the people. Thus we continually strengthened the people's confidence in and support for the struggle.

Within the Mozambique People's Liberation Forces themselves, the values of simple life and hard work – not comfort – were continually encouraged. Productive work was an integral part of political-military training. Productive work was not only aimed at creating better material conditions: its main aim was the transformation of man. We launched a constant battle against unprogrammed activity, idleness and laziness. We consistently fought personal ambition and the desire for comfort.

That is how the Mozambique People's Liberation Forces became strong and disciplined. Everyone knew his task and his responsibility. That is how the FPLM became the forge of national unity, forge of the revolution, forge of a new mentality, forge of the New Man. This is the very valuable experience of the national liberation struggle – experience that was not given its true value, was not taken up, when we won independence.

So what happened? When we won power, our forces had to advance to the areas where the enemy's ideology was strongly rooted. Our fighters had to face situations for which, in truth, they were not prepared and for which it would have been impossible to prepare them. On the one hand they were called upon to resolve all kinds of problems for the population within a social context whose complexity was new to them. On the other hand they had to face all sorts of seduction and blandishment.

In this phase there was a flurry of numerous problems and new situations that often demanded firm measures. In this phase, many commanders acquired a taste for comfort, for a soft life and even for luxury.

These factors opened the way to a slackening of discipline, to negligence and the separation of commanders from their soldiers. The need, within a short space of time and on the foundation of our guerrilla forces, to create a strong regular army capable of defending our country's borders under threat from the neighbouring racist regimes, made an already difficult situation even worse.

We had to expand our army rapidly. And our perspective was sometimes wrong. We did not pay enough attention to the soldiers' training. We put too much stress on technical aspects. When training our new officer corps, we did not give sufficient value to the criterion of class. We paid too much heed to levels of education – whether or not they had completed secondary schooling.

We did not establish a correct balance between the need for the army's technical growth and its political growth. We attached more importance to the technical aspects. As a result, we disregarded the need for the permanent purging of our ranks as a catalyst within the armed forces themselves. We thus opened the door to enemy infiltration into the ranks of our armed forces.

The situation we face today should not surprise us. It is the result of not making enough of the experience of the armed struggle for national liberation. It is the result of our having abandoned the profoundly popular methods that used to characterize our army. It is the result of not having maintained the close link between the army and the people. It is the result of not having always put politics in command. It is the result of being more concerned with the quantity than the quality of new recruits. It is the result of inadequate political work within the armed forces. These are deviations that must be corrected immediately.

When we analyse the causes that permitted infiltration in the rest of the defence and security forces, we find identical explanations. We did not have police during the armed struggle – the police were the population themselves; they were the people's militias.

When we won independence, the basis for the creation of the police was not the FPLM; was not the experience in organizing the population in the liberated areas: the basis was the colonial police.

We wanted to avoid a vacuum. We did not have the courage to accept a temporary vacuum, while creating a police force that was ours, with our methods, with our content. We preferred to use colonial capitalism's police, trained to repress and despise the people.

We used them, on the pretext that they had the technical knowledge. But for what? The technical expertise to oppress, to humiliate, to brutalize, to massacre the people. These individuals had a profound and extremely pernicious influence over the inexperienced young people who later flocked into the police force.

This explains why the methods, the concepts of the colonial police are still found in some of our police, despite the purge already begun.

With regard to security, during the armed struggle for national liberation this was a task of all the people. There were FPLM comrades who had specific security duties. But their main task was to educate and mobilize the people in vigilance. It was to teach the people to recognize the enemy in any guise. It was the people who detected the infiltrators and denounced them to our security, thus enabling us to neutralize them.

After independence we created a security organization, the People's National Security Service (SNASP), to correspond to the needs of the new phase of our fight, the intensification of class struggle in our country.

We defined it quite clearly: SNASP is people's security; it is security based on the people. We do not want secret police. We do not need them.

We have always said: the enemy can speak our language, wear our uniform, eat like us, shout *vivas* for FRELIMO, shouting even louder than us. What he can never do, and is incapable of doing, is to behave like us, to live by our political line. The enemy cannot abandon his characteristic vices: contempt for women, the desire for comfort, personal ambition and drunkenness.

He is incapable of respecting the people. He cannot stop being tribalist, regionalist, divisionist, confusionist, racist. These are the characteristics of the enemy.

He cannot lead a simple, modest life. He cannot abandon his arrogance, the cult of intrigue, slander, rumour. His morality, we repeat, his morality, his civilization, is corruption.

It was his conduct, his way of life, his habits, that enabled us to spot the enemy. However, in this sector, too, not enough was made of the experience of the armed struggle for national liberation. In this sector, too, priority was given to the technical over the political. Priority was given to quantity over quality.

For this reason we also find infiltrators in SNASP – and well entrenched in reinforced concrete shelters. We find elements who adopt the methods of capitalist secret police, methods conceived to oppress the people, to repress and humiliate.

In the defence and security forces in general, we find that numerical and technical expansion has not been accompanied by a corresponding political growth.

Another factor that explains the infiltration in our defence and security forces is that the rot has reached people in positions of responsibility. The failing of a soldier or policeman often goes unpunished because this soldier or that policeman knows too much about the life of the commander. And when the big fish are corrupt, the small fry follow their example. Networks of obligations, favouritism and nepotism are established. A state of godfathers is created, a state of personal favours, a state of accomplices. Networks are established with the aim of robbery, corruption, the violation of legality.

When the situation reaches this point, then ideological infiltration has already set in. And the conditions are created for physical infiltration. The door is open for the enemy. It is an invitation for the enemy to come in.

The Social and Cultural Dimension of the Problem

The situation we face now has a cultural dimension that must be taken into consideration. We must understand the complexity of the society bequeathed to us by colonialism.

During the armed struggle for national liberation, the population of our country was divided into three broad areas: first, the population of the liberated areas, where the embryo of the New Man was growing; secondly, the population of the concentration camps, exposed to corruption, brutalization, to the destruction of their integrity and personality – in the concentration camps the values of the tribe and the clan, polygamy and the inferiority of women were glorified; in the third place, the population of the zones unaffected by the war – in town and countryside – likewise oppressed and subjected to the political, ideological, social and cultural influence of the enemy.

In the towns, in particular, colonialism promoted drugs, pornography and prostitution. To promote moral degradation in the former Lourenço Marques there were the Pinguim, the Luso, the Aquarium, the Texas Bar, the Tamila, cabarets and brothels where women were sold to sailors, officers and soldiers of the colonial army, sold to the Boers. Even the Boers arrived. Every barracks had its brothel. There were prostitutes for officers, prostitutes for sergeants, prostitutes for ordinary soldiers.

The prostitutes also had categories. There were first-class, second-class, third-class and fourth-class prostitutes, reflecting the prevailing social stratification. This is what we found in Lourenço Marques.

It was in the towns too that racism put down deeper roots, where social stratification was more obvious. In the city of Lourenço Marques, only the Whites, Indians, mulattos, and assimilated Blacks had access to the 'cement city', while the overwhelming majority of Blacks lived in the 'reed' areas.

In the 'cement' area, the first-class Whites lived in Polana, Sommerschield and Ponta Vermelha. The second-class Whites, the Indians and the mulattos lived in Alto Mae and in Malhangalene. In the 'reed' areas people gathered in neighbourhoods based on tribe or region of origin.

In the countryside, colonialism concentrated mainly on repressing the growth of national values. To do this, it used tribalism, the traditional chiefs and the church. Young people from the countryside who are in the armed forces, in the police, in SNASP, still have these values today. They carry the burden of ignorance, obscurantism, superstition, subservience and fatalism.

We found the Catholic Church giving its blessing to these situations, encouraging submission to colonialism and the acceptance of its decadent values. It was the Catholic Church that blessed the murderous forays of the colonial army against our people. It was the Catholic Church that provided the moral justification: they killed in the name of Christian civilization; they discriminated and oppressed in the name of divine morality.

In this stratified society, each group had its code, was treated differently under the state and law. At the top of the scale were the Whites from Portugal – the first-class Whites. These were further subdivided according to their wealth, and each group was treated differently: the carpenter and the railway worker did not merit the same treatment as the doctor, the bank manager or the factory owner.

In the second place came the Whites born in Mozambique – second-class Whites. These were excluded from certain positions of responsibility.

In the third place came Indians from Goa. As they had assimilated the religion and culture of the colonizers, they were entitled to some privileges. They were usually the lower- and middle-level colonial civil servants.

In the fourth place came Indians from India. Many were wealthy, but even so could not aspire to any position of responsibility in the colonial apparatus. So they devoted themselves to trade.

Occupying fifth place in the scale were the mulattos. Here there was a further distinction between colour – based on White and Indian, or on White and Black, or on Indian and Black. They were also stratified in accordance with the social positions they managed to achieve.

In the sixth place were the assimilated Blacks. These received the smallest crumbs from the colonial banquet, the left-overs that no one else wanted.

Finally there were the natives, the vast majority. They had no rights or prerogatives, had no protection under the law. The only law applied to them was the Native Code. In addition they were subject to despotism from chiefs who wielded their small power as agents of colonialism, on behalf of colonialism.

This was Mozambican colonial society. Hatred and feelings of ill will were created and generated among these various groups.

All Mozambicans who joined FRELIMO during the armed struggle passed through Nachingwea training camp: this was the filter and the mould of consciousness.

The first thing that any Mozambican joining FRELIMO did was political-military training. Thereafter he went on to specialized activities. He might become a teacher, nurse, or doctor – but first, he underwent political-military training. That does not happen today.

Those who went to study abroad received training before they went and when they returned, in order to readapt themselves.

Political-military training was the forge of national unity, of a common way of thinking, of a patriotic and class consciousness. We entered Nachingwea as Makondes, Macuas, Nianjas, Nyungues, Manicas, Shanganas, Ajauas, Rongas, Senas; we came out Mozambicans. We entered as Blacks, Whites, mulattos, Indians; we came out as Mozambicans.

When we arrived, we brought with us vices, defects, egoism, liberalism, élitism. We destroyed these negative values, reactionary values. We learned to acquire the habits, the behaviour of a FRELIMO militant.

When we entered, we had a limited vision because we knew only our area. There we learned the scale of our country and revolutionary values.

We entered superstitious; in the confrontation between superstition and science, we gained a scientific viewpoint. We were disorganized, susceptible to rumour and intrigue, corruption, incapable of analysing and interpreting phenomena. There we learned to live in an organized manner, to interpret reality correctly and to act on it. We often arrived motivated only by feelings of resentment and hatred for the oppressor; we came away with a clear understanding of the aims for which we were struggling, with a clear definition of the enemy.

That is why we say that Nachingwea was the laboratory and forge of the Mozambican. Then we won the war, we gained independence. The entire people were liberated: the concentration camps ceased to exist; there were no longer areas controlled by the enemy. Different codes – codes for natives, for the assimilated, and for Whites – ceased to exist.

Today, from this great mixture, we have created a people who are all equal under the law and who all enjoy the same rights and duties. We all mixed together: we became just Mozambicans, Mozambican people, living from the Rovuma to the Maputo. Our area today starts at the Rovuma and ends at the Maputo.

In this area we all live together: those who passed through the purifying process of the armed struggle; those who were in the concentration camps; and those who lived in the area unaffected by war.

So today it is more difficult to draw the line. It is no longer possible to make a physical, geographical demarcation. More than ever before, the demarcation between us and the enemy is an ideological demarcation, a boundary line drawn by behaviour, by identification with the people.

However, the majority of young people who join the defence and security forces did not experience the process of armed struggle for national liberation, did not pass through Nachingwea, the laboratory of national unity, did not grow up in the liberated areas. Many of them grew up in the concentration camps, grew up in the towns controlled by colonialism, were educated and shaped by colonialism. Others came directly from the countryside, from traditional-feudal society.

It is they who swell the ranks of the defence and security forces, without having passed through a process of profound change. They receive a uniform, a firearm, without yet having freed themselves from the burden they still carry.

They are given the task of defending the country, but for many of them the country is still the tribe, not the nation. They have not yet overcome the tribe so as to rise to the concept of nation.

They are given the task of fighting the enemies of the revolution but in many instances they still identify ideologically with the bourgeoisie.

Today, we no longer have Nachingwea. We do not have centres for political-military training. So we do not have the forge of the new Man, and there is no serious fight against tribalism, racism and regionalism.

In the present military units, whoever enters confused, comes out confused; the tribalist comes out tribalist; the regionalist comes out regionalist; the racist continues racist. There is no genuine transformation. So they are confused about the enemy. When they meet the people, they are incapable of distinguishing between the enemy and the people.

That is why, when these elements act as members of the defence and security forces, we find the profound marks of their origin, of their past.

The marks of the past have remained. The hatreds, the buried resentments have not died, particularly among those who did not directly experience the process of armed struggle for national liberation. And this is reflected today in many sectors of society. We find these marks too on the defence and security forces.

The White of humble origin, who at school was humiliated by the doctor's son, today, if he is in security, takes delight in arresting and humiliating the one who humiliated him as a child.

The mulatto who is now a CID officer uses the opportunity to take revenge on the White family, or the mulatto but richer family, that would not let him marry the girl he liked.

The Black who is now in the police force enjoys arresting the White or Indian to demonstrate that he is someone now, that he has power now. He wants to take revenge for the hatreds, the resentment, the humiliation he suffered.

There is also the tribal problem among the Blacks who are found today in the police or militias. Someone from the south arrests people from the north or the centre, just to show his tribal superiority. But he lets off the real criminal, because he comes from the same tribe, speaks the same mother tongue. Even within the same tribe, there is rivalry between clans and families. Disagreements between parents, uncles, or godparents become motives for arrest, beating, ill treatment.

The native who could not marry the daughter of an assimilated Black today arrests him and insults his wife.

In all these cases, we find the use of our power – and here lies the problem – the use of our uniform, our weapons, to satisfy petty hatreds and personal resentment. This is not what we struggled for. We shall not allow this to happen in the People's Republic of Mozambique. We shall punish all these cases severely.

When we analyse the kind of abuses, despotism, violations of legality carried out by infiltrators in the defence and security forces, it is easy to detect in each such case the social and cultural origin of the culprit. Whipping and tying up prisoners were methods used by the chiefs. These young people learned this in the village. They come from the countryside and have not been changed. They brought into our defence and security force what they saw the chief and the native policeman do. They are the same ones who practise tribalism and regionalism.

But torture, the humiliation of prisoners, arrogance and racism are marks of the town, are marks of colonialism, capitalism and Fascism, are the methods of apartheid. This is the work of city dwellers, taking pleasure in other people's suffering. It is sadism. They learned this with PIDE, with the racist police, the colonial bourgeoisie in the towns. Since they have not been changed, they now apply these methods in the defence and security forces.

In both instances, they are enemy methods that reveal the enemy ideology infiltrated among us. We will make no pact with this. We shall not allow it.

The actions of these infiltrators tarnish the glorious traditions of our defence and security forces. The fight against this situation involves all of us. It is not the business only of the Ministry of National Defence, the Ministry of the Interior, the Ministry of Security, or the Ministry of Justice. It is not the task merely of the party or government, but one for the entire people.

Who are these young people who enter the defence and security forces? They are our children, our brothers, our nephews, our sons-in-law, our brothers-in-law, our cousins, our relatives. So it is we, the parents at home, who give our children their first education and teach them to take the first steps in life. In this way they bring with them to the defence and security forces their cultural universe: they bring their habits, vices and traditions. So all of us have a responsibility in the fight against the old mentality.

A Bibliographic Note

by Colin Darch

Since independence Samora Machel's major speeches have been widely published in the Mozambican media, such as the newspapers *Notícias* and *Diário de Moçambique*, the party journal *Voz da Rovolução*, and the army journal *25 de Setembro*. Such texts are sometimes not accurate transcripts. Some writings from the period of the armed struggle can be found in such periodicals as FRELIMO's English-language monthly *Mozambique Revolution*. For a fuller description of Samora Machel's writings and other FRELIMO materials, see Colin Darch, 'Published Documentation of the Party Frelimo: A Preliminary Study', *Mozambican Studies* (Amsterdam), no. 2, 1981, pp. 104–25.

This bibliographic note lists the authoritative Portuguese-language series, mostly published by the party's Department of Ideological Work, and the major publications in English of texts by Samora Machel.

Series in Portuguese

A. Colecção Estudos e Orientações (Studies and Guidelines)
The versions listed here are the most recently published. Earlier editions, especially in this series, have sometimes included different publications under the same series number. Nos 1–6 and 8 were also issued in a single volume under the title *A nossa luta* (Lourenço Marques: Imprensa Nacional, 1975).

1. *Produzir é aprender; aprender para produzir e lutar melhor* ('To produce is to learn: learn to produce and to fight better') (Edição do Departamento do Trabalho Ideológico, Maputo, 1978).
   Directives issued at the beginning of the agricultural season in 1971–72.
2. *Educar o homem para vencer a guerra, criar uma sociedade nova e desenvolver a pátria* ('Educate man to win the war, create a new society and develop our country') 1978.
   Speech to the second Conference of the Department of Education and Culture, September 1970.
3. *No trabalho sanitário materializemos o principio de que a revolução*

liberta o povo ('In our health services the principle that the revolution
frees the people becomes a reality).
Speech to a course to train nurses, November 1971.

4. *A libertação da mulher é uma necessidade da revolução, garantia da
sua continuidade, condição de seu triunfo* ('The liberation of women
is a fundamental necessity for the revolution, a guarantee of its
continuity, a precondition for its triumph') 1979.
Speech to the first Conference of Mozambican Women, 4 March
1973.

5. *Estabelecer o poder popular para servir as massas* ('Establishing
people's power to serve the masses') 1979.
Translated as Chapter 1 in this volume.

6. *Fazer da escola uma base para o povo tomar o poder* ('Make schooling a base for the people to seize power') 1979.
A synthesis first published in July 1974.

7. *Impermeabilizemo-nos contra as manobras subversivas, intensificando
a ofensiva ideológica e organizacional no seio dos combatentes e
massas* ('Let's make ourselves immune to subversive manoeuvres, by
stepping up the ideological and organizational offensive among the
fighters and the masses') 1979.
A synthesis first published in November 1973.

8. *O processo da revolução democrática popular em Moçambique* ('The
people's democratic revolutionary process in Mozambique) 1980.
Translated as Chapter 2 in this volume.

9. *Produzir é um acto de militância* ('Production is an act of militancy')
1979.
Translated as Chapter 7 in this volume.

10. An earlier edition of the following item.

11. *Transformar o Hospital Central num hospital do povo* ('Transform
the Central Hospital into a people's hospital') 1980.
Translated as Chapter 10 in this volume.

12. *Sobre os problemas, função e tarefas da juventude moçambicana* ('On
the problems, function and tasks of Mozambican youth') 1980.
Translated under the title 'A study of Mozambican youth', as Chapter 13 in this volume.

13. *Compreender a nossa tarefa* ('Understanding our task') n.d.
Text prepared for FRELIMO's political-military training centre at
Nachingwea, Tanzania, in December 1970.

14. *Organizar a sociedade para vencer o subdesenvolvimento* ('Organizing
society to conquer underdevelopment') 1982.
Translated as Chapter 9 in this volume.

B. Colecção Palavras de Ordem (Watchwords)
The earlier numbers of this series included various FRELIMO documents
from party bodies.

9. *Fazer viver a linha do Partido em cada trabalhador* ('Bring the party

line to life in every worker'), Maputo: Edição do Partido FRELIMO, 1979.
May Day speech in 1979.

10. *Organizemos os nossos recursos para resolver os problemas do povo* ('We must organize our resources to solve the people's problems') 1979.
Translated as Chapter 8 in this volume.

11. *Façamos de 1980–1990 a década da vitória sobre o subdesenvolvimento* ('Let's make 1980–1990 the decade of victory over underdevelopment') 1979.
Speech to a session of the Council of Ministers on 4 August 1979.

12. *Unidade anti-imperialista é a base do não-alinhamento* ('Anti-imperialist unity is the basis for non-alignment') 1979.
Speech to the Non-aligned Summit in Havana, 4 September 1979.

13. *Colher no 25 de Setembro força renovada para o combate* ('Reap from the 25th of September renewed strength for the fight') 1979.
Speech to the armed forces on the 15th anniversary of the armed struggle in 1979.

14. *Fazer do Niassa uma base sólida na construção do socialismo* ('Make Niassa a firm base for the building of socialism') 1979.
Synthesis of speeches made in Niassa province in October 1979.

15. *Reforcemos o poder popular nos nossos hospitais* ('We must strengthen people's power in our hospitals') 1979.
Translated as Chapter 11 in this volume.

16. *A vitório do povo do Zimbabwe é fruto da luta armada, da unidade e do internacionalismo* ('The Zimbabwean people's victory is the fruit of armed struggle, unity and internationalism') 1980.
Speech at a rally in Maputo, 23 December 1979.

17. *Fazer da Beira ponto de partida para uma ofensiva organizacional* ('Make Beira the starting point for an organizational offensive') 1980.
Translated as Chapter 3 in this volume.

18. *Transformar o aparelho de estado no instrumento da vitória* ('Transform the state apparatus into an instrument of victory') 1980.
Translated as Chapter 4 in this volume.

19. *Desalojemos o inimigo interno do nosso aparelho de estado* ('We are declaring war on the enemy within') 1980.
Translated as Chapter 5 in this volume.

20. *Na educação só investiremos em terreno fértil* ('In education we should only invest in fruitful ground) 1981.
Synthesis of two speeches in Beira in March 1981.

21. *As Forças Armadas de Moçambique devem participar na batalha económica* ('The Mozambique Armed Forces must play a part in the economic battle') 1981.
Synthesis of speeches made to the armed forces in April 1981.

22. *Desalojemos os infiltrados nas forças de defesa e segurança* ('We must

remove the enemy within the defence and security forces') 1981. Translated as Chapter 14 in this volume.

23. *Rompamos definitivamente com a burguesia para consolidar o poder popular* ('We must break decisively with the bourgeoisie to consolidate people's power') 1982.
Speech to a rally in Maputo on 22 June 1982.

24. *O apartheid é o Nazismo da nossa época* ('Apartheid is the Nazism of our age') 1983.
Speech to the Non-aligned Summit in New Delhi, 8 March 1983.

25. *Sindicatos organizarão os trabalhadores para matar a fome e a nudez* ('The trade unions will organize workers to put an end to hunger and deprivation') 1983.
Speech to the founding conference of Mozambican trade unions, 31 October 1983.

26. *Acordo de Nkomati: vitória da paz, vitória do socialismo* (The Nkomati Accord: a victory for peace, a victory for socialism) 1984.
Speech to a public session of the People's Assembly, 5 April 1984.

C. Colecção Unidade Nacional (National Unity)
Nos 2–4 of this series were all issued under the same title, although they contain different speeches.

1. *Consolidemos aquilo que nos une* ('Let's consolidate what unites us'), Maputo: Instituto Nacional do Livro e do Disco, 1983.
The proceedings of a meeting with representatives of religious groups, held from 14 to 17 December 1982. Includes opening and closing speeches by Samora Machel.

2. *A nossa forca está na unidade* ('Our strength lies in unity') 1983.
Speech to a rally in Beira, 17 June 1983.

3. *A nossa forca está na unidade* 1983.
Speech to a rally in Quelimane, 19 June 1983.

4. *A nossa forca está na unidade* 1983.
Speeches to rallies in Pemba, 2 July 1983; Montepuez, 4 July 1983; and Mueda, 5 July 1983.

D. Colecção Textos e Documentos (Texts and Documents)
The first volume of this series was a collection of articles from *A Voz da Revolução*.

2. *A vitória constrói-se, a vitória organiza-se* ('Victory must be built, victory must be organized'), Maputo: Edição do Departamento do Trabalho Ideológico, 1977.
Fifteen messages, 1967–1974.

3. *Unidade condição da vitória* ('Unity is a precondition for victory') 1981.
Text prepared for FRELIMO's political-military training centre at Nachingwea, Tanzania in late 1970.

4. *A luta contra o subdesenvolvimento* ('The fight against under-

development') 1983.

Anthology of extracts from speeches, 1974–1982, with linking commentary.

E. Colecção 4° Congresso (4th Congress)

Defender a pátria, eliminar a fome: tarefa de todos os moçambicanos ('Defending the motherland and ending hunger is a task for all Mozambicans'), Maputo: Partido FRELIMO, 1983.

Speech to a rally in Maputo, 21 May 1983, to explain the decisions of the 4th Congress.

Works in English Translation

This chronological selection omits works published in English in journals or newspapers, or issued in mimeographed form.

Mozambique: sowing the seeds of revolution. London: Committee for Freedom in Mozambique, Angola and Guinea, 1974.

A selection from the series 'Studies and Guidelines', with an introduction by John Saul, including biographical information on Samora Machel.

The tasks ahead: selected speeches. New York: Afro American Information Service, 1975.

A collection of speeches and one poem from the period of the armed struggle; includes several of the 'Studies and Guidelines' series.

Mozambique: revolution or reaction? Richmond BC: LSM Information Center, 1975.

Two speeches, 20 September 1974 and 25 September 1974.

Establishing people's power to serve the masses. Dar es Salaam: Tanzania Publishing House, 1977.

Translation of 'Studies and Guidelines' no. 5 (see above).

Our sophisticated weapon. Maputo: Department of Information and Propaganda, 1982. ('Building a nation', no. 2.)

Speech to the 10th session of the Central Committee, Maputo, 23 August 1982.

The enemy within. Maputo: Department of Information and Propaganda, 1982. ('Building a nation', no. 1.)

Translation of 'Watchword' no. 22 (see above).

Index

communism 6, 108, 158
competence 22
'comrade' designation reserved 160-1
concentration camps 195, 197
confessions, forced 188
conservatism 170
Constitution 185
    violations of 185-7
consumer co-operatives 127
contradictions 67, 106
contracts, penalty clauses in 84
co-operatives 31, 127-8
corruption xviii, 21, 27, 50, 74-6, 78, 93,
    113, 118, 121, 148, 183
cotton cultivation, forced xi, 9, 58
counter-revolution 81, 93-4
courts of law, shortcomings of 190
crime 83-4, 95
    by police 185-94, 197; by security
    personnel 185-90, 193, 197-8; by
    soldiers 185-94, 197
criminals, hard labour for 103
Cuba 4
cultivation by soldiers 51-2
cultural values, schools and 130-3

decentralization xxvii
decision-making 15-16, 49, 168
defence xxvi; *see also* armed struggle;
    Army; security personnel
democracy 3, 15-18
    economic 17-18; military 17
democratic: appointments 56; centralism
    164, 168; life, organization of 14-23;
    revolution xx, 34-6, 38-44, 53-5
democratization 25
deportation 6, 7
dictatorship 6
    of the proletariat 106
directors, provincial 125, 156-7
district councils 56
division of labour 3
divorce 138
dock strike 1963 9, 39
doctors 158-9, 166
    absence of 64
dos Santos, Marcelino xv-xvi
dos Santos, Pimentel 10
drugs 78, 174, 182, 195
drunkenness 173
Dynamizing Groups 74, 99, 116, 121-2,
    181

Eastern bloc 69-70
economic: democracy 17-18;
    independence 111; reorganization

58-60
education 38, 54, 60-2, 90, 177
    bourgeois 8; by public criticism 17;
    Catholic x; colonialist xi, 7, 138, 183;
    higher 61; ideological 60, 64, 133;
    party tasks in 132-3; speeches on
    xxiii, xxvii, 130-41; *see also* schools;
    teachers
egalitarianism 163-4
elections 18-19
élitism 165
enterprises: discipline in 97; enemy action
    in 122-3
exploitation xxii, xxiv-xxv, 8, 24
    Africanization of 11-12, 41, 57, 59;
    Church and 6; class 17-18, 41;
    destruction of 2, 11-12, 14, 121;
    imperialist countries' interest in 2, 32;
    of rural masses 58
exploiters 3, 170
    dictatorship by 5, 10, 12-13
exports 59-60, 128

family: extended 101, 130; sense of 173
farmers, African, displacement of xii
Fascism 40
fatalism 130-1
feudalism 5, 57, 104
first-aid workers 61
forced labour xi-xii, xxv, 6, 58
foreign exchange reserves 126
foreign workers 153-5
Free Methodist Church x
FRELIMO ix, xii-xx, 2, 105
    aims 29-30, 38, 143; Army and 51-3,
    196; attitude to Whites 47; Central
    Committee 13, 32, 36, 128; centres
    23, 25, 30-1, 33; Congresses: founding
    xiii-xiv, 37-8; *3rd* xx, xxiii, 128; *4th*
    xxv; democracy in 15-18; divisions
    within xv, xviii, 19, 39-42; external
    policy 66-70; internationalization of
    aggression against 32, 34; leadership
    19-23, 29-30, 79; Marxist-Leninist
    Party xx, 105-6; political line 13, 16-18,
    21, 31, 43-8, 63; training by 196-7;
    working methods 15-23

German Democratic Republic 108
girls, sexual abuse of 131
Gouveia, Teodósio Clemente de 7
governors, provincial 124-5
green belts 100-3
Guiné and Cape Verde, African Party for
    Independence of (PAIGC) 67
Guinea-Bissau Republic 67, 114

Muthemba, Mateus Sansão 41

Nachingwea 127, 196-7
Namibia 68
napalm 59
National Democratic Union (UDENAMO)
  36-7, 39-40
National Feminine Movement 73, 76, 93
national liberation movements 67-8
nationalization: health service and
  hospitals 147-9; opposition to 149;
  schools 176-7
NATO countries' aid to Portugal 2, 32,
  65-6, 71
negligence 118
  criminal 95
Negroes Association Centre of Mozambique
  37
Neto, Agostinho xxiii
Niassa Province 40, 59-60
nuclear weapons 104
Nucleus of African Secondary School
  Students of Mozambique (NESAM) 37
nurses 158-9, 166
nursing school 61
Nyerere, President xvi

officers' training 193
oilseed production 59
oppression 5-10, 24
Organization of African Unity (OAU) 68
organization of society 130, 141
Organizational Offensive 73, 79-80, 187,
  190
orgies 174

Palestine 68
Paris Commune 4
patriotism and Marxism xxvi
peace movement 107-8
peasants 23-4, 130-2, 136-40, 199
penal codes 17
people, Army's attitude to 50
People's: Democratic Revolution xx, 34-6,
  38-44, 53-5;
  Deputies 133;
  Hospital, Central Hospital's transforma-
    tion into 144-5, 147, 152, 155;
  Liberation Forces 48, 191-2;
  National Security Service (SNASP)
    185-6, 194;
  Power xxiv, xxvi, 32, 35, 119;
  democratic 3, 17; establishing, to
    serve the masses xxi, 1-14, 33; in
    Asia and Europe 4; in hospitals
    56, 163-4, 166, 168; structures of
    55-60, 79;

Republic of Mozambique 73, 77-9;
  Constitution of 185/violations of
    185-7;
  Shops 99-100, 103, 127; Tribunals 190;
    War 32, 44-8
Pereira, Custodio Alvim 5
personal struggle xxi-xxii
pharmaceuticals 62
planning commissions, provincial 128
police, illegal actions by 75, 185-90
  causes of 193, 198-9
political: consciousness 31, 112, 114-15;
  study 51; tasks 19
Political and Organizational Offensive 73,
  79-80, 187, 190
politicization of medicine 142, 155
politico-military: militants 53-5; tasks 52;
  training 196-7
polygamy 131, 138, 195
population growth discouraged 63
populism 163, 165
pornography 183
ports, efficiency of 98
Portugal: anti-war movement in 69;
  Communist Party 69; Constitution 6-7;
  underdeveloped world's actions against
    67; *see also* colonialism, Portuguese
Portuguese: army 55, 71/behaviour of 50/
  deserters 69; civilians 47; colonial
  Fascist regime 40, 66; language 20
power of human will xxi-xxiii
power-seeking 121-2, 158
preventive medicine 63
prices 102
prisoners, clemency towards 47-8
prisons as barracks for criminals 189
private enterprise 100
production 14, 18, 58-9, 64, 100
  an act of militancy xxv, 111; by soldiers
    51-4; camps 103; co-operatives 31,
    127; councils 79; increasing 111, 127;
    surplus 3, 58, 127; targets 126
productivity, low 112-13, 115-17, 120
professional ethics 157
profit-sharing 118
profiteering 58, 62
property, lack of respect for 18, 21, 31
prostitution 173, 195
Protestants x
provincial authorities 56, 128
  officials of 124-5, 156-7

Queiroz, Eça de 8

racial discrimination xii, xv, 144
racism 6-7, 73, 77, 86, 93, 120-1, 150,
  152, 154, 167, 183, 189, 195, 198